Catching Lightning
More Letters from Prison

Catching Lightning

More letters from Prison

Patty Prewitt

SOME
PEOPLE
PRESS

Published by Some People Press
PO Box 12453, Portland, Oregon 97212

ISBN: 979-8-9941977-2-1

Cover design by Harrell Fletcher and Laura Glazer
Book design by Laura Glazer
Editing by Harrell Fletcher
Copy editing by Kristi Garced
Proofreading by Gretchen Dykstra

The images on pages xii–xiii and 232–233 are facsimiles
of letters written by the author during her incarceration.

www.somepeoplepress.com
@somepeoplepress

Contents

Publisher's Note

Some People Press primarily publishes autobiographies by formerly incarcerated people who have participated in our weekly writing and publishing workshop at a minimum-security prison in Northeast Portland, Oregon. The writers work with us and their peers to draft and revise their manuscripts and, after they are released, we edit and publish their books with them. We have additionally produced a couple of other books that didn't develop through the prison workshop (and have nothing to do with incarceration), but in those cases, we still had long-term relationships with the work and the authors.

Catching Lightning (and its predecessor, *Trying to Catch Lightning in a Jar*) came to us in a very different way: professors who had worked with Patty Prewitt in prison in Missouri, and helped compile her letters into a manuscript, contacted us asking if we would take a look. After reading Patty's writing and being very moved by it, we decided to publish the manuscript in two parts.

This book covers the last twenty years of Patty's incarceration (the earlier book was from the first eighteen). Working with Patty through the editing and design process has been a pleasure. We are still amazed that she was able to endure such a long and painful ordeal yet remain productive and helpful to others throughout. Patty's writing and story are not what you would expect from someone who spent decades incarcerated, and that is one of many reasons her books are so compelling.

— Harrell Fletcher and Laura Glazer,
Some People Press

Foreword by Brian Reichart

I was a law student at Georgetown when Patty Prewitt changed my life. As part of a new clinic Professor Jane Aiken founded in 2010, I had the opportunity to draft a clemency petition on Patty's behalf. I had no idea I was beginning a fourteen-year advocacy journey—one that would expose me to both the profound pain of a wrongful conviction and the extraordinary strength of the human spirit that Patty embodies. These insights unfolded during a time of tremendous change in my own life. Becoming a lawyer, then a husband and, later, a father, I came to understand more fully the human stakes of Patty's long and unjust incarceration.

On a sticky August day in the confines of an air-conditioned law library, the trial transcript provided my introduction to Patty's case. I was disturbed by the obvious flaws in the case—reliance on discredited witnesses, key evidence as basic as fingerprints not taken from the crime scene, vital leads ignored including a neighbor's report of a suspicious vehicle near the Prewitt home on the night of the murder. As I learned more, I also realized how the prosecution used Patty's identity as a woman and a mother to influence the jury. They asked superfluous questions about the whereabouts of Patty's children during alleged affairs and asked Patty if she was a good mother, a line of inquiry difficult to imagine being directed at a man.

Despite these glaring flaws, Patty's judicial remedies had been exhausted decades ago. Our only recourse was to pursue executive clemency from the governor of Missouri. Unlike a judge reviewing an appeal, a governor considers not only the events that led to a conviction, but also the life a person had lived since. And what a life Patty had lived, despite facing the bleak reality of life in prison. I repeatedly heard strikingly similar accounts from women who served time with Patty. They entered prison at a low point in their lives with little sense of self-worth. Then they met Patty Prewitt. Patty urged, sometimes demanded, that they attend aerobics, theater and poetry classes, college courses, church services, community service—activities that reminded them that they had something to offer the world, even from behind bars. Others took note: state representatives, religious leaders, prison staff, and none other than the director of the Missouri Department of Corrections, who said, "Patty has accomplished more, given more, and touched the lives of more individuals than many of us outside prison will ever achieve."

But while she gave so much, Patty was suffering devastating losses. Her eighteen-year-old son tragically died in 1992. She later endured the loss of her father, mother, sister, and brother—all from her prison cell while her family mourned without her. Meanwhile her own children were having children of their own who would grow to adulthood without seeing Patty outside of prison. The letters you are about to read capture some of the pain, joy, and deep bonds Patty forged with those inside and outside of prison.

We tried to convey the compelling nature of Patty's petition to the governor's office across three administrations over fourteen years. There is no deadline for a Missouri governor to act on a clemency petition and so, as happens too frequently, justice was deferred. Supporters wrote, called, attended rallies, and published op-eds. Lawmakers from both sides of the aisle urged the governor to act. Journalists shined a light on the injustice of a clemency petition that languished for years. Patty's children pleaded with the governor to show mercy. I organized many of those efforts and spoke to anyone—inside or outside of the governor's office—I thought might persuade the governor to act. I even joined Patty on an episode of *Dr. Phil*, something I never imagined doing. We felt momentum and hope so many times over the years—and then nothing would happen. Until finally it did.

It was a chilly night in Pristina, Kosovo, just days before Christmas. My wife's work brought us to that newborn country with a newborn of our own. I was rocking, swaying, and coaxing little Elodie to lay down in her crib, but she wanted out! My phone buzzed. I answered to Patty's eldest daughter, Jane, sobbing; my heart sank. I feared we'd finally received an answer from the governor, but not the one we hoped for. Then I heard Patty from across the world, "Brian, I'm out!"

After thirty-eight and a half years, Patty was coming home. She and Jane drove out of the prison parking lot. My shouts of joy weren't exactly making Elodie sleepy, so I lifted her out of her crib and hugged her tight. That thirteen-month-old got to stay up much later that night after all, celebrating her unexpected reprieve from bedtime, while we rejoiced and toasted to Patty's long-awaited freedom.

A Chicago native, Brian Reichart is an attorney based in Boston, where he lives with his wife and daughters.

the start to point their

One strange entry
towels in my home.
I had towels the a
have thrown out, in
less-than-pristine t
tendencies. First, I
I worked right alo
our business and ou
we were raising fi
kids— who played ev
towels were used for
muddy volleyball. Clea
ness activity.

But why were de
the linen closet inst
Bill's murder? They

...re ...were... from
...jist fingers only at me.
...eemed the condition of
...e deputy noted that
...se housewife evidenc-
...ing that owners
...o indicate murderous
...was not a housewife,
...side my husband at
...farm. Secondly,
...children - active country
...sports. Many of our
...irthing puppies,
...up, and every other
...ties investigating
...of investigating
...ere too occupied digging

My Life Sentence Goes On and On

February 17, 2004

Dear Mary,

On Friday, I received my January property order. Three times a year, we are permitted to order certain items, although the rules as to what we are allowed change all the time. For example, a couple of years ago, the shoe ban came down. We are no longer allowed to order athletic shoes from a vendor like JCPenney. We must buy poor-quality shoes from the prison canteen. It's all about profit.

This year, the jacket ban was implemented. We can no longer purchase warm jackets. We are supposed to wear the thin, cheaply made state coats. That rule baffles me. We save the state money when we buy our own jackets, and we save on medical costs when we stay warm and healthy. Obviously, no one asks my opinion before inventing prison rules.

In all these years I've never ordered a necklace, although we can own one chain and one religious medal. Most of the girls have crosses, but I've never seen one so special that it made me spend the money on myself. It seemed like an extravagance, not a necessity like undies.

But this year, in a friend's Catholic catalog, I spotted and ordered a "Memorial Teardrop" necklace in sterling silver. "A teardrop to be worn in memory of someone beloved. The rose is a symbol of love that never ends." Inside the teardrop rests a silver rose.

It arrived just in time for the twentieth anniversary of Bill's death, which is tomorrow. The silver tear is for Bill and our son Matthew, symbolizing all the saltwater tears I've wept for them. Someday I'll save enough to buy ones for my daughters, too.

April 15, 2004

Dear Gary,

Just worked our monthly mothers and kids visit. During our last Christmas event, Mr. Rose, our activities coordinator, asked the kids to trace their hands on green construction paper and cut out the prints so we could tape them on the wall and make a Christmas tree of handprints.

As soon as the announcement was made, I looked over at this sweet little boy who has no fingers. I think he was born with none, but I'm not sure. I raced to Mr. Rose and before I could get an explanation out, he hurried over to the kid and asked for unique handprints to use at the top of the tree. I was so touched that I cried. Mr. Rose is special. I'm sure he won't stay long in this prison. The good ones move on.

Today I helped an overworked grandma take care of one-year-old twins. She's responsible for four grandkids under five. She was putting Coke in their bottles, so I scared up some milk. Obviously, no one plays with them. They didn't know peek-a-boo or pat-a-cake or anything! It took me an hour to get a smile out of any of them.

November 9, 2004

Dear Marsha,

Why is it that no woman in my family ever talked about menopause? At least no one ever told me about it. I've been trying to explain this to all my daughters without scaring them too much. When I was a kid, I'd hear the old women talk about "the change," but I didn't realize that it was very much the same as what werewolves experience under a full moon.

I also feel sorry for teasing Mickie and Donna when they suffered their "power surges" and mood swings. I didn't know what they were going through. It's yet another example of ignorance is bliss.

Yesterday, my big boss from Central Office was in the shop for a demo of the tracking system I've been creating for them. We sat side by side in front of my terminal while I, at the keyboard, explained the flow. Everything was going nicely until the mother of all hot flashes hit me right between the eyes.

I began the burn from within but soon was radiating heat like the molten-red back of a roaring wood stove. Without saying a word about my out-of-control physical furnace, I nonchalantly reached down and rolled my trouser legs up above my knees, then pulled my uniform over-shirt off onto the back of my chair. With one hand, I pulled my hair up off my neck and kept on explaining what function key caused what drop-down. My face had to be beet red, but Jim still didn't say one word. He didn't even glance at me.

I felt like I might spontaneously combust, leaving only smoldering shoes, but the fire finally subsided, leaving me chilly. I casually rolled my pants legs back down, dropped my hair, and pulled my shirt back on. Jim still acted like nothing weird was happening. Bless his heart. And best of all, he liked what I'd done with the tracking system for visitation.

January 18, 2005

Dear Nancy,

I haven't written anyone over Christmas or New Year's because I hoped to have good news, but this plan didn't work. Let me explain what's been going on.

In September, Phil Cardarella, one of my trial attorneys, called my daughter Sarah. He wanted me to file an application for executive clemency. I called Phil's office for clarification. When my application was denied by Governor Holden in the fall of 2003, the paperwork stated clearly that I could not file for three years.

Phil tersely explained that since the governor was going out of office, Holden just might sign my papers. He said it was worth a try, but that we must keep it all hush-hush. No publicity. He was looking for someone who knew the governor on a first-name basis to open the door.

I gathered together a work appraisal report stating that I'm a wonderful worker on my job and wrote a letter to the governor asking for mercy and slipping in the fact that the Midwest Innocence Project has been researching my case. I mailed the packet to Phil. In a week I called to see if he'd gotten it. He told me that the "interested party" had the papers. That's all he would say.

After the November election, I called Phil again to check on any developments. Determined to worm some crumb of info from him, I stayed on the line until he told me that he, Judge Bob Beaird, and Representative John Burnett had met with the governor and his legal counsel in October to plead my case. Bob had been appointed a judge by then. Burnett had helped Holden with his re-election campaign. As far as politics go, it seemed to be good.

During the Thanksgiving weekend, two women I know were informed that the governor had commuted their no-parole sentences to regular life sentences. They are paroling soon. The governor had actually done something. We were all on pins and needles.

Right before Christmas I received a card from Paula McCurren. I met Paula and her husband while I was housed at Church Farm near Jeff City. A pregnant inmate was desperate to find a family to care for her baby until she paroled, so I asked Father Behan. He found the McCurrens and they volunteered to care for her baby. They're wonderful people and brought Nik to see his mom every week. Unfortunately, the mom was never able to step up to the plate, and so the McCurrens adopted Nik, whom they love mightily.

Also, while we were at Church Farm, Michelle Dale battled cancer. It was so invasive that she was granted medical parole. (Medical paroles are only given to the dying.) Since she had no place to go, the McCurrens took her in. I called their house to talk to Michelle until she was no longer in her right mind. My Momma called the McCurrens "angels on earth." Indeed.

I haven't seen the McCurrens in years, but we still exchange Christmas cards. This year the note in her card blew me away. She's now the office manager for Rep. John Burnett! When he told her that he was helping an inmate with executive clemency, she asked who. When he mentioned my name, she just about fell over. After she pulled her jaw off the floor, she told him that she knew me, loved me, and that I was instrumental in them having Nikolas, the son they adore. She even wrote a letter to the governor and hand-delivered it. In her note to me, she told me to call.

So, I called her office at the Capitol, and we chatted like old friends. She told me that John worked in Beaird's office in the '80s and attended my trial. I called her house on the evening of January 5, and Paula told me that the governor's legal counsel had called Burnett that very day and assured him that my file was on his desk. John offered to go there to speak again on my behalf. Cosgrove told him that was unnecessary. They all knew where John stood. Paula was jumping out of her skin. When I said goodbye and walked back to my cell, my legs were like rubber. The inauguration was on January 10, the deadline.

On Friday the 7th, another girl on camp heard that her sentence had been commuted. She'd been convicted out of Higginsville on sodomy—had sex with a grade schoolboy while she was a teacher's aide. She'd received twenty years for that, and the governor commuted her sentence to fifteen. The newspaper stated that he'd commute no others, but I still held on to a thread of hope.

After lunch on Monday, January 10, I called Cardarella and got the bad news. Governor Holden commuted the sentences of four women (adding Shirley Lute) and forty-some men. He denied over four hundred.

I was kicked in the stomach and had the wind knocked out of me—once again. But I'm back.

Last year a state representative from KC, Jenee Lowe, filed a "lifer's bill" allowing for those of us serving no-parole sentences to apply for parole after serving twenty years. It was designed to take the politics out of the clemency process and look at the inmate's rehabilitation. I hope she plans to try again this legislative session.

And that's where we are now. Legislation seems to be my only way out. But my enemies not only fight me, they also fight the house bill. Several years ago, Janie went to a legislative committee meeting, and Bill's sister, Georgeanne, and Johnson County prosecutor Mary Ann Young were there in full battle gear. They killed that bill in committee only because it would have helped me. A couple of years later, Cindy Ostmann, a friendly state rep from St. Louis, sent me copies of the poison-pen letters Georgeanne's youngest son had sent to her and all the legislators. He doesn't even have the facts straight. It's so sad. I babysat him when he was a baby.

A year ago, all the legislators received notice from Springfield State Rep. Bob Dixon, a friend of Georgeanne. He hates me, too, by proxy. Sarah, who gets so upset with Georgeanne, emailed all the legislators her rebuttal to his rantings about me. After Bill's death, his family absolutely ignored our children. If they believed I was crazed, why would they leave the kids with me? Good Christians, as they report to be, would not leave five small children in the care of a madwoman—if they honestly thought that to be true.

If that weren't bad enough, Senator Delbert Scott from Appleton City, a tiny town south of Holden, works tirelessly against me. I found out from a friendly legislator that he owned a hardware store when we had our lumberyard. We shared a hardware salesman who told him how awful I was from the rumors of the time, so he's made it his personal mission to keep me in prison.

Supposedly, he met Bill and me at a hardware convention, but I don't remember him.

While I'm on the subject, this summer the *River Front Times* reporter called Kevin Hughes, the Johnson County cop investigator on my case. Hughes now lives in Montana or Wyoming and had his file on me sitting on his desk. Scary. He also writes long letters to governors and legislators about how I am the most cold-blooded, callous killer he's ever run across.

Bet you had no idea you are friends with such a horrible person.

Anyway, that's where we are now.

I apologize for not writing sooner. Thank you for all your support and love. Carli sent me a sweet thank you for the little gifts I'd sent her beautiful children. I'm awaiting an order of yarn to make a bedspread for Drew's second birthday. Still making teddy bears for orphans and charity, too.

Gary's great. His production company is working on a website for him. Don't know if it will be garykirklandsings.com or garykirklandmusic.com.

After we got the bad news, I urged Gary to abandon me and go on with his life. He's worked and waited for me for nearly eight years. He says he can't leave, and that no one else could understand him and get along with him like I do. I doubt that's true, but for now, he's still with me, bless his lonely heart.

My theater class is presenting Acts II and III of *Macbeth* next month. This time I play Banquo, Macbeth's best friend, whom he murders. I get to come back as a scary ghost.

I love you so! Have a ball with the kids!

February 23, 2005

Dear Gary,

Our theater troupe had just concluded the Q&A session, after presenting Acts II and III of *Macbeth* to my sister prisoners, when a smiling, thirty-ish, big-boned blonde approached me, explaining how much she enjoyed our performance and especially my death and resurrection as Banquo.

When I was killed, I rolled off the back of the plywood stage. For the next scene, two girls carried a long table covered with a big tablecloth (state sheet) to center stage for the banquet scene. I scrambled unseen under the sheet as they carried the table to center stage. There I huddled until it was time for me as the ghost to appear. Janiece, who played Macbeth, drew attention to herself, acting nuts at the edge of the stage, while I slowly rose from my crouch up to my stool behind the table. When Janiece turned and pointed at me in horror, the audience also gasped to see me there as a ghost. They had no idea how we managed it. But I digress.

I love the meet-and-greet part right after a performance for two reasons. First, the stage fright is over. We've made it through another performance. Whew! But the feedback from the audience is what I most enjoy. Their perspective is always fresh and satisfying to me—whether they have a history with Shakespeare or not.

That inmate hugged me as she cheerily explained, "Biker broads don't ever go to Shakespeare in the Park, but now that I've seen it's just a story—a story that I understand, with thugs and murder and ghosts...when I get home next year, I'm gonna gather up my kids and go to the festival. The kids will get a kick outta it. Until just now, I never woulda considered taking my Harley-riding ass to some uppity-up snooty type-a-shindig. I almost didn't come out tonight, but there was nothin' else ta do. Thanks. I was thoroughly entertained."

Others in the milling crowd offered congratulations, hugs, and pats on the back, but no one affected me as much as that self-described "biker broad." All the memorization, rehearsals, and hassle with the powers-that-be are now worth it. When that gal paroles, she'll be open to new experiences and will broaden her children's horizons, too. That's a prison miracle.

March 14, 2005

Dear Nancy,

Happy St. Patty's Day! The play is over. The girls did great. We start on Act IV on Thursday. I want to play a witch again. That was fun!

Enclosed is info on a house bill that was introduced last week. If it should pass, I'd be eligible for parole! Yes!

Carrie and Sarah brought Megan and Drew to visit yesterday. We had such a great time.

Momma is going to the doctor today about her bladder problem. She HATES to go to the doctor about anything.

Gotta run to dance practice. I'm part of a halftime show for a March Madness basketball game. I'm the token senior citizen! Ha! It's so much fun! Gary will be here on Friday. He bought a new bike, not a bicycle, a motorcycle.

July 16, 2005

Dear Nancy,

In February, after we performed Acts II and III of *Macbeth*, several weary members of the cast expressed interest in exploring something other than Shakespeare. Anything. So, on St. Patrick's Day, Agnes returned to us with Dale Davis, an energetic New York writer/producer/character, who told us that she'd written for *Rolling Stone*—only because they thought she was a man.

As Dale mesmerized us with her stories, she handed out typing paper and told us to write "I Am" poems right then and there. No torturous pondering. Just write. "What do you want? What do you pray for? What makes you happy? What makes you mad? What makes you crazy? Where did you come from? Where are you going?"

This fast-talking, middle-aged white woman cast a spell on us and made us tell the naked truth. The results were so phenomenal that we caught poem fever. Many of us had never checked out a poetry book in our lives and began scrambling for any poetry we could find to share, as well as scribbling our own. That's how "Spoken Word" was born and added to our repertoire.

Last week, our troupe performed Act IV of *Macbeth,* samples of our poetry, and works by famous women. My heart swelled with pride because it would have been difficult to distinguish the professional pieces, by the likes of Maya Angelou, from those of our fledgling writers.

One of my poems is a true tale of a young girl who stood at the barred window every Saturday morning for hours, desperately hoping and wishing that her mother would come to visit in her old blue Ford.

After our final performance on the big prison yard, a woman I've jailed with for many years expressed, "Patty, I really loved 'Old Blue Ford.' It was an old tan Plymouth for me." The hurt in her gray eyes caused me to hug her fiercely.

If I hadn't had the opportunity to share the story of my former cellmate, this woman would not have opened up about her own pain and disappointment. What we do is good.

July 28, 2005

Dear Marsha,

This is a quick note to describe some of the ripples caused by the plunk of our theater program in the prison pond. As a writer, I know you're interested in this stuff.

Last week, after a step aerobics class, Cindy, a boyish drug addict who keeps coming back here, stopped me with sweat still dripping off her nose and quickly blurted, "Patty, I really enjoyed your play and the poetry. And remember when you asked us to write an 'I Am' poem? I've been working on mine every night since then. But I keep changing it. Is it normal to rewrite every day?"

"Why not?" I replied. "We change daily—and if you're really soul-searching, you uncover different layers every day."

She seemed to appreciate my explanation, and as she walked away, she hollered, "If I ever get done, I'll show it to you. Thanks!"

This morning at breakfast, I sat across from an unfamiliar, middle-aged Black woman. Since I rarely eat my white-bread toast, I offered it to her. She looked hungry. When she shyly looked up from her tray to my face, she smiled and stated, "I really enjoyed the play. I'll never forget your poem either. It had so much feeling. I've been writing my own poem on scrap paper until it's right."

The do-gooder part of me began to plot how I can get a writing tablet to her. She obviously has no money for extras like paper. Dale Davis has started a poetry epidemic at WERDCC!

November 27, 2005

Dearest Gary,

Although you are far from computer literate, you know enough to get a kick out of this little story: "Has your grandma been Googling?"

That's what our caseworker asked Kris as she sat in the hot seat in his office. And Kris reported that all she could do was stutter, "Huh? What? Ahhh, Grandma, Grandma's in a, in a nursing, nursing home." Include a deer-in-the-headlights look to that.

It turns out that her grandmother had used the Google search engine to find an aerial view of our prison, printed out the map, and dropped it in a letter with this sweet request, "Kris, please circle where you live so I can feel closer to you."

Bless Grandma's computer-savvy heart. But the prison mailroom did not see the humor. They saw it as an escape attempt of some sort. Kris was mortified, scared—and a bit amazed and amused. Evidently, her grandma thinks outside the box.

When she returned to work and told the tale, we were all amazed and amused. Times have certainly changed! Before that day, I'd never heard those words strung together in a sentence: "Has your grandma been Googling?"

January 17, 2006

Dearest Gary,

While telling the other five occupants of our cell about her children, Nicole shared, "I try so hard not to *favoritize* my oldest daughter, but it's hard. I have a tendency to favoritize Lily because I feel closer to her. I guess it's because I've had her longer..." Favoritize.

The canteen now sells toilet paper, and we are limited to three rolls of state-issued toilet tissue a week. If we ask for more, some officers growl, "I suggest you buy yourself some." If we prove that we desperately need an extra roll, the exchange is documented. Officers are the keepers of the toilet paper dispensation records. Most of these girls are attempting to survive on the $7.50 prisoner pay.

And state paper is far from Charmin. The one-ply rolls are cheap and loosely packaged, so the roll disappears in no time at all. Because toilet paper has become a hot commodity, Recreation no longer keeps any in the bathroom. We must check it out at the equipment room. "Can I check out an exercise mat and a wad of toilet paper, please? Here's my ID."

Staff constantly grumble because we females use more toilet paper than the male inmates do. Duh! Have they given this difference any actual thought? You don't need a college degree to figure that one out. Surprisingly, we also use more sanitary napkins.

At the canteen, I overheard a disgruntled customer, "I refuse to spend my hard-earned money to buy toilet paper. The state wants my ass so damned bad...well, they can just pay to wipe it!"

March 1, 2006

Dear Honorable Governor Matt Blunt:

My champion, Dale Whiteside, recently advised me to send you an accounting of my activities for the past year. I keep so very busy in this prison that I have to sit back to think about what has transpired.

ISU: Of course, every weekday, I work at my job as a computer programmer/analyst and shop lead for our Information Systems Unit under supervisor Linda McBride. Offender programmers save hundreds of thousands of dollars for the state by providing extremely cheap but skilled labor. I also teach programming to new students to both maintain our prison workforce and provide marketable rehabilitative skills for our women who are paroled. I have worked industriously for the Department of Corrections Information Systems Unit since January of 1995 and am usually the first to arrive and the last to leave.

PPA/MACBETH: A few years ago, Prison Performing Arts from St. Louis came to this prison. In the last year, we performed the final two acts of *Macbeth*. In July, I was fortunate to earn the emotionally meaty role of Macduff, who finds out that the evil Macbeth murdered his entire family. Since I have lost both my husband and my older son, my broken heart provided much to draw on.

WIZARD OF OZ: In December, an independent group of us, under the guidance of Recreation Officer Jim Lingua, miraculously put on *The Wizard of Oz*. With paper and poster paint, the art department creatively transformed the gym from Kansas to Munchkinland to the Emerald City—with even a witch's castle. The handmade costumes rivaled the originals. Every moment of every performance was magical—a special Christmas gift to inmates and staff. I'm proud to report that I painted props and scenery and played the best Wicked Witch of the West this side of the Yellow Brick Road.

CPR/FIRST AID: Last Spring, I embarked on studies to become a certified fitness instructor. Last month, I was CPR/First Aid certified with the American Red Cross. We undergrads use AFAA (Athletics and Fitness Association of America) Basic Exercise Standards and Guidelines and are under the tutelage of an AFAA-certified instructor who comes in weekly to monitor progress. I will take my written and practical certification exam in June.

BLAST: Our BLAST (Better Living Awareness Support Team) organization, under Recreation Officer Brenda Lemler, does much rehabilitative good. When people learn how to feel good and healthy without chemical dependencies, they are much less likely to return to drugs/alcohol. I teach yoga, Pilates, and aerobics.

CHAMP: Our prison also boasts the first dog-training program in the state. A few years ago, when the CHAMP program first formed, I moved to that wing to be a supporter. Since I have a full-time job, I cannot be a CHAMP trainer, but I still cheer on the program.

RESTORATIVE JUSTICE: In my spare time, I crochet teddy bears for ambulance services to hand to children and the elderly. These stuffed animals are donated through our Restorative Justice Organization under CCA Sheri Hees.

PATCH: As a board member of PATCH (Parents and Their Children), I dressed as a Christmas elf and helped wrap and distribute gifts and toys in the visiting room over the holidays. Many of these unfortunate children would have little to no Christmas without the generous PATCH program.

MOMS AND KIDS: I'm also a charter member of the Moms and Kids committee. I work closely with the IAC's Bruce Rose and Shoshana Hill to provide monthly special visits featuring games, music, and treats in the visiting room. In January, we successfully teamed up to bring *The Wizard of Oz* to the Moms and Kids visit.

HALFTIME SHOW: Friday is our all-star basketball game, our own bit of March Madness. For the second year, I've signed on as a dancer in the halftime show. I'm the token OG (old girl). Wish me luck!

March 12, 2006

Dearest Nancy,

I WON!! Last night at mail call, I received an envelope from PEN American Center in New York. Last summer, I entered a few poems and an essay in a prisoner writing contest. Wouldn't have even known about the contest if Agnes hadn't brought in the entry information.

The letter from PEN Director Jackson Taylor began: "Congratulations! I am delighted to inform you that you've been awarded First Prize for Nonfiction/Essay in the 2006 PEN Prison Writing Awards for your piece, 'Contraband.' We are in the process of preparing to post the winning entries on our website at pen.org. They should be visible by May. Please use the enclosed envelope and form to tell us where to send the check for the award amount of $200—you may sign the check over to a friend or family member if you wish."

You should have seen my shocked face when I read that I'd won! I will forward the $200 to Prison Performing Arts to pay for scripts and such. That's only right. Full circle. After all, if it weren't for Agnes, I wouldn't have entered the contest.

The letter went on to say that as part of my award, they will match me up with a writing "mentor who can offer critical feedback on my writing." How cool is that? An honest-to-God writer to help me!

PEN also offers "public readings of selected manuscripts by committee members or well-known writers or actors." This season, they plan to read selected manuscripts over the radio.

I figure I won because that essay is humorous, and I bet most prisoners don't submit funny material. It's the nature of captives to tell mournful tales. Woe we know, humor not so much.

April 14, 2006

Dear Nancy,

Just when I think I've heard it all, I get wind of an incident that proves me wrong. Last week, while a female guard searched the contents of a locker, she stumbled on a folder containing recipes that Janet had been collecting for the last decade in preparation for her return to society and a kitchen. The officer quickly disposed of the contraband recipes.

She gave this reason for her action: the papers had been torn out of magazines and were "not in the original containers."

The original-container rule haunts us always. If I buy crackers, take them out of the package and place them in a plastic bowl with a lid to keep them fresh, I've broken the law. (Canteen sells "storage bowls," but it's against the rule to actually store anything.) If I stow and organize letters in a cardboard envelope box, I'm a rule-breaker.

In 1991, the canteen sold jalapeño peppers in aluminum cans. Upon opening the can, we would pour the pickled peppers into another receptacle—a recycled plastic peanut butter jar, for example. Everyone knows that food doesn't keep in open tin cans. An overzealous officer seized everyone's peppers, citing the original-container rule. Defiantly, Judy brought an open can of jalapenos to a PATCH board meeting and ceremoniously handed it to our superintendent, "Sir, I opened this can last night and used a few peppers. But I'm afraid it's unsafe and unsanitary to keep this open container in my locker, so you can have it. Do you like jalapeños?"

His face turned stony and reddened as if he'd tasted the contents of his gift, but he got the point.

I'm not sure this recipe-snatcher will get it, though. What if someone tears open a ramen soup and tosses the hard noodles into a bowl of hot water in that guard's presence? What about a spoon of instant coffee transferred to a cup of hot water? Soda pop poured over ice? Toothpaste squeezed onto a brush? Unwrapped Ivory soap stored on a soap dish? A scoop of detergent sprinkled into the washing machine?

Such scenarios are the seemingly preposterous but probable possibilities that prisoners ponder.

June 28, 2006

Dearest Momma and Daddy,

As soon as I got back to the dorm yesterday at eleven for noon count, I was called to the visiting room with Carlene and four other gals. Law professor Jane Aiken, a couple of attorneys, and two young female Washington University law students from their domestic violence clinic were there to meet us. I first met Jane last year at a *Macbeth* performance. Tall, elegant, and beautiful with razor-sharp intelligence—Jane is a pistol!

Although I don't fit the profile for the domestic violence legal clinic, Jane is looking for an attorney who deals with innocence cases to check into my conviction. She'd asked me before what the Midwest Innocence Project did in my case, and I was sorry to tell her that they'd disappeared with no word to me as to why or what they were doing or not doing. Through the grapevine, I heard that they'd moved their office and reorganized—but no one from there has contacted me in over a year.

I told Jane about my PEN-appointed writing mentor. Jane knows a woman who won a PEN writing contest, is now out of prison, and is getting her autobiography published. Jane said that the PEN award is very difficult to win and opens doors.

Anyway, just wanted to let you know that Jane is trying to help me. I thanked her, and she retorted, "I haven't done anything yet to help!" But she is investigating. That's more than anyone else.

I had two programming students, but only one survived the grueling testing. Kris is tall, model-sized, with long blonde hair. Her father is a computer programmer. I don't know the history behind the incident, but somehow in an out-of-hand domestic spat, Kris fatally hit her abusive boyfriend with a baseball bat about five years ago. She's a good kid, only twenty-four, and very smart and funny. She's serving twenty-five years and must serve at least 85 percent of that number by law. I hate these mandatory minimum laws.

The doc read my X-ray and decided my wrist isn't broken after all, but I have sprained it somehow. Nothing to do in here about

the injury but try to baby it. I haven't crocheted for six weeks—
except a tiny bit for Callie's fifth birthday. I gotta have gifts for my
grandbabies! No time to be wounded!

July 2, 2006

Dear Mary,

Carrie and Sarah, along with two of their sweet children, visited
me on Friday for my birthday. Carrie informed me that it's my
"Heinz" birthday since I'm 57. During theater class on Thursday, Agnes asked whether we had chosen our poetry for the next
performance, which is in a couple of weeks. YIKES! I explained
to her that I'd become the angry inmate when it comes to poetry.
Nothing I've written of late will pass the administration's scrutiny.
Our work is heavily censored.

August 4, 2006

Dear Doc Kayser,

The reason I'm bothering you is because our PATCH program
is gone. We've been told very little—just that the director quit,
that the PATCH Board dissolved, and that there will be no more
PATCH visits. I have no idea if you're still affiliated with PATCH,
but those of us here want somehow to resurrect the program. We
must start asking questions.

I figure we still have a lot going for us: the physical space and a
group of local volunteers in the community. We also have a group
of dedicated inmates and their families. What we don't have is
communication between us.

PATCH was formed in the early '80s and has filled a desperate
need for incarcerated mothers and their children until now. We
can't just let our mission die of neglect.

Joe, if you know anything or can help in any way, we will be most grateful. Right now, we are stunned.

August 9, 2006

Dearest Gary,

You asked about my prison day, so here's the quick overview:

4:00–4:30	Rise, use bathroom before rush, laundry, dress
5:00	Security/custody count
5:30–5:45	Count clear, dayroom open, make bed
5:45–6:00	Breakfast (except on Tuesday because I then teach a 5:50 am yoga class in Drug Treatment Housing Unit)
7:00–7:20	Ice detail (take coolers to D-wing's icemaker)
7:15–7:30	Work detail called, so I go to my job detail
11:00	Leave work to go back to dorm
11:25	Security count
12:00–12:30	Count clear, dayroom open
12:30–1:00	Lunch in chow hall with pat search upon departure
12:30–1:00	Go back to work
3:30–3:45	Leave work and go back to dorm
3:45–4:00	Go to gym or teach exercise class
4:25	Security count
5:15–6:00	Dinner, but I rarely go because I'm in the gym
7:00–9:15	Free (shower, eat, laundry, study, write, chapel service, class, rec)

8:00–9:15	Mail call
9:15–9:30	Security count
10:00–10:30	Count clear, dayroom open
10:30	Dayroom closed, must be in cells, lights out
10:30–11:00	Crawl into the bunk to sleep
11:15	Count (but we can be asleep, thank heaven)
2:25	Count (can still be asleep)

There you have it. A regular prison day. Weekends are similar except for the job detail. On Thursdays, I have theater class from 1:00 to 9:00 pm. Now that we're studying for our personal trainer certification, we have anatomy class from 4:00 to 6:00 pm on Mondays.

Count: We are counted at regular intervals all day and night. The reason is obvious. During counts from 5:00 am to 10:00 pm, we are required to sit on our bunks in our room, with the overhead light on, appliances off, absolute silence, and the door open. But if I'm at rec, the recreation officers count us there. We line up around the basketball court to be counted, then we can return to our exercise.

Officers count us, check their numbers, then phone the Control Center with the count. All places that have inmates (housing units, chapel, school, gym, medical, visiting room, etc.) call in their count number to the Control Center. Control Center then decides if these numbers add up to the magic number—the grand total of inmates who should be here behind the fence. Often, the count is inaccurate, and officers must count again. That's called a "recount," which about sums it up. Meanwhile, the girls in the dorms are sitting on their bunks for ages waiting—held hostage, as it were. If they must count a third time, it's still called a "recount."

That happens often because the Control Center does not possess the actual magic number. An inmate can leave for a host of reasons—like parole, medical trip to a hospital, court appearance—and no officer entered that departure in the computer. Or someone can

arrive from a medical or court outcount or county jail and no officer entered that arrival in the computer. When that happens, we
are in our cells for hours waiting. No inmates can "move" unless
count is "good."

That's another reason I keep peanut butter and crackers on hand.
I've crocheted a whole teddy bear during one long count.

I've spent so much time telling you about my schedule that I'm
running behind schedule.

October 3, 2006

Dear Marsha,

Unfortunately, I must report that I have gotten myself in hot water
and have spent ten days in room restriction and property impoundment. We call this particular punishment "going in white" because
when one is on room restriction, the gal must wear a white jumpsuit
at all times. And she must stay in her cell most of the time, except
for meals. All her "stuff" must be locked up, so she has nothing to
do, either. It's a serious punishment. The next worst punishment
is going to administrative segregation, aka the hole.

Since I had not gotten a violation in years, you might wonder
what heinous infraction of prison rules I accomplished to earn
this. It's a long story, but I'll give you the *Reader's Digest* version.

I teach a 6:00 am yoga class at the Drug Treatment Housing
Unit. Most of the girls there are just kids, and a certain officer
who has a horrible reputation has been assigned there on the 7:00
am to 7:00 pm shift. His nickname is Chester, short for Chester
the Molester. He was outside our door observing the shower area
while I held class, but his proximity caused the girls to confide in
me about his nocturnal behavior. Some have been awakened out
of their sleep with him looming over their bunks, touching them,
scaring them to death.

Most women in prison have been abused in their lives, as you
well know. One tiny, pretty child hung back and trembled as she

whispered that she'd been awakened by his hand on her face, and continued, "That's exactly how my stepdaddy used to wake me up when he...you know...wanted sex."

The girls are scared of him but even more frightened of what will happen to them if they tell. If we report sexual behavior/advances by staff, we are packed up and sent to the hole for "investigation." Cuffed and stuffed. And can be there for months. Do you see why few report problems?

With a heavy heart I left the girls and wrote an impassioned report to our Training Officer. It was hardly the first time either. I cannot sit by and watch injustices without voicing my opinion. (This has been a lifelong problem. My late husband used to call me Crusader Rabbit.) The next evening at mail call I received Waybright's reply, "I relayed your concerns to Major Hurley and feel confident this will be addressed."

The next afternoon, I was called to Treatment and given a big fat double-whammy conduct violation for both "insulting behavior" and "creating a disturbance." Written by the Functional Unit Manager: "After a thorough investigation of an IOC dated 9-12-06 from offender Prewitt to William Waybright; Training Officer, I have found no basis for her allegations that Officer Capp is 'well-known as a pervert.' This is a slanderous statement that serves no purpose other than to harm Officer Capp's reputation. This also places offender in violation of rule #19.4."

In my defense, at my hearing I argued that slander is a falsehood. Among the women in this camp, Capp *is* well-known as a pervert, defined as someone who is doing wrong sexually. No other officer in history has sent more women to the hole for protesting his invasive frisks, and no other officer has had more complaints against him. These facts are documented. Therefore, my statement is not false, not slander, and not meant to harm the reputation of a man who already has earned a bad reputation.

I went on to ask, "If we are to be punished for reporting wrongdoings, does that mean that the administration does not want to know what's going on? Administration and custody staff cannot be everywhere. We inmates make reports to ensure the safety and security of all persons within the confines of the compound." Also, I brought in four reliable inmate "witnesses" to write their reports of the officer's behavior and reputation. I could have called 1,000 if they would have let me.

But my caseworker said that the verdict had already come from "up front" and his hands were tied, as it were. So, I spent ten days sequestered in the room teaching my cellmates yoga and Pilates. I got out of "white" Saturday morning. In fact, I taught two step aerobics classes and participated in another that very day. Felt good to be out and exercising. The sun on my face felt like a hug from an old friend.

But it's not over. I want to write to legislators about our problem—I just don't know who may be sympathetic. We need a non-Department of Corrections "watchdog" group to assist us. The officer's conduct was investigated—but the investigation was conducted by the DOC. It's not a good idea to let a fox oversee your chickens.

October 4, 2006

Dearest Momma and Daddy,

Last night I received the strangest IOC from Associate Superintendent William Beall. It chastised me for my CDV in an odd manner: The note was kinda in outline form, but these are the words: "Ms. Prewitt, the merits of your guilt are documented by the CDV. Honest? I don't believe so—not with what you've said and written about others. A leader? Not a positive leader—letters and CDV documentation. Suggestions—develope [sic] positive leadership skills by learning & practicing daily moral, ethical values to develope [sic] integrity."

I went to bed thinking of the harsh, judgmental tone and inaccuracy of his note—this stranger to me who has my incarcerated life in his hands. Then I woke up to a news story about the Amish in PA who just experienced a brutal attack on a group of innocent school children. A crazy man killed four or five young girls. The story this morning was about forgiveness. The Amish live by the New Testament and have already forgiven the shooter and his family. The TV talking head was obviously taken aback by the forgiveness of the Amish community. This certainly doesn't happen every day. TV crime reporter Nancy Grace must be appalled.

I live in Grudge World. Everyone holds onto thoughts of revenge—whether the hurt was slight or enormous. Everyone who goes to the parole board is grilled to atone for their sins. Crime victims come to rant and rave for more punishment. Inmates plan revenge because someone had the audacity to be using the micro-wave when they came in from recreation. In your world, motor-ists kill each other over infractions of traffic etiquette. It's all the same insanity. Bill's sister, Georgeanne, and her offspring spend countless hours and enough energy to keep New York lit, just so I stay locked up.

I read once that: "To hold hate in your heart is like taking a spoonful of poison every day expecting the one you hate to die from it."

"What would Jesus do?" is a cutesy Christian catchphrase—but rarely does anyone actually take that sentiment to heart. Rarely does someone do what Jesus or any spiritual leader would do. We'd rather do what Genghis Khan would do.

I applaud the Amish community. They've been struck a hard blow and have shown their sweet, loving, spiritual faces to the world. We can all learn from them—especially the Department of Corrections.

At recreation last night two fights broke out, and the gym had to be evacuated because of the mace in the air. I fear that our rec time will become restricted. We are way too overcrowded, and overcrowding causes tension. And we are getting more and more young meth heads in prison—redneck, wild gals with nothing to lose. Doing time is fine with them. They have nothing waiting for them at home except responsibilities that they don't want—like kids.

"A man's character is the reality of himself. His reputation is the opinion others have of him. Character is the substance; reputation is the shadow." We put that thought-for-the-day on the board with female pronouns.

I love you all with all my heart. You two are so very special! I'm proud to be your firstborn baby girl. God bless.

October 5, 2006

Dear Sarah,

A bit before ten, I was called to the visiting room, stripped, and changed, and in the "confidential" room found Doctor Joseph Kayser and another man smiling at me. Doc, who is a successful chiropractor and community leader in Jefferson City, was the former PATCH board president when I was housed at Renz. His friend is Representative Bill Deeken, a Republican from Jefferson City.

Let me back up and tell you that this summer, our PATCH program folded with a whimper. No one told us why or how, so I wrote Doc Kayser to see if he had any insight or ideas about how to get PATCH back. That letter must have reminded Doc that I'm still in prison, because he wrote that he wanted to make some phone calls and see if he could get legislative interest in my case.

Rep. Deeken asked me a bunch of questions about what I did in prison, so I gave him the ISU, BLAST, and PPA commercials. When I told him that six BLAST members had paroled and were employed as fitness instructors, but that I didn't certify with parole in mind since I'm not leaving, he stopped me mid-word: "Don't say that. You *are* getting out."

He asked me about my kids and if my incarceration had affected them. LORD, YES!! I fought tears and expounded for a long time about that!

He knows Joe Bednar, late Governor Carnahan's former chief counsel. Rep. Deeken's daughter's school friend married Joe. He knows former legislator Larry Rohrback from California, who was on our PATCH board when we were at Renz. He knows Rep. John Burnett, who was in Bob Beaird's office during my trial, and Burnett's secretary, Paula McCurren, who adopted an inmate's baby years ago.

In the middle of our visit, Rep. Deeken turned to Joe and commented, "She's exactly who you said she is. I'm in 100% and will do all I can to get her home to her family."

I had never had the chance to thank Doc for all he did for us at Renz, so I took the opportunity to thank him for treating us like human beings and working tirelessly for us. As I tried to express my gratitude, tears welled up, and I noticed that Joe's sweet eyes had the same problem. Then I saw that Rep. Deeken was also teary-eyed. He then said that a man who can't cry is not much of a man and went on to quote Herbert Hoover about crying.

I informed him that seeing a man cry really touches me, and I told a story about Daddy, who is afraid he won't live to see me free. While visiting one time, Daddy talked about his feelings and a single tear fell from his good eye, rolled down his cheek, and hit the table. Rep. Deeken softly replied, "You tell your Daddy not to go anywhere. You *are* coming home."

Rep. Deeken said that he has names to call and would get right on it. He told me that he's known Matt Blunt since Matt was knee-high to a grasshopper and that he might ask Blunt to jump in the car and come visit me. Picturing that scenario, I chuckled. I doubt anyone has that much juice!

That's the end of this report. It's my pleasure to send out good news for a change!

November 21, 2006

Dear Marsha,

At mail call last night, I received notice from PEN American that RICHARD GERE and his wife will read an excerpt from my "Contraband" essay next week in New York at a conference about justice in the USA!

Gere's wife, Carey Lowell, played a prosecutor on *Law and Order* years ago. Tiny brunette with short hair. CAN YOU BELIEVE THIS? RICHARD GERE!

Don't have much other news. Our dryer has been broken for a couple of weeks, so laundry is an issue. Our microwave went out Sunday. And we have no hot water. I don't think they love us.

We went to canteen at 10:00 and waited—only to be kicked out at eleven because One House was "fixin' ta hava Code 70." (Code 70 = simulated fire drill.) Then we went into an early count at 11:15. Then count cleared at 12:15 and at 12:30 I went to chow. Then I went back to the canteen to try to get my stuff.

When I left the canteen at one, I headed back to the dorm, but once inside the rotunda, a big fight broke out on D-wing. The guards were too excited to pop our doors, so bunches of us were stuck in the rotunda. I watched as a small, young, male guard was knocked around in his feeble attempt to stop two Black girls from killing each other. I watched the old man officer rush around to the door of D-wing and hit it hard because it was locked. A dozen of us stood and watched as another guard in the rotunda hollered for us to all go back to our wings. I watched as several hollered, "We can't. The doors are locked."

Finally, an old guard showed up, popped the doors, and broke up the fight. We were ordered to go to our rooms until the fighters were cuffed and taken off the house. Then I finally got back to work. Lord only knows what the rest of the day has in store for us.

November 21, 2006

Dear Bell Chevigny,

Late last night at mail call, your letter was handed to me and eagerly I opened it. Mail with the PEN return address has always been good news. But I didn't wear my reading glasses to mail call and had to hold the letter at arm's length to read. (Couldn't wait until I got upstairs to my cell.) Turning to a friend beside me, I pointed to your letter and asked, "Is that Richard Gere?" WOW!

Winning your contest has been a royal hoot! But I only reported the truth. I don't have to make up material. Every prison day provides inane prison stories.

Enclosed is a semi-short bio. Feel free to edit it as needed, of course.

Thank you for all your interest, kindness, and support. If I ever get out of this hellhole, I'd love to meet you all.

Life And Times Of Convict Patricia Prewitt

Luckily, I was born and raised on a cattle ranch east of Kansas City amid a multi-generationally, diversely educated, loving, free-spirited family. Sixteen years after my high school sweetheart and I were married and had five children, he was murdered, and I was attacked in our rural home.

I did not kill my husband, and refused to accept a plea agreement, but was convicted of capital murder a little over a year later, April 1985, and sentenced to "life with no parole for fifty years." Immediately after the trial I returned to my home, family, and community on appeal bond. In April 1986 I lost my appeal and was deposited in prison, where I remain to this day. My first parole consideration hearing will be in mid-2036. If I'm a good old lady, I should be free when I'm in my late eighties.

Although my story is sad, my life is not. I refuse to suppress my natural, joyful nature and work to make each day as productive as possible. Although I'm far away from my children and grandchildren, I mother, teach, and guide them through letters, phone calls, and visits, and take my role seriously. My family is a wellspring of joy and strength for me.

I write to vent, to inform, to make changes, to help, to tell. I write to prison administrators, legislators, family, friends, editors, organizations. I also write software for the Department of Corrections at my daytime gig and teach exercise classes (I'm AFAA certified) as a sideline. At 57, I may be the oldest living aerobics instructor!

Sometimes my words land me in trouble. Recently, I served ten days of room restriction and property impoundment for writing a memo reporting a guard who makes sexual advances to scared young inmates. But I always write the truth—and have accumulated enough to publish a book.

I wrote "Contraband" in lieu of hurling my scrawny body on the concrete in a hysterical screaming fit of frustration. I chose the road less likely to land me in solitary.

December 29, 2006

Dear Nancy,

At 9:30 yesterday morning, I was called to the visiting room for a "legal visit." Turned out to be Rep. Barbara Wall Fraser from Clayton. She said this is her last week as a state legislator, and we've been corresponding for eight years, so she had to meet me. She wore the bracelet that I'd made for her.

We had a nice chat. She's a Democrat, and of no use to me, she says. When Governor Carnahan died, she and the rest of my supporters were all so crushed that they never could get back on their feet. Governor Holden was *not* Carnahan. Barb hopes that Bill Deeken can help. She says we need more Republican help, but I don't know how to corral Republicans.

Yesterday I ran to my dental appointment at 12:30 pm. The crotchety old dentist put a temporary filling in the molar. It's like a piece of fabric that he poked in the hole. He told me not to put floss around that tooth because it will pull the "filling" out. He reported that I'm on the list for fillings, so when my name comes up, I'll get a real filling then. I turned to the tech and mentioned that I have been on the dentist list since June and was told then that it was a six-month wait.

The technician smiled, "Yes."

What? I counted on my fingers: June, July, August, September, October, November, December, "So, it's much more than a six-month wait now?" I asked.

"No, you're on the list. We might get to you in May. Try not to eat on that tooth. Hunk of it will break off."

"But I can't chew on the other side. I have no bottom teeth on that side."

He replied, smiling and chipper: "Like I said, Ms. Prewitt, don't chew on that bad tooth. It might not make it until your name comes up. But you're on the list! Bye."

"Excuse me, but this felt like he just poked toilet paper into the hole. That won't make it five weeks, not to mention the other cavities that need to be filled."

Perkily and vacantly, like the Stepford technician, "You're on the list. Now bye! Baby that tooth, hon!"

"Listen. I love my teeth and want to keep them, but I can't when they break off in hunks."

"Ms. Prewitt, like we told you. You're on the list. Next."

This morning, I noticed that the "temporary filling" is already gone. I must have eaten it with supper!

December 25, 2006

Dearest Momma and Daddy,

Merry Christmas. I don't think I'll get the opportunity to call you today. Not only are the lines for the phone extremely long, but the service is screwed up. We can't hear who we called, but our callee can hear us. That makes for a frustrating conversation.

All in all, the new phone system is a blessing. Not only are the rates fair, ten cents a minute, but we can buy phone minutes at the canteen. That means we aren't required to call collect. And because of that, we can call cell phones. This is a first!

You know yourself that the collect phone rates for prisoners have been horrid for all the years I've been incarcerated. It was around 60 cents a minute to call out of state with a $3 hook-up charge. Many families could not afford to take calls.

Well now some girls are doing without food items at the canteen just so they can contact loved ones. They budget and fret about how many minutes they can buy with their $7.50-a-month state pay—and still buy hygienes and laundry detergent.

Yesterday, as I trudged up the stairs to my floor from aerobics class, Georgia hollered that she'd spoken to her brother on the phone for the first time in three years. She was beaming. We both cried. He only has a cell phone and wouldn't take collect calls. She left instant coffee off her canteen list and bought phone minutes in hopes of hearing her brother's voice.

Because of her lifestyle choices and troubles, Tammy gave her children up for adoption many years ago. Her college-aged daughter recently made contact, and last week Tammy spoke to her on the phone. It was a heart-wrenching conversation for both of them. Tammy also budgeted so she could afford to call this girl, make her explanations, and become acquainted.

Faith's daughter was in labor with their first baby. In Texas! Faith scrimped and saved and got to listen to the baby's birth. That could never happen before. The capability of calling cell phones has opened up a whole world for us. We can check on our families as they are en route to visit us. We are no longer bound to land-lines and collect calls only. Yippee!

January 12, 2007

Dear Mary,

Got the results this week. We all passed the AFAA (Athletics and Fitness Association of America) step aerobics certification that we took in December. We are now studying to be personal fitness trainers.

I may have told you that my temporary filling fell right out, so I dropped three more MSRs (medical services requests) but only received little notices that said I had to wait until my name came up on the never-ending secret list. Grrr. So, I wrote a memo to the dental people and copied my FUM (functional unit manager) and the superintendent. I was called to the dentist today.

The tech was snippy with me right off the bat, "Mrs. Prewitt, we cannot and *will not* keep putting temporary fillings in this tooth. You have two choices. We can smooth down the jagged edge OR put in another temporary filling. But when the temporary filling comes out, we *will not* fix it."

I asked, "How about option #3, fill the tooth?"

"That is *not* an option. You must wait your turn on the list. We will probably get to you by summer." The whole time she was glaring at me.

Sweetly I smiled, "I love my teeth. I have served twenty years and have thirty more to go. I want to keep my teeth. Do you understand? Evidently you went into the field of dental hygiene because you like teeth."

"We understand, but that does not change the fact that there is a six-month waiting list."

"What about the girl on the bench out there who has served three months and is getting the stitches removed from her gums? Was she on the six-month list? I've been on the list since June." Glaring. More glaring.

So, the shaky old dentist with the tuft of goat-like white hair on his chin put a different type of filling in the tooth. (He shakes so much that the little mirror ra-ta-ta-tatted on my tooth while he looked back there.) This filling is not felt fabric. It is white and gooey and set up in about an hour. He accused, "Do you floss this tooth?"

"Yes, my dentist back home, Dr. John Yoder, told me to only floss the teeth I want to keep."

Glaring. As the goat-tuft wiggled at me, he warned, "Well, do not floss *this molar*. You will pull out the filling, and we *won't* do this again." I expected him to bleat, "That would be *baaaaaaaad.*"

While waiting to see the billy-dentist, I met a middle-aged woman from Ohio. She came to St. Louis for a business convention, had a couple of drinks, got into a traffic accident on the way back to the hotel, and killed the driver she hit, leaving three toddlers orphaned. This gal is very nice, smart, and has three grandkids. Isn't that a shame? She told me, "This has had a profound effect on my whole family. And I will never get over the fact that three children lost their mother because of me."

I also met a baby meth-head, who had lost all her teeth by the age of eighteen. She announced, "I've been here since November, and I leave Friday. I'm so ready to go home."

Dryly, I replied, "Everyone here is ready to go home. Even staff."

She went on to explain her vast criminal record, all because of her addiction to meth. I warned her, "Whatever you have done to get in trouble with the law, stop doing it. That's all there is to it. You cannot outsmart the authorities. They have hair-analysis tests that will show if your momma smoked pot in 1967. Do you understand?"

She told me that she'd heard there's a special shampoo sold online for $60 a bottle that will prevent the hair test from being accurate, and rumor has it that hair color will also thwart the test. I scoffed, "Do you really think that the scientists who designed the test didn't think of detergents or superficial chemicals? Testers cut down into the hair shaft past the hair gel, spray, and grease for the sample. This is the twenty-first century. You can't beat them. You can't fool them. If you don't want to keep coming to prison or OD, quit. That's your only option."

A girl on the bench up the hall added, "Amen, Sista."

February 17, 2007

Dearest Gary,

I just heard that my old caseworker from Renz passed away. I worked closely with Nancy at the old prison, and as grandma would have said, "She was a corker!"

I've never known a more generous Department of Corrections employee. Nancy made sure that the girls who had nothing did not go without basic needs like soap and shampoo. She quietly donated hygiene items and paid for them out of her own pocket. I know this because I secretly provided her with names of the truly needy.

Every year Nancy sponsored a Christmas decorating contest, and we'd go all out. I'll never forget the gorgeous nativity scene we fashioned out of cardboard boxes, poster paints, and scrap cloth. (Nancy would not be happy to learn that we prisoners are no longer allowed to decorate in a Christian Christmas tradition. That changed in 1998 when they opened the new prison.)

Nancy refrained from judging the decorating contest, but she always threw a party for the girls who lived in the winning dorm. She brought in summer sausage, cheese, crackers, dip, cookies, and punch, and served us on festive paper plates. Nancy even bought colorful Christmas paper napkins. She knew that the holidays are difficult for prisoners who are away from their families, so she did her level best to brighten our lives.

Nancy also was a loving face we could find in times of trouble. In 1992 when my Matt died, Nancy clutched me and sobbed with me. The family unit was very important to her, and she never treated us like children of a lesser God. She loved us like family. We hated to see her retire in 1995, but we could see how her battle against "the powers that be" was taking a toll on her health.

I will always hold Nancy dear to my heart. "Memories are like stars in the dark night of sorrow." I will hold on to my sweet memories of Nancy Carr.

May 17, 2007

Dearest Gary,

I WON! I WON! I'm still in disbelief even though I have the appeal response in my hot little hand! I WON!

Our grievance officer called me over just now and handed me the response from my grievance against my conduct violation last fall, which resulted in me languishing in a white jumpsuit in my cell for ten long days. The assistant division director of the Division of

Adult Institutions agrees with me. Here's what she wrote on May 5:

"I am in receipt of your grievance appeal request of 12/22/06 regarding your request for a conduct violation issued to you on 9/15/06 for Rule #21.1—Insulting Behavior, to be dismissed and expunged. You claim that you wrote the statement/letter to Williams Waybright, WERDCC Training Officer, regarding COI Capp's (alleged) behavior based on facts and not hearsay. I have reviewed your complaint and pertinent information. After further review and consideration, I am directing via this response for the above noted violation to be dismissed and expunged. Since this is the remedy that you requested, I find this matter resolved."

In essence, she agrees that the officer is indeed "well-known as a pervert." That statement is fact, based on information that the Department of Corrections has.

Of course, the pervert officer in question still works for us. He has not modified his behavior one bit. The only change is that I am vindicated—and the violation will be removed from my record!

But I'm too elated to worry about the big picture. I want to bask in this little victory. One tiny step against Chester the Molester. I WON!

May 22, 2007

Dear Jane and Yeena,

I wish I had a video of Shellie Hendrickson Saturday evening. My housing unit had just come back from dinner, and I was in the bathroom when I heard a voice announce, "Patty Prewitt! Carlene Borden! Shellie Hendrickson wants you and says it's important!" Knowing exactly what she wanted, I pulled on my gray uniform shirt and quickly exited. We can only leave the house during certain times and luckily it was outside smoke break.

As soon as I emerged into the sunlight, I spotted Shellie right outside the chapel—way out of bounds. She lives on the other side of the camp. I jogged toward her, which is also a no-no. A pat search officer walked to her while I ran. She was jumping all over the place, with her hands out in front to protect herself like he might try to catch her, and breathlessly she was assuring him, "It's really important. It's really important!" Then he saw me racing and turned away like he didn't want to be around for these many, blatantly broken rules.

Shellie grabbed me up off my feet in a big bear hug, another infraction of rules, and shouted, "It passed! It passed! I called Joe, and it passed! I know I'm way out of bounds, but I had to come and tell you and Carlene. I just got off the phone, and it passed!" I've never seen Shellie so excited and happy and bursting with good news!

As she turned to leave—to try to get back where she belonged with no trouble—we heard Carlene shout. She was walking as fast as she could toward us. I ran to her, grabbed her arms, and told her that the bill had passed, "You're going home, Carlene! You're going home!" Her mouth fell open, then she slumped in my arms and let loose. Tears everywhere. With an arm around her (more rule breaking), I guided her back to the dorm.

We asked the rotunda officer if she would call Ruby out (she doesn't live in our wing), and the officer agreed since she knew this was something big. Carlene blubbered while I explained to the officer what had happened. Ruby never showed up, so I spotted one of her friends and asked the girl to fetch Ruby. In a few moments, the girl came back to tell us that Ruby was in the shower. I then asked the girl to give Ruby a message. Carlene and I made our way into the dayroom of our wing while a crowd gathered asking questions. Carlene mostly cried and babbled during our "press conference" while I assumed the role of her spokesperson.

Since it was close to time for evening recreation to be called, I ordered Carlene to change shoes so we could walk the track. We certainly couldn't sit down right then! An hour later when we returned, I spied Ruby in the dayroom and motioned for her to come to the rotunda. The same nice officer let us talk. As I told Ruby what Shellie had reported, Ruby began to visibly sink. Thank goodness a chair was handy. Ruby slumped in the chair, closed her eyes, and let the news sink in. She told me that she was in the shower when her friend gave her my message, and she became so flustered she didn't put a towel on her head. It's a wonder she didn't come out of the shower stall stark naked (which would have broken yet another big rule!)!

Ruby is not normally demonstrative, but she pulled me down for a big hug right in front of the officers, then pulled Carlene down. I can't begin to describe to you the joy and relief on their faces. We did a good thing! We pulled off a big prison miracle! The Missouri legislature passed a bill allowing these women to use domestic battering as a defense and therefore be able to have a parole board hearing and parole.

Our next campaign must be to get both Ruby and Carlene ready to see the Parole Board. In Missouri, legislation goes into effect on August 28, so I think they should see the Parole Board on August 29. What do you think? Do you have a game plan to convince the Board of their history of abuse? Please let me know if I need to do anything toward that end. I'm at your service!

We are really going to miss you both. You are the Legal Eagle Dream Team and pulled this off. You should both be very proud of yourselves. When you come to talk to Carlene and Ruby, I hope you call me out, too. I'd love to see your sweet faces and share in our victory! God bless.

June 12, 2007

Dear Mary,

Sorry it's taken so long to get back to you, but things here have been on the hectic/strange side. What's been happening is hard to explain to "outsiders," but the bottom line is that our rooms have been "tossed" or "trashed" or "searched" every day for the last week...perfume.

The guards are looking for perfume.

Perfume is contraband in this camp, but women being women

find a way to procure colognes and perfume oils. It's my understanding that friendly staff supply the smelly goods, but I don't know that for a fact since I haven't worn perfume for many, many years—and am not about to go to great lengths to gain expensive contraband. And another venue is the transfers from prison at Chillicothe. Perfume is sold there, so the girls who transfer always have plenty to share or sell.

Some plastic eyedrop bottles of perfume were found in a room upstairs in my wing. Uh oh! I knew we were in for it. Then one more was found sewn into a dog toy downstairs in a "dog room." We have a dog-training program on my wing which has been just lovely—it's great to play with assorted breeds of canines after so many years away from all animals, but that's another subject entirely.

This was the search from hell. The unfortunate residents of B-wing sat in the dayroom yesterday from 2:15 until 5:30 while a team of officers searched everything we own. The team tossed photos, clothes, blankets, letters, magazines, food, plastic bowls, pillows—everything you can think of—out into the hall. When the search was over, a few inmates were chosen to sweep the spoils into trash bags before we were allowed back into our cells to assess the damage.

Rox helped and reported that someone had opened a jar of pickles and thrown it into the hall. So many photos and papers were ruined by the juice. One of the nicer officers warned Rox to watch her step and not hurt her knee again. (Rox had surgery last year.)

Tearfully, girls told me that their photos of their children were gone. Delila's son is in Iraq, and they threw out the only photos she had of him because they were "computer-generated." I tried to explain to the sergeant that most all photos and mail is now computer-generated, but he refused to comprehend, since this was an on-the-fly rule of which he was proud.

Some of the girls called home in tears, so their mothers called the prison to ask what the heck happened. Those calls earned the ear of the administration, so two of our superintendents showed up. Tammy was crying and trying to mop up her area when one super arrived to see that the searching officer had maliciously poured a big tumbler of coffee all over her photos and bedding. That super ordered the officers to go pick through the trash and return our stuff—at least the stuff that was salvageable.

Today all the dogs were loaded up and taken home. The kennels were removed to the warehouse. All signs of the dog training program have been removed. Even the photos on the bulletin board. Several of the trainers keep crying. Their hearts are broken. We all will miss our wet dog kisses. Instead of punishing the offending party, they have opted to punish everyone. But I didn't really expect anything less.

July 1, 2007

Dear Marsha,

The PEN American people wrote and asked if I'd answer some questions about my writing for them to post on their website. As a writer, you might be interested in my responses:

What was the spark that made you begin writing in prison? When did it occur?
When I was sent to prison in April 1986, my five children were ages eight to sixteen. As soon as I was allowed to purchase paper and pen, I began writing poems and stories as a means to communicate with them—as an outlet of my love for them. Collect phone calls are expensive and visits short (and not private); therefore, I suppose the writing "spark" was separation from my dear family. In my free life, I owned and operated a lumberyard-hardware store, ran a small farm, and drove kids all over creation to rehearsals, meetings, games, lessons, etc., which left me with no time to creatively put pen to paper.

Which authors influenced you? Do you gain benefit from studying their work, or do you feel that your influences come from a different place?

I was raised in the loving arms of a huge extended family on a ranch east of Kansas City. In the '50s TV was a mere novelty, and my paternal grandparents, both University of Missouri alumni, owned a huge collection of books—a room full. I cut my teeth on the classics but also found a stash of trashy Frank G. Slaughter novels hidden in the attic. So, it's difficult for me to point to any one particular influence.

My paternal great grandmother, a retired literature professor, babysat my brother, sister, and me often and had us act out Shakespeare scenes as a way to manage us. It wasn't until I reached high school that I realized she didn't make up that stuff.

I grew up with three special girlfriends. Two are professional writers and one is a corporate attorney. I'm sure our dedicated teachers had something to do with that outcome, although they cannot be blamed for my bad end!

What have you learned from writing?
I have learned that when I feel the most helpless, I am not. As long as I can report, I have power. I have raised my children with words of encouragement and love. I have made changes in the public perceptions of prisoners with words. My words have changed rules, policies, and laws. Words can console, shock, teach, persuade, touch, hurt, move, enlighten, lift, guide, and change us all. It is a pleasure and a privilege to choose my words carefully.

Describe your process of writing in prison. What philosophies and thoughts help you sustain the drive to write? Are you able to share your work with anyone? What are the most challenging aspects of creating in prison?
Everything good in prison is a challenge. For example, a few years ago I mailed a copy of a huge manuscript to a friend-of-a-friend editor/author for his opinion. (Copies were ten cents per page— not to mention postage.) He graciously red-penciled pages with suggestions but, by prison mail policy, could not mail it back to me in the three big clasp envelopes in which I'd sent it out. We are allowed to receive only five enclosures in one envelope—that means

five pieces of paper that are not a "letter." Sending the edited book back to me became a long, drawn-out, expensive ordeal. In the end, he sent me only the pages that held comments, to save postage.

Prisons are extremely noisy day and night. Heavy doors slam. Loudspeakers squawk. Overcrowded women holler over the din. Concentration skills are acquired. I can now tune out whole riots if I'm really into my work. Mothering five active children, while running a home, business, and going to college, was a good start at becoming a professional blocker-outer.

I write to vent, to inform, to rectify wrongs, to entertain, so I share my writings with anyone who's interested—and sometimes even when they're not. Also, if anyone, staff or inmate, needs an important letter, grievance, or proposal composed, I'm their gal. In the Land of Illiteracy, my communication skills keep me busy. Recently I penned a piece of state legislation that was actually passed and will free four deserving women who were prevented from presenting evidence of spousal abuse at their murder trials.

Do you feel that writing has become a permanent and necessary feature in your life?
As long as laws need to be created or changed, injustices plague our prison, daily life gives me stories to tell, my scrawny hands can grip a pen, and I have breath in my aging body, I will write.

Do you have access to a library? What books are there?
Because of my long-houred work schedule, prison overcrowding, and the limited library hours, I rarely get to hang out in the library anymore. I am fortunate to be a member of Prison Performing Arts, our "theater class." My instructor, Agnes Wilcox, brings in literature, poems, quotes, books, postcards, and all sorts of stimulating information. Not only do we perform plays, like *Macbeth*, *Crowns*, and *Midsummer Night's Dream*, we write and perform our own poetry.

Fortunately, friends often run to me, "You've *got* to read this book! Right now!" So, I get a novel without the library hassle. Our librarians are dedicated to offering a variety of books for our wide variety of needs, reading skills, and interests, and they sweetly honor sincere requests.

Are you able to read and study in prison, or are there major obstacles preventing this?

Like I said before, noise is a concentration deterrent. Also, many staff members seem to disapprove of inmates gaining education. Our study guides and papers are lost in shakedowns, or we are harassed trying to even get to class. Recently, two folders of information in regard to a personal training course I'm taking were lost in a cell search. All we can do is grin and bear it. Persevere!

I'd love to take correspondence courses, but they're expensive. Some of my friends are taking college courses through the mail—but getting their textbooks in, taking proctored tests, and mailing the books back out have proved to be a struggle for every course. Few tackle such a mountain of problems even if they can afford tuition, book fees, and postage.

My prison job, for the last twelve years, is writing computer software for the Department of Corrections on the IBM AS/400. In prison terms, I'm well paid, and that skill has allowed me to purchase a typewriter, expensive ribbons, and paper. Base pay for most inmates in Missouri is $8.50 a month if you have your GED, $7.50 if not. Basic hygiene needs are not met on such a stipend. Those girls can hardly afford the luxury of a pad of paper and pen.

Do you believe there is a certain type of responsibility for writers who have some connection with incarceration? Do you have themes that you return to?

I only write the truth. I have no need to embellish. The truth is awful enough. I feel a responsibility to report not only what happens but how we feel about what happens. My stories and poems are simply about my life in prison. I guess that's my theme, since it's what I know. But I leave certain subjects alone, at least for the time being, because of the risk involved. If I reported certain taboo happenings, I would live in jeopardy. In other words, I would get slammed in the hole under investigation for many, many months. "Cuffed and stuffed." Until I'm free, I must edit what I report. But if I ever get out of here, Katie bar the door!

Feel free to share anything about your work that is not reflected in the preceding questions and answers.
Thank you to PEN American Center and all the dedicated, involved individuals who have created an outlet for incarcerated writers. Gandhi said, "Be the change you wish to see in the world..." You obviously live by that mantra. Thank you for the opportunity to share myself with an ever-widening circle of friends.

July 5, 2007

Dear Nancy,

You haven't heard from me for a while because I've been too busy to answer right away. My theater group has been working hard to prepare for and perform *A Midsummer Night's Dream*. Getting anything done in prison is NOT easy! But we pulled it off.

We performed two shows Tuesday, June 26, for visitors and staff, which was great fun. We were strip-searched six times that day. I also had four costume changes, so you can guess how many times I pulled shirts over my head! I played Theseus, the Duke of Athens, in a conservative navy blazer; Tom Snout, the Tinker, in overalls; and Oberon, the King of the Fairies, in flower-child hippie garb and a headband.

Gary came to the evening show and even went out to dinner with a group of Prison Performing Arts supporters, who were mostly Washington University professors and scientists. He had a lovely time and made new friends. (Gary's been busy with hospice and loves to entertain the families at the Hospice House in KC.)

The next day we had to lug the stage and everything to the gym, and we performed for the R&O's (Receiving and Orientation—new girls.) There are over 200 of these new kids. No one had informed them that they were there to see a play. As I handed out the playbills, I heard many grumbles, "Hey, I came here to play volleyball!" But thankfully after our performance, those same gals sought me out to tell me that they really enjoyed themselves. It never ceases to amaze me how many prisoners have never, ever seen any kind of live play or been to a theater. The TV and video generation.

Thursday afternoon we performed for the Drug Treatment girls. We had a small crowd because rehab gals pay in some way for doing anything out of the usual "treatment" routine. We were very thankful after the show when one announced, "This was worth missing a smoke break and a happy nap." That's saying a lot!

That same night a big crowd of our friends from "general population" came to the gym to be entertained. They were a great audience: laughed at the funny parts, cried at the heartfelt poems. And we really hammed it up for them.

I'm exceptionally proud of my sister actors. None had ever acted before, and certainly none had any prior contact with Shakespeare. With guidance and clarity from our instructor Agnes Wilcox, they threw themselves into their roles, memorized pages of words. They overcame their stage fright enough to dig in.

Our new assistant warden does not approve of our poetry and wants us to just study published poets, but Agnes convinced him to allow us to also write *if* we use a "real" poem as our inspiration. We had to read our poems to him prior to the show. He had a problem with Robin's poem about her father's sexual abuse because she used the word "bed," as in, "when he came to my bed." Our censor doesn't ever want any mention of sex no matter how tastefully it's done. Missouri prisoners are G-rated creatures and never had any sex, wanted or unwanted.

Sunday, the 24th, my youngest daughter Carrie and her hubbie brought Callie and four-year-old Drew here to visit for Callie's sixth birthday. We got permission for them to bring in cupcakes for our little party. Carrie mentioned that my fifty-eighth birthday was close to Callie's, but I could tell that Callie was not eager to share the spotlight!

A bunch of our BLAST (Better Living Awareness Support Team) girls have gotten in trouble and are on recreation restriction, so a handful of us are covering all exercise classes. I have to fill in for Shellie's Shell-Bo class. It's a spin on Tae-Bo. I told the class that this was "My-Bo" now!

PEN American, the organization for prison writers, asked me to answer a slew of interview questions to be posted on their website since I won their writing contest last year. I mailed that off last night.

Saturday an officer was escorted off the premises and is under investigation for charges of rape. He's been a problem for many years. Good riddance to bad rubbish. That makes two in the last six months. The Department of Corrections *knows* about their problem guards, but they turn a blind eye until their behavior gets out of hand. I'd write a poem about it, but the assistant warden would *really* hate that! Ha!

On Tuesday, for my birthday, I was spoiled by the young girls on my dorm. They fed me prison pizza and prison cake. It's amazing how creative prisoners can be with canteen food. I appreciated their efforts. Most have not the best mothers, so I mother them all.

Yesterday, for the Fourth of July, we BLAST girls hosted "Olympic" games. I ran the horseshoe toss. We can't have stakes of any kind or metal horseshoes, so we toss rubber horseshoes into hula hoops. I played a W.C. Fields carnie all day, "Come here, little girl. Everyone's a winner." One girl told me that I was the most fun! I knew I was the most outlandish!

On Monday I called Dale Whiteside, who's going to visit the governor's chief counsel in a week to talk about clemency for me and a couple of other gals like me. Sweet Dale has been trying to free us since the early '90s.

In regard to our nightmare big search of June 11, several of the officers got chewed out for their behavior, which is small consolation, but a severe scolding may make them think twice before they destroy photos and mementos. All in all, this place is a zoo. Ya gotta keep your sense of humor but not laugh at the "handlers."

August 8, 2007

Dear Sarah,

Thirty-nine years ago today, two scared skinny college kids, high school sweethearts, were married. His parents were upset and pouting because the kids refused to endure a big lavish traditional wedding, so the groom's older sister and her husband met the young couple at the First Methodist Church after work and stood up for them. The bride's brother and sister were too young for such responsibility.

The groom stood darkly handsome in his black suit trousers, a short-sleeve, white cotton shirt, and a narrow, blue-striped tie that matched his eyes. His brown-eyed girl wore a lavender mini tent dress with a white Peter Pan collar. His short-cropped and her waist-length straight hair were the same shade of mahogany.

She was so nervous that she messed up the vows—couldn't simply repeat after the minister. It was so hot. She wore nylon stockings on her long, thin, tan legs. No A/C in churches in those days. And no bare legs.

No reception. After the brief nuptials, his sister snapped a photo of the kids, and they hopped into their candy apple red '67 Mustang convertible. With the white top down, of course. Sailing out of town, her long, dark hair waved goodbye to their hometown as they plunged, fender first, into their young marriage.

Never looking back, they headed east and south toward Branson and made it to Clinton by dusk. Found a beautifully seedy motel on the main drag that boasted cool air-conditioned rooms. Times Square Motel. Had a dinner plate-sized clock that didn't work, frozen in time, mounted next to the flashing neon "Vacancy" sign.

Greasy drive-in burgers and fries eaten in the car for their wedding dinner. They were too young, scared, and green to be anything but happy. It was an adventure. Too naïve, unworldly kids out on their own. They weren't old enough to purchase alcohol, but they did buy a pack of Winstons. The motel provided free "Times Square" matchbooks in clear glass "Times Square" ashtrays.

As the newly hitched couple shyly perched on the edge of the double bed and choked on the smoke, they burst into laughter. They really were free and not free—all at once. Free of their parents and forever bonded to each other.

I will always miss your Daddy, Sade.

August 27, 2007 (Sarah's 36th Birthday)

Dear Nancy,

I called Gary right before the 11:30 count today, and he told me that Danny Kohl, Washington University professor friend who's trying to help me get free, had just asked about my history with the Midwest Innocence Project. Well, funny he should ask. This weekend, I got some interesting news.

Get this: Saturday night, while I folded my laundry on the dryer, a middle-aged Black convict slid into the laundry room to show me a news clipping about a wrongfully convicted man from South Carolina who had been freed with DNA evidence. She then went on about how the Innocence Project was working with her and how she would be free very soon. I asked her which Innocence Project was helping her, and she answered, as I feared, "MIP, The Midwest Innocence Project out of Kansas City."

Putting my hand on her shoulder, I advised kindly, "Hon, don't get too enthused over that bunch. A couple of years ago, they dropped me with not so much as a 'see ya.'"

Her eyes grew wide and she gasped, "Oh my gosh! My MIP investigator told me that he'd called the Innocence Project about eighteen months ago to offer his free help, but no one ever responded. He then nosed around and found out that the office had been left empty for a year. The attorney who ran it up and left with no notice. So that's probably what happened in your case. You have got to write those people. I'll give you their address."

Left with no word! I'd never thought of that scenario. After all, I never heard back from them, and I took it personally. Thought they hated *me*.

Every Sunday morning, I cook up a big batch of my famous red-hot beans and rice for the occupants of my room, and we six eat together Sunday night. It's my weekly treat to them. And I cook early because I'm busy all day. Yesterday was no different. At 7:00 am while I fried diced summer sausage in the microwave in the dayroom, Bertha called me over to the phone to talk to Charlie Snyder, the investigator she'd mentioned to me the night before. I gave him a fast run down of my case, while Bertha watched the meat cook. Charlie promised that he would nose around the office and see if the previous bunch had left any files on me.

Turns out that former MIP attorney Phil Gibson opened a law firm in Blue Springs (just East of KC) after he dumped the Innocence Project. And the new Midwestern Innocence Project no longer uses law students, which is a good thing. (To students we are homework—and they only work a few months on a case.)

Back in January 2004, I was told to call my attorney. Since I don't have an attorney, I called the number provided with trepidation. Attorney Phil Gibson with the Midwest Innocence Project answered the phone and told me that out of over 800 applications, they had chosen me.

Gibson stated that he was privy to the late Governor Carnahan's plan to commute my sentence, and he went on to say that he also knew that in October Governor Holden had denied my application for executive clemency. He promised that a wrongful convictions class at the UMKC Law School would research my case.

Sometime after that, we arranged a conference call with that class. I was in the caseworker's office trying to speak about the worst event of my life while my caseworker kept coming in and looking for stuff. What an ordeal.

Then, some months after that phone call, Gibson visited me with attorney Mark Thomason, who planned to investigate. Mr. Gibson was really mean to me that day. Grumpy. He even told me that it bothered him that I had had trouble answering all the students' questions on the phone. He thought that I should know all of the events of 1984 and '85 with no hesitation. I guess he has no clue how some of us shovel dirt over the dead past—and don't dig it up easily.

Gibson also said that they chose me to investigate, only because some rich "bitch" MIP board member had pushed the issue. He didn't like my case since I had no DNA evidence. Yeah, he was a sweetheart that day. Shoot, for all I know he was having a breakdown, then left the MIP shortly after that.

Mark even met with my family and promised to investigate the case in Holden and get back with them, but he didn't.

In the middle of all that, the MIP dropped off the face of the planet to us. It was not until Saturday night that the mystery was solved for me. So, we'll see...

My folks are going to Hannibal for their honeymoon this weekend—dining and dancing. They'll visit me Sunday. Daddy can't drive after dark, so they will taxi from the motel to the riverboat. Gary will be here this weekend, too. He loves to visit with them.

September 25, 2007

Dear Nancy,

I really hate to always be the bearer of bad news, but here I am again. On August 28, your birthday, Governor Matt Blunt denied my latest bid for clemency. I just received notice from the chairman of the Board of Probation and Parole at mail call. We are never given a reason. The chairman did mention that I can reapply again in three years. I've lost track of how many tries I've lost. This is the fastest denial so far. Just applied in December.

I also feel sorry for Representative Bill Deeken. He had written to me this summer that he planned to approach the governor when he's close to going out of office. He never guessed that the governor would sign my denial papers so quickly.

So here we are. Back at the drawing board. I read that Thomas Edison said failures bring us one step closer to success, or something like that. But it sure doesn't feel that way.

January 11, 2008

Dearest Gary,

Can't wait to see you tomorrow, although I know you are extremely weary of prison visiting. But even the most stubborn Scotsman would tire of this particular, suppressed activity, after nearly a decade.

This week I single-handedly wrote every prisoner in the state who's under the same prison sentence as me. The sentence of "life with no parole for fifty years" was only on the books from 1978 until 1984. It's labeled as capital murder, but capital is for the death penalty now. I'm hoping to create a grassroots campaign to rescind our old, outdated sentences. I decided to rattle all their cages. There are a number of sharp legal eagles in the men's prisons.

Oh, and everyone loves the big mule head I crocheted for *Midsummer Night's Dream*. As I entered my wing, the rotunda officer asked what was in my bag. Looking him straight in the eye, I honestly informed him that I was "dragging my ass home."

February 3, 2008

Dear Jennifer Whitney,

Received your JPay email Friday night at mail call. Although I wonder how you plan to tell my story in photos—since my husband was murdered 24 years ago—I'm always willing to help a student. So, count me in.

I have no internet access, but I did alert my daughters this weekend and gave them your online addresses. Getting to a phone in this prison is not easy. We have three phones for around 85 women—and we can only call during specific times, so it's a battle.

I attempted to call you Saturday night, but my youngest daughter Carrie reminded me that you just don't call college students on Saturday mornings. Sorry. I was not thinking.

The only lawyer who has worked on my case in ages is law

professor Jane Aiken. She was with Washington University but moved up in the world to Georgetown University. She's wonderful!

If I put you on my visiting list, you would not be allowed to bring a camera in. There are strict rules for visitors. In fact, the administration doesn't even like cameras. I believe you will have to call the prison and ask for my caseworker, Jennifer Raspberry, to get the ball rolling—to acquire an interview time and date.

Also, we have a new phone system, so I can now call cell phones and pay for the call myself. You cannot send me stamps, but don't worry. I work as a computer programmer and make a very good wage (by prison standards). It's true that most prisoners make $8.50 a month, the base pay, but I'm now making $275 a month. (I've worked hard to be well paid.)

My theater class, sponsored by Prison Performing Arts out of St. Louis, is performing the middle part of *A Midsummer Night's Dream* in the visiting room February 19 at 1:00 pm and 6:00 pm. If you want to attend, call Office Manager Dan Martin or Director Agnes Wilcox and explain your mission. Dan can put you on the list. We perform for administration, visitors, family, PPA members, etc. in the visiting room on that Tuesday—then take the show to the gym for the prison population on Wednesday and Thursday. And we perform our poetry, too.

I'm mailing this in case I don't catch you on the phone. I look forward to meeting you and hope that your master's project gets you a big fat A!

February 26, 2008

Dear Agnes, Beth, and Dan,

Senator Joan Bray's intern, Tracy McCreery, came to our PPA performance and met me. We corresponded last year when we were trying to pass that bill that eventually was tacked onto a house bill.

Tracy sent me a sweet note that I must share with you: "Dear Patty, a big congratulations and thank you to the entire cast of *A*

Midsummer Night's Dream. The whole evening was very special. I really admire how the poets were able to open up their souls. I was so moved by Mary Oliver's poems that I requested a book from my library."

So, our poetry mission with Spoken Word is affecting more people than we even thought about. Isn't that cool?

Gary mailed me the loose pages of Callie's book, *Kalamazoo Zoo.* Dan, you did a wonderful job putting my story and her drawings together! Thank you so very much. At mail call, the whole dayroom full of women were oooh-ing and ahhh-ing over it last night. Callie is ecstatic and thinks she's published!

Saturday my daughter Carrie told me that Callie had finally asked about me being in prison, so Carrie gave her the six-year-old version of events. She then warned me that Callie had questions for me. Before we left, Callie culled me from the herd, bored into me with those big brown eyes, and leaned in whispering, "Granny, Momma told me about her daddy and why you're in prison. But why did they think it was you?"

I told her that the police didn't believe her mother and Aunt Sarah because they were so young. I added, "Has a grownup ever failed to believe you—even when you're telling the honest truth?"

Wide-eyed and deadly serious, Callie nodded. "Yes, Granny, it happens all the time." That seemed enough for her, but I'm sure there's more to come. This was not my first grandchild conversation. We digest these matters in small bites.

April 13, 2008

Dear Sarah,

I'm almost too tired to write this letter. We performed *Grease* all week. It was fun, but we did like eight shows over four days. Lots of dancing, too. Janiece directed and created a bunch of the choreography. I ended up playing Cha Cha, the "fast" girl, only because the dress fit me and no one else! Isn't that wild? I wonder how many parts are doled out just because the costume fits?

The dress fit me, but it was cut way too low for prison. I ended up with a piece of white state sheet stretched across my bosom as camouflage.

Anyway, I had a solo, too. I sang, "Look at Me." I wish they would let us perform in the visiting room for you all, but we're working on it for the next play. Moving the set from the gym to the visiting room would be a major pain, but it would be worth it. I'll enclose a playbill. You can see the white bodice-covering sheet in the picture.

June 1, 2008

Dear Janie,

Play rehearsals in our prison can be hectic and unfocused. The women have appointments elsewhere, some don't show, some sneak out to catch a smoke, and some have their attention drawn elsewhere.

One Thursday afternoon in May, as Bottom the Weaver, I curled up with my Titania at the front of the rehearsal room—entwined in a very G-rated way. We feigned sleep while other actors emoted behind us. At least I was pretending to slumber. Tracey, a healthy Black woman, who must have been very weary, became heavier and heavier on me, pushing my slight bony frame into the concrete floor as she snored softly in my ear. Tracey wasn't acting.

I tried to ignore my physical discomfort, which bordered on excruciating pain, by working on my next lines in my head. Completely into my next scene, or at least my brain was, my senses were shocked when a big, wet tongue dove deep down into my ear canal. What? Had Tracey lost her ever-lovin' mind? Jerking upright, and thereby startling my sleeping Titania, I whirled around to look squarely into the happily panting face of Hobo, the pup.

We have a dog-training program at our prison called CHAMP. Inmate trainers work with service dogs for handicapped clients and work with rescue dogs salvaged from the death row of kennels. Rescue dogs are cleaned up, given a minimum of manners lessons, and adopted out. The charming, untrained Hobo, a pitbull mix, was the responsibility of one of our actors and joined us at rehearsal to entertain us all.

Everyone enjoyed a good laugh. The other actors had been observing Hobo slowly sniffing and sneaking his way toward Tracey and me and shrieked when he unexpectedly stuck his wet tongue into my defenseless ear. Professor Beth Charlebois, a Shakespeare expert who's helping Agnes produce *A Midsummer Night's Dream*, got the biggest kick out of Hobo because she adores him and thinks he can do no wrong, while I keep a watchful eye on him. Don't need another doggie ear wash like that again.

June 11, 2008

Dear Beth,

I called Carrie last night about getting glasses for Janiece, because she has no one in the world to do it. I had written a whole story to Carrie to explain and called her last night to see if she would buy the glasses. When she answered, she started right in, "Momma, as soon as I got your letter, I ran out to Walmart and checked prices and frames. And Janiece is *blind*! Her prescription is off the charts. Literally." (I love my kids!)

She expressed concern about choosing the frame style and size, and I admitted, "Well, Janiece is not small. Do you remember her from the play?" Carrie then replied that she had a picture of her. That's when I found out that you had already emailed the photos.

Also, I mailed the lion headdress and paws that I'd made to Callie and Drew. Carrie reported that when they arrived, Callie put them right on and never spoke the rest of the day. She only roared. I think she's a method actor.

A baby was born in a housing unit bathroom last Thursday. Friday morning, I was standing in the dayroom waiting for the call on the loudspeaker to go to work when a woman walked up to me grinning from ear to ear, "Patty, last night I was called out of bed to go to 4-House to clean up blood (that's her job—bodily fluid cleaner upper). I was not happy about it and stomped all the way over there. When I walked through the door to the wing, here comes an inmate on a stretcher wheeled by EMTs, and she had a baby in her arms!"

That doesn't happen every day—I actually can't remember it ever happening before, and I've been locked up for over twenty-two years. Work was called, and as I walked to my job, I saw 4-House girls waiting outside the canteen. Pam Fann has glow-in-the-dark dyed blonde hair, so I hollered, "Canned Ham, did you deliver a baby last night?"

Pam turned to me beaming, "No, I didn't, but this little girl did."

The young white girl next to her could not hide her pride and awe, "Yes, ma'am, three of us did, and Sgt. Taylor helped."

I pressed on for the story. It seems that the pregnant gal had "self-declared" twice that day complaining of pressure and pain. The nurses sent her back with, "This is your first baby. You'll know when the time comes."

Pam mentioned that when the newborn first cried, every woman on the wing cried, too. My eyes water just writing about it. People die in here. Death seems a normal element in hell, but the miracle of new life right here in this awful place *is* a *miracle*! Everyone in camp seemed lighter that day. More loving. Touched by goodness and hope.

I also heard that the new mother plans to make Taylor the baby boy's middle name, thanks to the officer who helped bring him into the world.

This morning as I walked through the rotunda on my way back from breakfast, the rotunda officer stopped me, "Ms. Prewitt, I have a question for you." I stopped because I have to, not because I wanted to. We have history.

A few years ago, I taught yoga in the Treatment housing unit at 6:00 am. I saw this perv guard leering at girls in the shower, reported it, and was written up. I spent ten long days in punishment and filed a grievance which I eventually won! But he didn't lose his job. Dozens of grievances have been filed against him. Hundreds of complaints, but, as he puts it, he's Teflon. Kevlar. Untouchable.

That particular guard recently moved to the midnight shift of my housing unit. He stares at me as I sit waiting for breakfast. I stare back fearlessly. I know he's plotting a way to plunge his word of retaliation into my tender underbelly. The game began this morning.

Two other officers stood nearby, so he whispered, "Ms. Prewitt, I have a question for you. I know you're a member of the legal team."

Puzzled, I replied, "No…" I spoke loudly enough to gain the attention of the two officers.

"I mean, Ms. Prewitt, that you do a lot of work in the law library on cases and law."

I looked at him like he had two heads, "No."

"Ms. Prewitt, weren't you a lawyer before?"

I was done with this game. Curtly, I pronounced, "No, I write software."

As I headed for the door, he leered, "Oh, I must have the wrong person." I kept walking. Try as he might, he can't push any of my buttons. Talking to him is dangerous. He's looking for a reason to cuff me and take me to the hole. I do my best to make sure he and I are never alone. He could easily lie that I said something and take me down. That's what he wants.

My Gary didn't get to attend our performance because he was in Northern California. He gave away the bride, his goddaughter, and learned how to fly-fish trout. He leaves today for Georgia. He and his siblings are moving his mother to Topeka soon, since his father passed away.

The big talk of this camp is anger because makeup has been banned. No one knows why, of course. So, these insipid guards are walking up close to girls and eyeballing their eyes to see if they are wearing the dreaded eyeliner or eyeshadow. Someday I will laugh at this, but it won't be today. It's *so stupid*! This is a maximum-security prison. Makeup has been sold for decades at the canteen. Suddenly makeup is big contraband. Don't they have anything important to do? Like stop fights or drugs?

The girls who have tattooed eyeliner are constantly harassed. It makes my asshole pucker. (My old heroin-addict friend Mickie used that saying, and it fits.)

July 15, 2008

Dear Bob and Jan,

I love your handcrafted belated birthday card. Gorgeous. And the sentiment brought tears to my eyes. Bob looks great. I like the white beard. My hair is salt and pepper now—more salt.

Thank you for your prayers. They mean so much to me. I have supporters who are attempting to convince the outgoing Governor Blunt to commute my sentence before he leaves, but I have so many who work just as hard to keep me inside. Prosecutor Mary Ann Young and Sen. Scott, along with my sisters-in-law, are tireless about it.

The kids are great. The girls live in Lee's Summit, and Morgan recently moved to a place outside Pleasant Hill. Janie's fighting her cancer as best she can with no health insurance or money.

My parents soon will have been wed for sixty years, and the family is throwing a wingding on Sept 27. Momma didn't want all the fuss, but I told her that when she and Daddy fell in love and started this family, this party was inevitable. I'd sure love to be there. I miss out on all the fun.

July 17, 2008

Dear Senator Matt Bartle:

My mother, Ann Slaughter, informed me that she recently called you asking for your assistance in procuring inmate Roberta Carlene Borden a parole board hearing date. I want to thank you and your staff for your prompt attention to that matter and inform you that yesterday Ms. Borden was indeed issued a hearing date. She's scheduled for her parole consideration hearing on Monday, September 15, 2008.

The entire prison, inmates and staff, were jumping for joy and crying yesterday when we got the news. Carlene is still in shock. October 17 will mark thirty years of incarceration for her. You can't imagine how she feels. The possibility of returning home after three decades is overwhelming.

Last evening I called my parents with the news, and Carlene was on the other phone calling her family. There were whoops of joy at both ends of the connection. Carlene's family can't wait to get her home. Her son and daughter were teenagers when she left—and now Carlene is a great-grandmother.

Three other longtime incarcerated women who qualify under the law were also provided with the same hearing date. These four women were not allowed to use domestic violence as a defense at trial and will now find justice. It took you, your staff, and a gaggle of attorneys to pull this off.

Again, thank you and your staff for your assistance in urging the parole board to honor the provisions of the house bill that was passed and signed into law last year. Your intervention is very much appreciated.

July 24, 2008

Dear Mary,

Today at 4:20 pm when count was announced on the loudspeaker, Heather scurried in, threw herself on the bunk, and sobbed into her pillow. We five cellmates averted our eyes to offer her a bit of privacy. She will confide—if and when she wants.

Only twenty-three, Heather has bunked in my room for nearly a year, and although she's never acted like this before, I have a hunch I know what prompted her breakdown. This weekend she's taking the mandatory-to-pending-parolees ICVC class: Impact of Crime on Victims Class.

The curriculum is designed to heap shame and guilt on offenders and force them to not only name all the people they hurt but also take responsibility for their crimes. It's tough. Unrelenting. Hopefully, the class knocks some sense into some girls, but for the wrongly convicted, this class is an instrument of torture.

Heather was a college coed who came up pregnant. (So far, this story is not unusual. Girls have succumbed to this fate since the first day university doors opened to females.) As a single, proud new mom, she was forced to quit school and find a job to support her bundle of joy, but she made the fatal mistake of relying on the babysitting help of the baby's daddy, who already had a couple of kids. If she had known what was truly in his heart, she would never have allowed any of this to occur. But we mortals can't peer into the hearts of others. We are all just guessing here.

One sad day, she returned from work, he concocted a lame story, and her unresponsive baby was quickly rushed to the hospital. Sick at heart, frantic with worry, and without a clue, she was questioned by white-coated staff. Since abuse had never existed in Heather's world as an adored only child, she didn't readily see where these questions were headed.

I can sympathize. Many summers ago, my towheaded toddler Matthew tripped and sliced open his brow bone on the sharp brick hearth—while my mom was watching him and the girls. Upstairs from the tub, with shampoo lathered into my Cher-long hair, I heard the scream. In hindsight, I must have looked a crazed mess with dried suds stiffening my windblown, fright-wigged tresses as I leaped into the emergency room while pressing my profusely bleeding and loudly screaming diaper-clad boy to my heaving bosom. Get the picture, Mary?

The ER attending grilled me like a hotdog, "Taking care of little ones who get into everything is not easy. Miss, do you anger easily?"

"What? Anger? Yeah, when some kid doctor thinks I could hurt my precious baby boy! More stitching and less talking, please, Doc." I might have looked mad, but I wasn't mad at Matthew.

When Heather's truth came to light—that the baby's daddy had brutally beaten the infant—Heather was beside herself with waves of anger, disbelief, grief, betrayal, panic, desperation, and mostly pure, white-hot rage. And to make horrible matters worse, the authorities were eyeing her as an accomplice—as if she would ever, ever harm a hair on her sweet daughter's angelic head.

The next months were a haze of hospitals, doctors and nurses, police, social workers, and lawyers. A mother's worst nightmare. In the end, the baby-beater copped to a plea of six short years. Heather was bull-headed for a jury trial, when someone finally crammed reality down her throat: "A jury here in the heartland will eat you alive, little girl.

You had a baby out of wedlock. Strike one. With a biracial man. Strike two. Your baby was hurt so badly that she'll never live a normal healthy life. Strike three. You're out."

So, Heather reluctantly accepted the plea agreement for "child endangerment" and got three years. She left her injured daughter with her mother and went to prison. She will serve two years or more, then parole to her mother and daughter. But there is actually no "happily ever after" after prison for the misfortunate who must falsely endure their punishment.

The bottom line is that she did *not* make the decision to commit a crime that would bring her to prison. Neither did I. I'm not saying we are angels, but we are not criminals. And those of us who are not guilty of breaking the law do our prison time in a different way than anyone else. We are loners. Friendly loners, but loners, nonetheless. We don't fit in. We just learn to blend in.

We can't relate to the murderers, because we didn't take a life, although I totally sympathize with battered women. (As my cowboy daddy commented years ago after I explained that one of my prison friends had killed her abusive spouse, "He was asking for it.") We have no connection to robbers, armed or otherwise, because we thieved from no one. Heather and I never did, sold, or manufactured illegal drugs. We never passed bad checks or ran filched credit cards. We never stole cars or cattle. We never cooked anyone's books or embezzled money. We never assaulted anyone. We never destroyed public or private property. Neither one of us was ever issued one DUI, much less the multitude required to bring one to prison. We never pledged membership or affiliation to a person, gang, or group that broke the law. We never dreamed of leaving our children in a hot, locked vehicle while we threw back shots in a bar. In fact, we never even shoplifted (called "boosting" in here), although I once absentmindedly walked out of the dime store with a spool of thread in my pocket. (I knew the couple who ran the store, and we shared a laugh about it the next day when I paid. Case closed.)

I feel Heather's anguish. She will always and forever be branded as that woman who broke the caregiver code of motherhood and hurt her own baby, then served prison time for it. Always. Forever.

I will always and forever be that woman who took her husband's life, although in truth, I obviously did not kill my husband, nor was I an accomplice to the crime. But that doesn't matter now. Labels are stickier than convictions. If a miracle occurred that completely exonerated Heather and me, our "name tags," our marks of disgrace, would still adhere. We'd be known as the bad women who manipulated and finagled a break.

Only a handful of loyal supporters, who know me and know I did not and could not murder anyone, exist. Only those who are close to me know that, unlike Heather, I unwittingly refused plea agreement offers. The rest of the world only reads my label:

murderer—evil, lowdown, killer who preyed on her peacefully slumbering, unsuspecting mate.

And nearly as bad is the fact that we are perceived as unrepentant. We don't beg for forgiveness and thus fail to display the appropriate sorrow for our heavy sins. But we do indeed regret unfortunate life choices that allowed fate to deal us these losing hands.

When the count cleared, and our cellmates exited to the dayroom, Heather was ready to talk. We discussed the stigma of a wrongful conviction. The "baby-abuser" and "murderer" hunched across the cell from each other on steel state bunks, but it was two innocent women who shed salty tears of suffering.

October 1, 2008

Dear Nancy,

June wrote that Danny Kohl wanted her to get my permission before receiving any letters from my family. Does he not know that you and June *are* family? My kids have known you all their lives, and have known June since 1986, since she ran the PATCH program, which is most of their lives!

I think my kids are reluctant to get their hopes up. The year that Carnahan died, his chief Counsel Joe Bednar personally called my daughters several times and convinced them that clemency would be given—only to call again to say that their aunts protested too much and that their mother would not be coming home. That was the most hurtful weekend of our struggle. They can't go through all those emotions again.

But my kids had to chuckle at Kevin Hughes' mean letter to the governor swearing that I'm the evilest woman on the face of the earth. (He was the county detective who lied on the stand at my trial.) I was hardly a spendthrift. I was wearing hand-me-down shoes that belonged to Mary Englert's twelve-year-old son Shawn. I gardened and canned our food. My wardrobe consisted of three pairs of Wranglers and free, logo-clad tee-shirts that were promotional gifts from the Pepsi man. (My favorite was the Orange Crush.) We had no credit cards, much less credit card debt. Our house was furnished with refurbished finds. Even the trampoline was purchased for $100 from the high school. Our lumberyard trucks were hardly sporty. How Hughes would get "lavish lifestyle" from the home of two hippies is beyond us. We were living off the farm as much as possible. In fact, in one of the police reports, he had commented that in our linen closet I had "ragged towels that the average housewife would throw away." Does that sound like a prima donna? Sheesh!

My folks' 60th wedding celebration was a lovefest according to everyone. I'm thrilled you and Tom attended. Speaking of Tom, what a sweetie. I know your dad is loving him.

The September 25 issue of *The New York Times* ran an article about our 4H program here in prison. Here's a quote from it: "Visitation rules during the monthly meetings are far more relaxed than during traditional visits, according to participants and their family members. Physical contact is allowed, children can play freely, and the environment is more nurturing than punitive, said Carrie Melton, who brought her son and daughter, ages 5 and 7, to visit Patricia Prewitt, Melton's mother. Prewitt, 59, is serving a 50-year sentence for the 1984 slaying of her husband in Johnson County, a crime she and her family insist she didn't commit. 'Normally, they're walking around yelling at you nonstop,' Melton said of the prison guards' conduct during traditional visits, 'You have to sit still, you can't move—they treat us like inmates.'" (Can you see, Nancy, why I got a violation that day?)

October 15, 2008

Dear Mary,

You need to come watch one of our PPA plays. Live theater can be crazy. For instance, last semester, I performed *A Midsummer Night's Dream*, and Janiece, my adopted prison daughter, played

Theseus. Janiece works as a coder in my shop, and I dearly adore her. She calls me her white momma when she's not mad at me. Ha! Anyway, as a duke, she was delighted to get a knockout costume. Agnes picked out a quarter-length sequined jacket befitting a tall, beautiful Black duke. The sequins were metallic yellow, orange, purple, and gold. Best of all, Janiece said she felt like royalty in it. That feeling doesn't come around often for prisoners—if ever!

As Janiece waited off stage in the sun coming in from a doorway, she ran a hand over the sequins and whispered, "Look, Patty." She pointed to the disco ball reflection on the wall. At that moment, she felt a string hanging from the jacket and pulled it. Horrified, I pointed silently at the waterfall of sequins falling to the floor. Janiece looked just like the naughty little kid I bet she was. But there's no time for catastrophe in live theater. I shook her to see if all the sequins would fall. They didn't, so I walked back on stage with Janiece. We discovered that walking didn't disturb the sequins, but if anyone touched the jacket, sequins stuck to that hand. Thank heaven, the jacket made it through the performances without too much balding.

November 2, 2008

Dear Nancy,

Sarah, Carrie, and Sarah's kids came to see me today. Abbey has lost more teeth, Megan is so smart, and Will is a dimpled doll. The guards were so mean to the kids who were acting like kids, not rocks, as they would have preferred. Then Sarah sat close and put her head on my shoulder. I yearned to pull her into my arms and comfort her—but because we're in this awful place, I pulled away and took her hand. Handholding is legal. Cuddling is not!

Tiny Megan bored a hole through me with her blue eyes and grilled me like a hotdog, "You're not coming to live with us, are you? You're not coming home. You say you are—no, Momma says you are, but you never do. Why don't you want to come stay with us?"

Carrie reported that recently, when I sent a letter to Callie, Callie ripped it open, read it, then got really sad, "I thought Granny was writing that the mayor was going to let her come home."

So now we refer to the governor as the mayor.

December 23, 2008

Dear Beth,

What a great surprise, on a horrid night, to receive your letter. It's horrid because the new prison at Chillicothe has opened, and they created a lottery to decide who will be uprooted, shackled, chained, and transferred there. The phones are off just in case one of the lottery losers knows the A-Team and can call for help. And on top of it all, we had two fire drills back-to-back with the temperature in the teens. But in the middle of all that turmoil, I was handed a card, a letter, and poems from my favorite professor.

I love the poem you wrote for us, and thanks for the William Carlos Williams clipping. You know how much I adore him and his chickens. Emily Dickinson is full of crap. Hope is not a sweet bird. She is a vulture. My shoulders sport bloody claw punctures where she keeps gripping me for dear life. When I call home, I listen for the tone of the loved one who answers for a clue. Someone at some time will know the answer—will know my fate. So far, hope just keeps gouging me with her talons, pecking me with her sharp black beak, and beating me about the head and shoulders.

I haven't called Danny, but I bet his head has already blown off with worry and anticipation. It's nearly Christmas. Time is running out.

This letter is stupid, but I can't seem to gather my wits about me nowadays.

My kids are all dealing with our wait differently. Carrie is ignoring it. Morgan doesn't know what to think. Sarah and Jane are on pins and needles like Danny is.

I can't complain. I couldn't have asked for a better spokesperson than Jane Aiken. I trust that she did everything possible to drive home her points. Don't know if you know her, but she's a force to be reckoned with.

I haven't learned my lines as Malvolio yet. My brain is fried! I can't allow myself to think about the outcome either way.

January 4, 2009

Dear Beth,

Are you attending Obama's inauguration? Looks like it will be quite a party—and you're in the neighborhood.

Friday night, Jane Aiken sent me some letters so I could see what's going on. Jane is working so hard to free me. I've never had a lawyer more committed. What a godsend. We have until the governor's inauguration on the 12th for word on the clemency application. Oy vey! (I think I'm becoming Jewish under Danny's influence!)

On Friday, Gary planned to bring my oldest daughter, Jane, and her son, Jace, who will turn seventeen that day, but something was wrong with one of his truck wheels, so they had to abort the mission. Everyone is disappointed. My daughter Sarah asked, "Why is it, in our family, that you must reach your eighties before you can afford a reliable vehicle? Grandpa has the only good car." True.

Yesterday, I called my old friend Father Hugh Behan in Florida, where he's semi-retired and teaching college philosophy. He was our prison chaplain for ages. When I mentioned that the governor's chief of staff asked for documentation in regard to the gunpowder residue test that I took hours after my husband's murder, Father got all Irish on me—mad, "Do you mean to tell me they took a test, and that wasn't brought up at trial?"

I had no answer. I was stupid then.

January 13, 2009

Dear Beth,

I feel so bad that I disappointed everyone with my executive clemency denial. I fear I'll cause Danny an early grave. My kids are crying—brokenhearted. I've had no chance to sob. Must keep a stiff upper everything in here. Only Janiece and Heather knew what I was up to. And right after Christmas, they stole Heather away to the new prison in Chillicothe.

Two girls did get clemency from Blunt, and I'm genuinely happy for them. One of the women I've known for decades was just plain evil about Stacey's good news. I took her aside and told her she was being ugly. "You run to every church service and want to play as if you were sitting at the right hand of Jesus, but you're mad that Stacey gets to go home? I don't understand it!"

I get wanting to go home, but overt jealousy needs to be kept under wraps, if you ask me. I haven't spoken to her about my bad news, but she's very happy I didn't get good news. That, I don't understand either.

Jane Aiken called Gary and wanted to speak to me, so I called her in DC after chow. I love Jane. She plans to compile a convincing argument for innocence and present it to Governor Nixon this year. She knows people close to him. She also wants to compile an article we both wrote to submit to national publications like *The Atlantic* or *Rolling Stone*. She has a ton of ideas.

Since she's in DC, I asked how she'd get all the footwork done in Missouri, but she has her WashU volunteer students, she says. She's a force to be reckoned with.

Just wanted to drop a note to assure you that I'm fine—and excited to see you on the 26th or 27th. When I told Dana and Janiece you were coming, their smiles were genuine, and their eyes lit up. You are much loved by us, the worst women in Missouri.

February 23, 2009

Dear Nancy,

Did I tell you that Jane Aiken has assigned her two brightest law students to dig up gender bias in my transcripts? She also wrote to Gary that she *loves* his CD that he sent to her.

I'm taking a "Keep Your Bobber Up" course with Michelle Moe, a realtor from Independence. The bobber is a fishing bobber on a light chain. If you hold it over your open palm, positive thoughts cause the bobber to circle, and negative thoughts cause it to pendulum. Our workbooks hold daily quotes and affirmations for both morning and evening to ponder and meditate on. The course is based on the Law of Attraction. We are all energy. Like energy attracts like energy. When our energy is high, our bobbers are up, we are attracted to people who are the same. If we are depressed and our bobbers are down, we are attracted to like energy.

To me, in its simplest form, think of how you feel when someone approaches you in a positive way and how you feel when you're approached in a negative way. Someone can say, "You need to move your car" in a polite, friendly, non-threatening way, and you respond in kind, "Oh, let me move it right now. Thanks." That same sentence can be said in an attacking mean way, and your response would also be negative, "Oh, yeah, who's gonna make me?"

To me, our goal as humans is to let positive energy flow from us, through us—no matter what energy is around us. Our health, relationships, wealth, and everything else depend on our energy. What do you think?

On Thursday, Gary brought my folks for my quarterly food visit. Momma had colored her hair for years until the day before our visit. It's not completely silver, but cute. She's not entirely sure about the gray. She's eighty and still doesn't like gray hair. I held my Daddy's hand most of the time, and Gary's so sweet to allow me to almost ignore him when he brings my folks.

March 22, 2009

Dear Mary,

One of the organizations is having a drawing contest with a spring theme. I told Janiece that I want to sketch a frisk with the guard's hands on the prisoner's breasts. That's what spring means to me. Getting felt up even more.

But there's no freedom of artistic expression in prison. I bet the entries will be an array of pictures of flowers and trees drawn from memories of the free world, not what we actually experience here in prison.

April 13, 2009

Dear Beth,

My brain! I was on the phone for ninety minutes with Jane Aiken and two of her law students this morning—going over all the details of my husband's murder and the gobs of questions they sent me. Exhausting. We had talked Thursday morning, but we only had an hour due to the 11:30 am count.

After that conversation, I called my old pal Mary. She plans to call a few other old friends for more insight. See, I had asked her what the police wanted to know from her husband, Jack, and she told me neither she nor Jack had ever been questioned by the police. I was shocked. Jack was my husband's best friend, and Mary went to the crime scene just hours after the murder to gather clothes for the kids. We were on the same coed volleyball team and hung out together. The cops took no fingerprints at the house, but I just assumed that they spoke to everyone in our circle. Wrong.

October 13, 2009

Dear Momma and Daddy,

On Thursday, I received a cute letter from Callie and Abbey with drawings of me in their rooms. Callie wrote, "Abbey and I made these for you to show you what your room would look like if you lived with us. And if you did live with us, you would be able to see my toad in person and not just in letters." I'm going to now draw myself in the free world doing exactly what I long to do with my family and friends.

I chose a book to read for Storylink today called *Jake O'Shawnasey* about a seagull who could not fly—until he was given the *secret* of the Cliffs of County Cork. Jake learned he could have always flown. All he had to do was *believe*! Belief in himself and not doubt. My heart smiled because I'd selected a great book for the kids about believing in themselves—and the book had a message for me, too! I must *believe* that I can and will be free and come home. I can't fly unless I totally believe and have confidence! My grandkids are great teachers.

Gary visited today. We misfits fit perfectly.

Our *Wizard of Oz* production has distracted me so much that I haven't written a decent letter in a month. But we had a successful run. We fulfilled a dream for the kids who dropped out of school and never got to be in a school play. We provided a platform for many who'd never known success or completed a project. That's quite a gift. I'm proud of being a part of it. I'm also happy for a reprieve. Hammering out computer code all day, then teaching aerobics after work, then rehearsing all evening filled my days. Now I'm back to just coding and exercise classes.

October 18, 2009

Dear Mary,

This summer, Georgia, Danny Kohl's Washington University science collaborator, asked me to crochet a travel angel for a friend. This friend was a Hudson Bay survivor—a passenger on the plane that pilot Sully brought down safely after geese clogged the engines. Georgia reported that her friend's travel angel is in her luggage at the bottom of the river, so I made a little angel. Her friend sent me a commemorative coin in appreciation, but I can't keep coins and had to send it to Gary. So, the friend bought me a subscription to a *wonderful* literary magazine called *The Sun*. It's chock full of *great* writings! I'm in heaven. One of the stories, "Confessions from a Conversion Van," mentions *A Course in Miracles,* which was given to me in the '80s by an Italian violinist from New York who taught a music appreciation class at the Chillicothe prison.

The author of the confession story also mentioned a hundred-year-old book, William James's *The Varieties of Religious Experience,* and wrote that the chapter titled "The Religion of Healthy-Mindedness" reminds him of the course so much that he wonders if Helen Schucman might have read it, too. I must find that book someday and see for myself. He quoted a paragraph: "To recognize our own divinity and our intimate relationship with the Universe is to attach the belts of our machinery to the powerhouse of the Universe. One needs to remain in Hell no longer than one chooses to; we can rise to any heaven we ourselves choose; and when we choose so to rise, all the higher powers of the Universe combine to help us heavenward." Right on!

Moe assigned the class to create storyboards of what we really desire—when we are free. As an overachiever, I cut out magazine pictures and did 3-D drawings—very colorful! I sketched my family outside the gate, and me running to them. I put in a hot air balloon, a bag of money, and my book with *NY Times Best-seller* on the inside, horses, cowboy boots, a log cabin, a business card with Patricia Prewitt—Personal Trainer, vegetables, fruit, an airplane for travel, trees—a huge oak tree rising up from acorns in the center. That's me! Moe liked it so much that she photocopied it. I had fun creating it—finding images that are important to me. I felt free juices flowing while I worked on it. Great exercise!

I called my folks yesterday and got to talk to Morgan. That's a huge treat! Then Carlene, Roxie, and I went to an event where a basketball "handler" amazed and entertained us as well as a singer from Texas who used to have her own radio show. In the afternoon, we three (and Rox's lab) went back to see the middle-aged woman from South Dakota do her ball act and heard a young girl from Puerto Rico sing and tell her story. We were bundled up since the weather is cold.

Yesterday at eleven, when I taught aerobics to the Treatment girls, I encouraged them to make storyboards, too. Moe calls them "vision boards" and says they're like creative prayer. Powerful medicine.

A few of the Treatment kids said they'd try to bring their storyboards to the gym next week, but transporting such things can be a problem in prison. It depends on the officers whether it's considered contraband. The girls in Treatment must be very careful. They can easily get in trouble and get kicked out for a minor infraction. If they are kicked out of the program, they'll have to serve more time. More time away from their children. I wouldn't want to be the cause of that!

October 24, 2009

Dear Marsha,

Sarah and Carrie brought Callie, Abbey, Megan, and Will to the 4H special visit. In our meeting, as I read aloud from a children's book about the origins of Halloween, I noticed a mild disturbance within my clan, but I read on. When I came back to our table and sat down, Megan proudly showed me the hole in her gum and the tiny white tooth she'd wrestled out of its moorings. Never a dull moment with my crew. It's a circus, and I love it!

December 28, 2009

Dear Gary,

"Believe to Receive." An ex-con named Peggy wrote me that in her Christmas card. That's a great bumper sticker sentiment, but tornadoes, earthquakes, hurricanes, and tsunamis don't care if you believe or not.

Christmas has come and gone. We did our best to make it merry. I gave gifts, helped with our on-the-dorm Christmas program with scripture and song, and called home to see what was going on in their blizzard. We all had a white Christmas.

Carrie, Tom, Callie, and Drew drove across the heavy snow to be with me the day after their hectic Christmas. Our 4H visit was scheduled for the day after Christmas, but even with the bad weather, several families made it, and we had great fun. Tammy, the 4H director, is talking to George Lombardi, the head of the Department of Corrections, about 4H. I think she gave him a three-minute DVD of me speaking, with photos of my grand-kids rotating in a slideshow. George is always behind programs that help society—like CHAMP, the dog training program. He liked CHAMP so much that he brought a similar program to all the other prisons. Puppies for Parole is the name, and prisoners train rescue dogs from death row.

February 18, 2010

Dear Mary,

Today is the twenty-sixth anniversary of Bill's murder.

I've been staring at that sentence for a long while. I don't know what to say about it—except it weighs heavily on me. I'm sure it weighs heavily on the kids, too. Carrie and Bunky don't remember him. I try to keep his memory alive, but I'm not sure I'm succeeding. The kids will never know what a good athlete he was. He played baseball and basketball as a kid. He was a gymnast in college. As an adult, he played on a softball team called the Hazbins, and of course, we played coed volleyball with you and Jack.

Our foreign exchange student, Ehab from Egypt, taught him soccer, and in exchange, Bill taught Ehab to play guitar. He loved to run, too. Bill was so smart. After earning his bachelor's, he tried teaching high school, but it wasn't a good fit. We bought the lumberyard because he knew that business from his years with McKee's. Also, we wanted to be active parents. If we owned our own business, we could attend school events. We could have taken high-paying jobs in the city, but we were determined to be with the kids as much as possible.

During a recent prison visit, I told Carrie and Sarah that their dad and I planned to foster kids when they all grew up. Carrie's mouth flew open, and with great emphasis, she blurted, "More kids? Were you two nuts?" I had to admit that we were nuts and that we did love raising kids. That reminds me of another Carrie story. After Bill was killed, we took a road trip south. I was cruising the main strip in Springfield, looking for a cheap but not-too-cheap motel when I saw a neon sign that read, "Kids Free." As I pulled in, eight-year-old Carrie cried, "Oh, no! We don't need more kids!"

February 27, 2010

Dear Marsha,

Carrie, Sarah, Abbey, Callie, Megan, and Drew came for our monthly 4H visit today. I'm relieved that I could make it. I've been trying to pass a kidney stone for most of the week. It's been crazy! Finally, the pain was too much, so yesterday morning around four, I "self-declared" and made my way to medical. To "self-declare" we must convince the officer in the rotunda that we are in desperate need to leave the house and walk to medical. This wasn't difficult. The guy took one look at me and wrote the movement pass with no argument.

Once inside medical, I tried to explain to the officer why I was there. He just stared at me, so I walked back to where I might find a nurse. There was none to be had. The officer finally spoke, "You gotta come back when they call sick call."

Sick call is announced any time between seven and nine. I answered simply, "I'm not leaving." And I didn't. I ended up writhing in pain on the floor right in front of the officer's desk, while he simply gazed out the window patiently waiting for his end-of-shift at seven.

I knew the exact moment the stone passed, because the pain passed, too. I heaved a sigh of relief, got up off the dusty tile floor, and walked back to the house. That whole episode is exactly the way medical cares for us: little to none.

July 20, 2010

Dear Beth,

Last week, Agnes brought in David Clewell, the Missouri Poet Laureate from Webster University, and he is wonderful! Although the chapel was not packed, we were a rapt audience as Mr. Clewell read several of his own published poems. Those of us from the Spoken Word class smiled to hear poems that we'd studied this last semester recited in the author's voice and with his emphasis and rhythm. His first and most important advice to budding poets is to "read as many poems as possible." He also admonished us all to read poetry slowly and pause at the ends of lines, because that's what the poet intended. After his readings, Mr. Clewell opened the floor for questions and comments.

During the discussion, he urged us to write what we really feel, and also, if we use the pronoun "I", it doesn't mean the piece must be factual or biographical. "Personal is not the same as actual, but it must seem like it really happened." We must create a world in a poem, and can use any speaker we want. Mr. Clewell mentioned that poetry is a solitary act, which makes it very meaningful for prisoners.

He also pointed out that a poet wants his/her readers/listeners to say, "I never thought of it that way before," and "It seems so right." Poets must use the freshness of approach with concrete particulars in language. What is the inspiration for his poetry? He can use a word, a phrase, a chunk of conversation, or an image. In fact, he really doesn't know where he's going when he starts. He quoted poet Richard Hugo, "I'd rather end up meaning what I said than saying what I mean."

The two-hour seminar flew by, and most of us were loathe to leave and return to our cells, but both closed-movement and count-time loomed like twin buzzards causing us to scurry away. He was great!

For my birthday, my brother brought my folks to visit, and we were in hot water the whole visit for hugging too long and laughing too loudly. My loved ones have been visiting me in prison for so many years that the grumbling of guards washes off them like rain off a yellow slicker. We always have fun.

On Saturday evening, I called Gary, and the first thing he said was, "Have you called home today?" My heart froze. He then told me that my seven-year-old grandson, Drew, has been at Children's Mercy in KC since Thursday. They don't know if he has MRSA or regular staph. No one knows how he got it, but it's contagious. Carrie's living at the hospital with him, while Tom drives back and forth. Sarah is keeping nine-year-old Callie. Carrie says that Drew's a trooper, though, and in good humor. The doctors are trying to grow a culture so they can treat it with the correct anti-biotic. Breaks my heart to think of sweet Drew in trouble.

I have yet to hear a word from anyone about the clemency petition that Rep. John Burnett and the Democratic Caucus gave Governor Nixon in February. I have a feeling that nothing is happening.

I started training a new group of fitness instructors and just typed up their first quiz. I don't want to scare them too much but the written exam for the certification is no joke, so I'm making the quizzes difficult to get them prepared. They're not happy with me right now, but someday they'll be glad I pushed them this hard.

I'm also making them work out every single day. Being a good fitness instructor is not for the faint of heart.

August 1, 2010

Dear Janie,

On the evening of July 28, my roommates returned from smoke break with the news that Clementine Jones had passed. We were all in shock. Sherry Mitchell came to my door trembling while mopping up a flood of tears. It didn't seem real to any of us that Miss Clem could be gone.

I had seen her at the beginning of summer at medical. (She'd been sequestered at the Transitional Care Unit for ages. TCU is far from caring. If you're too ill to be in general population, they slam you there, where no one can visit.) I was leaving the dentist when a woman in a wheelchair grabbed my arm. My heart froze, because everyone knows Officer Shepard has zero tolerance for both physical contact and conversation. I looked down and recognized my friend Clementine, but she was not the shiny, well-kept, happy lady I remembered. I was looking at a dull, gray, lifeless individual with wild, nappy hair. Also, my old Clem weighed in at over 350 pounds and sported enormous breasts. This Clem was half that size.

As soon as I recognized her, I exclaimed, "Clem!" She hugged my arm, "Patty-Cakes! How are you?"

Shepard was zeroing in on us like a heat-seeking missile, but with wild abandon I bent down and gave her a big hug, "Take care of yourself! I miss you. We all do."

Then I fled like the big chicken that I am. The image of sick Clementine came to me as soon as roommates told me she'd died. She was only in her fifties, and her loving personality was as big as the woman herself. We slumped down at the cell table to share the adventures of Clem in a feeble attempt to somehow keep her alive.

Clementine was most famous for her huge breasts. No one I knew ever saw bigger. They were legendary. Around a decade ago, the X-ray technician confided in me that it took ten separate plates to mammogram one of Clem's breasts. She held up the biggest plate to show me. (She was using the tiniest plate for me at the time.)

Around the turn of the century, the LTO (Long Timer's Organization) sold cans of Mountain Dew as a fundraiser. Clementine, who could walk but traveled distances in a wheelchair, needed help picking up her soda, so I volunteered. (Why, I don't know. I'm not exactly a heavyweight.) With all I had, I pushed her heavy-duty-wide-load wheelchair to the Music Room. When we arrived, it occurred to me that I had not made plans on how to carry the two whole cases back to the house. But Clem had plans of her own. That was not her first rodeo. She raised her thunderous bosoms and ordered me to stack the cases on the space she'd cleared on her ample lap. She then settled the "girls" down and forty-eight sodas disappeared. I was impressed. I might add that it was all I could do to force the load back to the housing unit. Clementine teased me the whole huffing, puffing trip that I lacked enough "ass" for the job.

When we first opened this prison in '98, Clem had to sleep with her mammoth breasts in a chair beside her bunk. I can't imagine that she got a good night's sleep trying to keep her breasts from slipping off the plastic chair. Maintenance finally built her a wide bed by bolting another steel bunk to the original. Her bras were constructed especially for her by a local artisan. Her "girls" were past the point of mortal sizing. I think they ran out of alphabet letters.

Years ago, Roxann Earles and I used to take her to the gym to slowly walk the treadmill, but that got to be too much for her, and she sank further into the sedentary lifestyle of the handicapped. Clementine suffered from many health issues associated with obesity and that somehow fueled monumental eating binges. Clem could easily eat two boxes of macaroni and cheese as an appetizer while cooking a meal.

What I remember most about Clementine Jones was her good humor, booming laugh, and expressive, big, beautiful brown eyes.

I don't even know why she was in prison with me. (I can't worry about a friend's past. Today's what counts.) I do know that her family loved her very much and visited often. I picture her in the visiting room grinning from ear to ear while proudly patting the diapered fanny of a sweet grandbaby on her shoulder. I hope they have good cuisine in heaven. We have sent a sweet, loving angel ahead to check out the kitchen.

September 26, 2010

Dear Beth,

I'm not too happy with myself right now. I was just called to the visiting room to receive a conduct violation. Rats! They wrote me up for hugging my daughters *twice* at the end of the visit. This means that I will be allowed no more 4H visits until next year (ninety days) and won't be able to read a book on tape to my grandkids. Those are the two activities that require us to be ninety days violation-free.

The officer mentioned that she'd given me a warning in July about excessive hugging with my Daddy. I even blogged about it, and Sarah posted it on Facebook. I compared the staff to Nazis. It's the truth, but they evidently don't agree with my analogy.

Did you hear? Carlene gets to be *free!* She's beside herself! I can't tell you how happy I am for her and the other two girls. There was a big article in the *St. Louis Post,* and Danny emailed me a copy.

Thanks for the love and support! Between Danny, Jane A, Gary, and everyone else, maybe I can go home soon! I've spoken to the two third-year law students on the phone: Brian and Greg. They are so sharp. I'm trying to give them a crash course in how difficult this is. There's no regard for a governor who grants clemency. This is politics, and we have to find the payoff for Governor Nixon.

Yet Another Commutation Application

December 11, 2010

Dear Momma and Daddy,

I have news! The Georgetown Law students and Jane Aiken plan to visit me on the 16th. They're flying from Washington, DC that morning. Then they'll meet with the chairman of the Board of Probation and Parole, Ellis McSwain, the next morning and hand deliver my clemency petition. We are all praying that Governor Nixon will see fit to commute my sentence and send me home. I can't become too elated, because the fall back to Earth is extremely painful.

Speaking of painful, Gary came to visit me today and I managed to break the law within the first thirty seconds of my visit! Yes, and I got a conduct violation, too! After the perfunctory strip search and check-in at the desk, I walked over to Gary, who was talking to that one guard with the bad skin. Gary turned to me and asked, "Have you ever tried these chips?" He then shook the little package to allow a chip to peek out. I reached up, plucked the chip, and popped it into my mouth. That guard exclaimed, "Did you eat that?" Since I was only a couple of feet from her eyeballs and still chewing, I didn't feel it necessary to corroborate.

She then went on to explain that "we" have a new visiting room rule that came out today prohibiting inmates and visitors from eating from the same package. She said that if we want to share the chips, we must spread out a napkin and then spread out the chips on the napkin. That is to keep us from hiding drugs in the chip packages, or at least that's what she said. Then she proceeded to write me a conduct violation right then and there for breaking the rule.

The moral of this story is…is there a moral to this story? The moral to this story is to never trust a guard who might easily spring a brand new, unposted rule on you at any time.

February 20, 2011

Dear Nancy,

Have I told you about my cellmate Amy, who's around the same age as Janie? Because of her drug addiction, Amy passed through prisons for a couple of decades. I knew her during every incarceration and warmed to her readiness to see humor within the darkest of prison days. During her confinement in '98, not long after we were transferred to Vandalia to open this new prison, she gave birth to a son. He was the one she gave up entirely. She was finally mature enough to know she couldn't provide a child with any kind of stable life. Her two daughters weren't so lucky.

A few months ago, I spied her across the chow hall at breakfast. I hadn't heard she was back. Self-disgust radiated from her slumped shoulders and bowed blonde head, so I ambled over to hear the sad story of why she was back. I'd worried for her when she was freed after the birth, because she was paroled on *homeless status*. Yes, Nancy, they send these kids out with no plan and no help, then they act either surprised or disgusted when they fail to thrive.

Amy was put on a bus and spent that night under a bridge in a cardboard box. I think most citizens would be appalled to know that this is how the state treats parolees. Her story of failure was familiar to me, but at the end she sighed that she would have to spend twelve years in here before she would be eligible to parole. She'd racked up two seven-year sentences, plus two fives running wild. That's twenty-four years. Amy is required by law to serve half of that sentence. Prison sentences can be run consecutively (aka wild) or concurrently. Every felon tries for concurrent sentences, but it's up to the judge, and evidently Amy's judge wanted to "lay her down."

As she told me her story, my heart ached for her and all the broken-winged sparrows who fall from freedom into this hellhole. Amy interrupted my musing, "Ya gonna eat that toast?"

While she gobbled, I asked where she'd landed, what wing. With a sour look on her face she answered, "A wing. And it's loud, disrespectful, a trap house zoo. Plus, they put me on a top bunk above this rude, loud-snorin' bitch with boils all over her butt. Boils! She says a spider bit her, but I bet it's staph. No self-respecting spider would put his mouth on that ass!"

That very morning, I talked to Ms. Raspberry, my caseworker, about the possibility of moving Amy to the one empty bottom bunk. (She's only 4'10" on a good day, so a top bunk is a struggle.) I had only known Amy by the name "Amy Banks," but Ms. Raspberry informed me that there was no one by that name in this prison. I sat stunned across the desk. Had I hallucinated that whole conversation? I'd known Amy for decades. Who did I talk to?

While I sat mute, Ms. Raspberry was clicking away on her keyboard and announced, "Oh, you mean Amy Sherrill on A-wing." She then showed me her intake picture. Ms. Raspberry was right. She's smarter than me and had looked up aliases. Then I swore that Amy would be a good fit. We have the CHAMP dog training program on our wing and don't allow inmates who would not respect the dogs and the trainers. And that's how Amy became my kid.

Since she owes thousands in unpaid parole fees—felons must pay the state for the privilege of parole—she got a position at the clothing factory, the only job that pays almost a living wage. Since she owes the state, all her monthly earnings except for $5 are taken to pay her debt. They let the girls have $5 to buy all their necessary items, like shampoo, lotion, detergent, toothpaste, and brushes, etc. Of course no one can purchase these items for $5, so I help her. (Around Christmas, Carrie and Tom ask me for three or four prisoners they can send money to. Easily I find kids who have nothing and secretly get their names and numbers from their uniforms. When Amy's state debt is paid, I'll add her to the mix, but I can't now. The state would grab their charity.)

May 26, 2011

Dear Momma and Daddy,

One of my cellmates, Leann, is from Joplin. We didn't know about the tornado until Monday morning. I was in the dayroom around 5:30 am heating coffee water and caught the story and pictures on the national news. That's how devastating this huge tornado was—CNN was covering it. Leann was still sound asleep, and I wasn't sure if I should rouse her. She's from Joplin and is part of a huge family that has resided in that area since before the Civil War.

I paced back and forth from our cell to the dayroom. I must have had three cups of coffee before I built up the courage to wake her. Amy and I just adore this kid. When we were performing our last play, we'd drag in about ten minutes before the late count to find that Leann had a paper-wrapped, hot, *cheap* burrito waiting for each of us on our standup lockers. A cheap burrito, in my book, is simply rehydrated and heated refried bean flakes inside a wrapped-up wheat tortilla. This may not sound so appetizing to you, but when you're in prison and only have time for either a quick shower or a meal—not both—those cheap burritos are lifesavers. Also, you've probably only seen refried beans in cans. In prison, we purchase them as flakes in plastic resealable bags. (Someone might use a can lid to slice someone.)

I softly touched Leann's shoulder, and when she opened her eyes, I whispered, "Joplin got hit last night by a tornado." That's all I got a chance to say. She leaped out of her bunk and raced to the wall phone in the upstairs dayroom. I busied myself making her a cup of coffee while she tried every number she knew, then she wailed, "There's no service! No one is answering! No one!"

Can you imagine how awful that was for this kid? She has grandmas, grandpas, her parents, aunts, uncles, siblings, nieces, nephews, cousins, not to mention lifelong friends in Joplin. Of course, the prison has been no help in contacting anyone for her. But this morning Leann ran all the way out of bounds to my shop to report that she'd finally made contact.

They'd had little warning, but three of her older brothers raced to grandma's house, scooped her up, and practically fell down the basement steps just in time. When the deafening roar subsided, one brother climbed up and pushed through rubble where the door had been. He said he'd lived in that neighborhood all his life but there was nothing left—no familiar landmarks. He felt completely lost. Every building, every tree, every bush, every vehicle was gone. Not until daybreak did they have a true picture of the swath of destruction.

But the great news is that none of her family died. All the injuries were minor, but everything they had is gone. They have not one worldly possession. Only the clothes on their backs.

Leann told me her brothers and cousins are stupid. They made a big plywood sign on the highway that reads, "Don't send water. Send beer."

July 5, 2011

Dear Beth,

On my birthday I awoke to find signs and pictures plastered all over the wing—in the bathroom, laundry room, everywhere. The kids were so cute about me and had worked so hard to decorate the place. The artwork and announcements stayed up until our stern guard, who we call Cratchit, tore them down during the noon count. "Ladies (which is code for bitches), we can't put up with such nonsense in this institution!" No, we'd never allow nonsense inside these fences.

Last week I came back to my cell from aerobics to find it torn up. Just my area. The girls informed me that the lieutenant spent forty-five minutes going through every piece of paper. I had no clue as to why until I called Gary on Sunday. He reported that Brian had forwarded an email to him from Father Dorn stating that a VIC (volunteer in corrections) from here had circulated a petition in support of my clemency application at Mass on Sunday in a free-world church, and a staff person from here had reported her. The VIC cannot come back to the institution now while they investigate.

I don't know who this VIC might be, but I sure hope I don't get thrown in the hole as part of the investigation. Agnes will kill me if I miss the play. I know the rules and never talk about my personal legal struggles at church services. We only have a few minutes to chat before Mass, and Father Judge won't allow visiting while he's doing his thing. I feel sorry for whoever is in trouble.

April 23, 2012

Dear Beth,

My eighty-three-year-old mother fell over a puppy and broke her leg on the 17th, so the whole family has been running. She's now in a rehab center at a retirement village, and my brother and sister are taking care of Daddy and transporting him to Momma's side every day. I'm so blessed to have such a wonderful family who will drop everything and rally. I'm the worthless one, but hopefully not forever.

Momma's doing better but at first she balked at physical therapy like Amy Winehouse, "They want me to go to rehab and I say no, no, no!"

I call Daddy each evening to get an update. He's so proud when he can find the right button to push on the phone. He's blind. Spending his days in the hospital is wearing him out, so I gently advised, "You know, Daddy, you don't have to go there every day." Daddy quietly but sternly told me, "She's my woman." 'Nuff said.

Law professor John Amman, a friend of Jane Aiken from SLU, is working to pass the geriatric bill that Jane's students originally wrote. It's HB1175, and I pray it passes.

Last year on my twenty-fifth anniversary of incarceration, your students at Saint Mary's held a rally. I'm still in awe of them! I know you're terribly busy with the end of semester. Take care of yourself and don't overdo. Take Mary Oliver's advice and enjoy the mysteries.

May 12, 2012

Dear Nancy,

Today is Gary's CD release concert, and practically my whole family will be there to celebrate. *I miss out on everything!* (I just had to get that out!)

My Momma (piano), Daddy (guitar), Frankie (bass), and Doug (mandolin) contributed to the CD. Gary said that working with Momma was like herding cats. She's an excellent piano player, but as soon as they finished a song, she'd talk—say something like, "How was that?" Gary tried to explain to her that they needed so many seconds of quiet after the music ended, but Momma failed to obey—take after take.

Gary was paying for the studio, and time plus money were slipping away. He and the other musicians silently looked to Daddy since everyone knows he's the only one who has influence over her. Daddy quietly informed his wife that as soon as we get a good take, we'll all go out to eat. The next take was perfect. Momma waited the prescribed time before she spoke, and then this is what she said, "Don't people in this city ever eat?" And they did!

May 20, 2012

Dearest Mary,

Warning! This paragraph may be too graphic for you. In the chow hall, a girl with a mohawk jumped up hollering at a young kitchen worker, "Hoo, hoo, hoo! Look at *you!* Come here, baby, and wipe down my table!"

Then mohawk reared back and screamed at the top of her lungs, "i'll suck ya til yo cross-eyed!" In case the object of her affection didn't understand, she reiterated while trying to sound seductively inviting. Screaming, "Did ya hear, hot thang? I promise i'll suck ya puss-a til yo cross-eyed an dry as uh muh-fuh!"

I glanced at the victim to see if the loud display was embarrassing her. Most kitchen help are fresh, scared little kids. I had no need to worry though. Under her white kitchen shower cap-looking hair cover, she was a peacock preening from the attention. Her dimpled face showed a big toothy smile with gold flashing. Dinner and a show.

This next story is not icky at all: At chow, a young girl sat across from me. (I've been here so long that none of these kids were born when I came to prison.) I told her that Bonnie Hamilton, the geriatric master crochet teacher, was very proud of how quickly she'd caught on during the crochet lessons. The kid is far from the brightest bulb on the Christmas tree and smiled her almost-pretty (if it weren't for the chewed-up meth teeth) vacant smile. Another girl asked, "Have you ever crocheted before?" The dim bulb sweetly responded slowly, "No. But I thought about it once."

June 11, 2012

Dear Gary,

I know I'll see you next week with the kids for the 4H visit, but today is Amy's birthday and during the noon count she told me the horrible story of her father's death. I can't sleep thinking about it. Maybe if I write the story to you, I can unload a bit of this burden.

When Amy was just a little kid, her father had her and her older sister at his place for the weekend. He was taking them fishing, and he told the girls to run out and wait in the pickup. They waited and waited until Amy couldn't stand it any longer. Disregarding her sister's protests, Amy raced back into the house to holler at him.

When she burst into the living room poised to yell, "Daddy!" she choked. His limp body lay crumpled across the rusty-orange shag carpet, a ragged pool of red blood oozed from where the top of his head had been, the smoking shotgun muzzle still stuck in his gaped mouth, hunks of brain tissue, blasted across the wall, lost their grip and splatted on the console TV.

I realize that her father had to have been in terrible pain to do what he did, but how selfish to do this to his little girls. I don't want to judge him, but I guess I do. I just hate that it happened so much for Amy. No wonder she turned to drugs to numb the pain.

I'm going to try to fall asleep now. Good night, sweetheart.

July 10, 2012

Dear Beth,

Brian wrote that he takes his Illinois bar on the week of the 24th, so I responded that he'd better keep his nose to the grindstone and not worry about traveling to Missouri for an inmate play! Brian is such a sweet kid. I know he has a great life and career ahead of him.

Agnes gave me three huge blank canvases and a bag of paint pens to create our Greek graffiti backdrop for the play. With the help of my buddy artist Katie, who's not in this semester's production but agreed to help me, and a handful of actors, we did it!

I made a bunch of sketches of characters, lettering and quotes in Latin and English, and sweet-talked the rec officer into allowing us to work in the gym during aerobics. Then Katie and I transferred my sketches onto the canvas with pencil, and for four afternoons we invited the actors to come and paint-by-number. Several pitched right in. I worked so hard that I nearly caused permanent nerve damage from hunkering on my hands and knees for so long, but it's worth it because Agnes will be blown away. We've outdone ourselves. Can't wait to show her Thursday.

At first the actors made excuses, refusing to put paint to canvas, but I forced some to give it a try. I explained that it's graffiti and can't be hurt. Why are some so afraid of new experiences? The ones who gave it a try were grinning from ear to ear. Creating is liberating and spiritual in my book.

Gary is bringing my oldest daughter Jane and her grown son Jace to both shows on the 19th, then will come back the next day to really visit. After that he's flying to Oregon to visit his adopted daughters. Many years ago, Gary's best friend died in a house fire while saving his children. The girls see Gary as their father and are anxious for him to visit again. It will be good for Gary to have a big fuss made over him. Also, he talked about visiting your part of the world in the fall.

Somehow the chest freezer in my parents' garage came unplugged and everything melted, so Sarah and Mary spent last Thursday afternoon cleaning up the mess. What a waste since it was full of frozen blackberries the kids had gathered in their woods, and their big white dog had rolled in the river of blackberry juice. Daddy's blind and Momma hadn't been outside, so no one had noticed the blue dog and blue concrete patio.

Take care and pluck the day. Our Greek professor, George, told us that "carpe diem" is not Latin for "seize the day." It's "pluck the day." The poem from which it comes is a story of a man wanting a young woman so badly that he yearns to pluck her like a flower, and therefore "deflower" her. Ancient erotica. So, pluck the day!

October 13, 2012

Dear Marsha,

Sorry, I'm on the late freight. I missed your birthday!

So, you're curious about strip searches. Let me inform you. Let me provide you with the naked truth. Nakedness is a requirement, of course. Thus, the term "strip." But, removing every piece of clothing and brazenly standing a foot or two from the prying eyes of a guard is just step one of a strip search. Once you're in the buff, there's specific choreography that has changed over the years—but this is the current method: First, bend over, shake your hair and mess it up. No braids are allowed, and heaven forbid you arranged your hair to try to look cute or simply presentable for your visitor. The first time I was ordered to do this, I tried to joke to the guard that my hair won't even hold a curl so how can it hold contraband…but she was unmoved. Before you can progress from step to step, the officer must approve. "Yes" and "OK" are the most popular positive reactions.

Now push the end of your nose to expose your nostrils. "Yes." Open your mouth really wide and wiggle your tongue and press it to the roof of your mouth while the officer peers in. "OK."

If you wear dentures or partials, they have to come out—no adhesive allowed. I'll never forget the fear in Amy's face when she realized her top plate was firmly buried in her vending machine hamburger. Her visitor wore the same expression.

Ears next—show both inside and behind. Good thing ears are rubbery.

Now we are moving south. No one has ever asked me to lift my breasts, but if you actually have breasts, you must pick them up to show that no contraband is pinned on the underside. Raise your arms to show your armpits.

If you have any other skin folds that might need to be repositioned for a better view, now is the time for show and tell. While still facing front, open your legs to display the inner thighs. When this move was implemented, I doggie-lifted my leg way high and was chastised for revealing too much. No points for exuberance or flexibility.

Now turn around, widen your stance, grab your butt cheeks and pull them apart, drop into a low squat and cough—all at the same time. This pull, drop, and cough must be accomplished simultaneously three times—sometimes more if the guard believes you are not giving any of these components the proper intensity. Their theory is that any wads of drugs you've stuffed up your "purse" will shoot out on the floor from the force of these motions. Don't know if that's ever happened, but at my age, I must do my best not to dribble!

While still spreading your butt cheeks, fold way over, bottoms up, to reveal as much of "down there" as possible without turning this routine into a full cavity search. And if you don't know what a cavity search is, just think about it. Cavity. Search. Speculum.

You're in the homestretch! Lift your feet, one at a time unless you're exceptionally talented, to show the soles, wiggle your toes, and you're done...IF your dance is deemed a success. Every officer rates differently and can require a repeat. Some guards are really into it and seem to be checking every inch of me for melanoma. Others step farther back and hurry me along.

One guard told me she wanted at least three of the twelve-inch floor tiles between my feet. I gave it my best shot but then couldn't squat deep enough to suit her. I wanted to ask her who in this particular hellhole could do that, but I refrained. It's prudent to keep most of your questions and comments to yourself.

This striptease comes before and after visits, upon arrival to and exit from the prison, and any other random time we are ordered to. After a short time of incarceration, we lose any shred of modesty. I could strip *in* the visiting room if that's what it took to see my loved ones.

A guard once commented on how quickly I ran through the motions, so I remarked, "Yeah, I'm a professional stripper."

Her eyes widened, "Really?"

While she grilled me about moves, Velcro, G-strings, and costumes, I kept trying to interrupt, "No, no, no! I'm kidding! Look at this body. Would anyone *pay* to see this?"

One more tip—from personal experience. Strip humor is almost always lost on the stripping, searching officer. "How many assholes have you seen today?" is not appreciated. Keep it to yourself.

November 1, 2012

Dear Carrie and Tom,

Amy nearly lost her life last night—on Halloween! That is a bit dramatic, but it was close! These people have no sense of humor.

We had been ordered to not celebrate Halloween in any fashion, which did not sit well with some of us. For example, I bought cheap candy for trick or treaters because Amy and I like celebrations of any kind. This is a prison, not a convent.

In defiance, Amy fashioned a bowler hat out of paper and cardboard and smudged mascara above her top lip. She then ventured out to stroll the hall like Charlie Chaplin. She was in the middle of an award-winning imitation when over the loudspeaker, we heard,

"You! In the hall! Come here now!" I was in our cell at the time, so I reached out, grabbed Amy, jerked her into our cell, licked the mascara off her face, shoved her into her bunk, and covered her up. The guards yelled more, but no one gave us up, and the guards were too lazy to come up the stairs. When we thought the coast was clear, I announced that I would be giving candy to trick or treaters in the safety of the laundry room—first come, first serve. I made sure Amy stayed hidden. Later after the 9:30 count, Amy whispered, "You licked me! You licked the moustache right off my face." I whispered back, "It was an emergency." With that we giggled like idiots until a cellmate grumbled that she had to work food service at two in the morning. Just another day in paradise.

March 6, 2013

Dear Janie,

At church last night, I had such severe chest pains that I leaned over to Jeanie and whispered, "I think maybe I'm having a heart attack." Why I confessed this, I'll never know. I guess I thought she'd smile and keep on listening to the sermon without going nuts. I was wrong. Jeanie leaped into action screaming, "Oh my God! Patty's dying!"

She then ran out of the chapel, still screaming, and came back in with a super-sized wheelchair. Horrified, I protested getting in, but Jeanie wrestled me into the chair and proceeded to bounce the chair off the door jamb several times before she threaded the wheelchair through the doorway. She was still screaming, I was screaming *noooo*, and others joined in with their version of *oh no!*

Medical is down a hill from the chapel and because Jeanie is so short, she lost control of the chair long enough for me to quickly roll, unsteered, for a while. Somehow, I missed the huge light pole halfway down, but the random little girl racing with us hopped into the double-wide with me for fear of her life. I hung onto her, and we didn't die.

Jeanie gained control while still screaming and wheeled me straight through a crowded med line to the nurse in charge. After a few hours, during which Amy and several others showed up (out of bounds) to check on me, and while the nurse read the directions on the package, she did an EKG on me. I was fine.

Somehow, I ended up spending a restless night in TCU (Transitional Care Unit), but the next day Deputy Warden D. J. Miller came to see me. Amy had called Gary, who called D. J. Gee whiz! I was fine. The day nurse told me it was probably just indigestion, which I'd never had before. But if I ever have indigestion again, I will keep it to myself!

September 20, 2013

Dear Nancy,

That play I wrote was actually performed at the Kennedy Center last month, the real Kennedy Center! Danny Kohl, Beth, and Brian attended! So cool.

I'm sending the script to you. I didn't before, because I wasn't sure it was good enough. Oh, the actor who played me wrote and asked if this actually happened. I had to chuckle a bit. I'm not a fiction writer, but outsiders have no idea the range of atrocities inside prisons. Maybe this play will open some eyes. Agnes doesn't like the ending. Tell me what you think, please.

CLARITY

One male corrections officer with a Midwestern drawl, one 30-ish female prisoner. Bare stage except for one chair. She, sitting in chair, is looking down thoughtfully. Guard bursts in.

Guard: Cat got ya tongue?
Girl: No.
Guard: Good, good. Afraid ta talk?
Girl: No, but I suspect that anything I say will be used
      against me.
Guard: That's a goodin', gal. I like you. I have this feeling we
      gonna get along real good. Real good. Stand up. *(Girl
      remains sitting.)* I said *stand up! (She stands, warily.)* Ya
      see, sweetheart, this is how it goes. Ya call me boss and
      do exactly what I say when I say it. When I say jump, ya
      politely ask how high. It dat simple. Piece a cake. You
      can make yo time here really hard or keep dat "hard"
      right where it belongs. *(Grabbing his crotch.)* Get it?
      (Menacingly.) Now, don't get too skittish on me, Missus
      Patricia Ann Prewitt number two six six seven, widow,
      black widow. I read yo file. Ya no innocent baby. Ya

been round the block a time or two. We not talking
here 'bout nothin' you ain't done afore.

Girl: *(Softly)* I don't want any trouble.

Guard: *(Overly sincere)* Me, either. Ize all 'bout no trouble. This
iza "no trouble" zone, gal. I like ta keep things simple.
Real simple. So, how much time ya doin'?

Girl: You tell me. You read my file.

Guard: See. Like I said, yo a smart one. I like dat. *(Steps up
close to her face.)* Fo-fuckin-evah. Dat's what yo doin'.
Fo-fuckin-evah. Life without parole, ya life-doin' bitch!
Ya got nothin' ta lose. *(Steps back and softly continues.)*
Or so ya think, but you be wrong. Dead wrong. Der is
perks when ya follaw da program, don't make waves,
cwoperate. *(Pause, then friendly)* Ya got kids?

Girl: I'm sure that's in my file, too.

Guard: Yeh, smart gal, yeh. Five. From eight ta sweet sixteen.
Three pretty gals, too. Just like they mama. An I know
ya wanna see em. No sweet visits when ya buried in da
hole for "failure ta cwoperate." But smart gals don't have
ta worry bout dat. Smart gals know who be in charge,
who got all da cards. Like I said, ya do have lots ta lose—
if ya don't cwoperate. *(Pause, steps back close to her face)*
Am I clear so far?

Girl: *(Silent stony stare.)*

Guard: *(Nose to nose)* Am! I! Clear?!

Girl: Crystal.

Guard: Good, good. Ah knew ya was a smart gal. My job is ta
show ya da ropes, an I gotta thick, stiff rope right here.

*(He starts to laugh but when she turns and walks away a few steps,
he gets serious again.)*

Don't turn yo back ta me, smart gal. That uh di-rec orda.
Ya hear, Fresh Meat? Ya *must* obey uh di-rec orda. It a
rule. Sure would hate ta hafta write ya up fo failure ta
obey uh di-rec orda. Got it, smart gal? Got it?!

Girl: *(Turns to him)* Got it, boss.

Guard: *(Friendly)* Aw, smart gal. You knew prison was gonna
suck. Guess ya didn't know ya would suck, too. *(Mean,
short chuckle.)*
(Moves close) Ya got pretty hair. *(Strokes hair)* Soft. No
girly shit in da hole. I bet ya like ta read, too. Smart girls
like ta read. No liberry when ya buried deep in the hole.
(In her face speaking rapidly) No canteen, no coffee, no
visits, no phone calls home. No shit! Gals tell me da
worst part of being in da hole is da once-a-week showers and once-a-week changes of clothes. Pretty gals like
yo like ta clean up every day—specially in dis heat. In
nother month, dis place gonna be a hot box, an da hole
fuckin' hotter. *(Chuckles at this line)* Hotter than a fresh
fucked fox. All lone in dere...cookin' in ya own juices—
like uh turkey at Thanksgiving *(merrily snorts at his own
analogy)*. But you a smart gal. You know what side yo
bread's buttered on, don ya. You *want* ta cwoperate. Ya
want ta be a model inmate. Yo big city lawyer told ya ta
be a good girl, din he? Keep ya nose clean. Stay outta
trouble, if ya *ever* wanna get back home ta ya lovin'
family. Ya need ta take vantage of all da things dat make
yo time go by easy. I know ya really want easy. "You can
do yo time or let da time do you." Smart gals learn that
fast. Listen, babe, I gotta special private place ta show ya.
Only my special gals, my smart gals, get ta see it. You a
smart gal, an we gonna get along just fine. We got *years*
ta-gether. Years and years. *(Pause, smiles.)* Ya may turn
out ta be my favorite. Come on.

(Guard freezes while the girl addresses the audience.)

Girl: Dear God, what can I do? What would *you* do? What
would you *do*? He's right. I'm fresh meat. I've been in
prison a matter of days and don't know what he'll do to
me if I resist. And I *am* all alone in here. There's no one
to help me. Not Daddy, not my brother... That "big city

lawyer" warned me that "innocence is the worst possible defense," which means I'm defenseless. Completely defenseless. Again. Still. *(Loud and crazy.)* I wanna scream like a banshee and tear my hair out while slamming my head into the concrete wall…or the steel bars. Somebody! God! Jesus! Somebody, help me!

(Begins a hysterical scream but cuts it off by slapping her hand over her own mouth then wrestling with herself for a beat.)

Would he leave me alone if he thought I was a raving lunatic? I *feel* like a lunatic. It wouldn't be a stretch. *(Rationally)* But he already thinks I'm homicidal and that doesn't bother him. If I tell anyone, it's my word against his. I know how that worked in court. Liars with badges have all the credibility. Dear God…*(Drops to knees, looks up with arms raised)*. Are you even here in this forsaken place? *(Fights back sobs)*.

(Stands, shakes it off, takes a deep breath, squares her shoulders)

Get a grip. Get a friggin' grip. You cannot lose your head in this asylum. You cannot lose it now.

(Guard unfreezes, turns to leave, and motions her to follow).

Guard: Come on.
Girl: *(Quietly)* I don't think so, boss.
Guard: What?
Girl: I don't think we're going to get along at all.
Guard: *(Steps to her yelling)* Don't make a big mistake here!
Girl: *(One step forward to him defiantly with her arms pressed to her sides for support)* Let me make this clear, boss. *(Another step to him)* I'm good, real good at making big mistakes. But I'm bad, real bad at getting along with slimeballs like you. *(Pause glaring, then presses her wrists together for handcuffs.)* Do what you have to do.
Guard: *(Through clenched teeth with balled fists)* Yull be sorry. I promise. Real fuckin' sorry, ya piece-a-shit

life-doin'-bitch. *(Inhales, steps back, regroups)* But dis is
yo lucky day.

Girl: Yeah, I'm the luckiest girl in the world.

Guard: *(Nose to nose)* I'm not gonna take ya down *today*. But I
will take ya down. Ya can count on dat. Yo can guaran-
damn-tee dat! I will make yo miserable life more miserable dan yo ever thought possible. Is dat clear!

Girl: *(Quietly)* Yes, boss.

*(He exits fuming while she sits warily watching. She sits because
her legs are apt to give out. Quivering slightly, she announces to
herself.)*

Crystal clear.

Fin

September 21, 2013

Dear Janie,

Attached is the copy of that play I promised to send you. The director is great and has written me several times to make sure she's getting it right. I'm still blown away that I've had two plays performed at all, anywhere—much less at the Kennedy Center! Crazy, isn't it? Don't worry. This one is a comedy, and the funniest thing about it is that it's true. I've simply reported the conversation nearly word-for-word. And people think prison is morose.

THE PLOT

When scene opens, caseworker is sitting at desk riffling through papers. One chair on other side of desk is for the inmate. Inmate talks to audience and caseworker, but caseworker only addresses inmate.

Inmate: *(Enters talking to audience)* As a prisoner I can tell you that it's extremely stressful to be called to the caseworker's office when you have no idea why. Out of the blue. You're minding your own business when over the loudspeaker, the rotunda officer announces, "Prewitt. To the back. In full grays. Your caseworker wants you."

First, your mind races through what prison sins you may have recently committed. What might seem like a minor infraction to you can be a big deal to them. Then you worry about who in the family might be dead. (Yes, they sometimes give you news from home.)

I start my worry list with Daddy, the oldest, and work my way down to the littlest grandkids. Seriously, you could be called for any reason. There's never a heads-up. We forge blindly into each situation. Like a summons to the principal's office. It's rarely good news. The only thing worse is to be called to see the investigator. That's *never* good.

(Takes breath) Well, here goes...

(To caseworker cordially) Hello, Ms. Simmons. You called for me? Prewitt?

Caseworker: Yes, yes. Of course. I know who you are, Prewitt. Have a seat.

(Inmate sits on the edge of the chair tensely while CW shuffles papers. Inmate glances at the audience as if looking for support. CW finds Chadwick's clothing catalog, leaves through it while inmate glances back at audience.)

Here. Here it is. Which of these do you like best for the bridesmaids?

Inmate: *(To audience)* Yikes. Nobody ever really wants to know what I think. They just want me to co-sign their opinion. So, which one would *she* like?

Caseworker: *(Interrupts)* I like that one, the green with the puffy sleeves, but in lavender. *(Points)* Our wedding colors are lilac and buttercup. That's a very pale yellow. Won't that be beautiful?

Inmate: *(Smiling)* Oh, yes, lovely. *(To audience)* Thank God she pointed out her pick, because I felt the sand shift under my feet.

(To caseworker) I can see the wedding party now. Lovely. So spring-y.

Caseworker: I'm glad you agree. Some people think it's awful to pick the dresses out of a catalog, but I don't have time to travel to the city and shop. I wouldn't even know where to begin! And this is my only daughter. I want to make sure her wedding is spectacular.

(Pauses dreamily) Every young woman should have the wedding she's always dreamt of since she was a little girl. A fairy-tale wedding to remember forever...

(Sadly) We eloped, and I'll regret that to the day I die.

(Sad pause, then lightbulb and sharp inhale) Which reminds me...listen, I didn't call you back here for your fashion opinion. I called you 'cause I want to run this great idea past you. I've been thinking about this for quite a while. And I want your unbiased opinion. Be honest now.

Inmate: *(To audience)* There's that quicksand again. Do you feel it?

Caseworker: Tell me exactly what you think of this.

Inmate: Of course.

Caseworker: *(Leans in and announces her idea proudly)* We should put a cemetery out behind this housing unit. *(CW pauses in anticipation, but inmate sits mum)* We could have flowers and maybe even tombstones. The flat kind that maintenance can mow right over. Did they have those back when you were free? The flat ones? *(Inmate nods slowly)* We can't plant trees or bushes, ya know. For security reasons. Wouldn't want anyone hiding out in the cemetery, now would we? That would never do.

Inmate: Of course not. *(Still looking befuddled)* But, Ms. Simmons, exactly who will you bury in this flat cemetery?

Caseworker: Oh, I guess I didn't make myself clear. I brought this idea to *you*, because it would be for *you*—and all the ladies who will *die* in here. You know. Like Carlene, Miss Ruby, uh, Connie Flowers, Miss Verna, Ms. Copeland, Mrs. Tidwell...you know, poor Mrs. Tidwell is in her eighties and not in good health. Doesn't she have diabetes and a heart condition? I noticed she's in a

wheelchair now. Is Ms. Copeland in her eighties, too?
(Inmate nods) I thought so. We need to think ahead.
And with Henrietta Tidwell and Faye Copeland, this
will not be far in the future.

Inmate: *(Stupefied)* I never thought...

Caseworker: *(Interrupts)* Exactly! No one thinks about it, but
everyone dies. You need to make plans. *(Pause)* And
you old lifers could get the area prepared and all dolled
up in anticipation. It would be yours! Ms. Prewitt,
you're so creative. I wanted to bounce this off you, especially since you will benefit from it!

Inmate: *(To audience, rises to pace)* I never saw this coming.
Did you? She wants to bury me out back—behind this
building. In the rick-racked shadow of the razor-wire
perimeter fence. Talk about digging your own grave!
She wants to bury all of us serving life with no parole.

The only difference between life without parole and
the death penalty is that the state *must* wait us out. No
cheating and hurrying along the process with lethal
injection, hanging, electrocution, firing squad, behead-
ing, or whatever other tricks they hide in their murderous state execution bag.

In the '70s, my sentence was called "natural life," meaning that your life "creeps in its petty pace from day to
day" behind bars, removed from society until you die
naturally of "natural causes." Lack of both adequate
medical care and proper nutrition are perfectly natural. But there's nothing at all natural about the slow
decay of your heartbroken flesh as prison officials wait
patiently (or impatiently in this case)—as they bide
their time, and yours, in hopes that you will give up
your ghost, much sooner than later. Prison rot is inevitable and terminal.

Personally, I'm not near ready for...permanent placement in a prisoner's plot.

(Pause, breath) OK. At least I'm not in trouble and no one in my family has died. But I sure never guessed this subject would rise from the grave.

Caseworker: *(Interrupts, so inmate sits down)* Ms. Prewitt, I see your wheels turning and can tell you're already plotting on this. *(Giggles)* Plotting! Get it? As in burial plots? That's funny and I didn't even know I said it. *(Giggles some more.)*

Inmate: *(Attempts to chuckle)* Yeah, you crack me up, Ms. Simmons.

Caseworker: Hey, it just hit me! Why can't the students in the Building Trades class construct the pine coffins? That would be a good trade for them to learn. I imagine there's a serious need for coffin carpenters in the free world. It would be rehabilitation for them! The Department of Corrections is all about rehabilitation.

Inmate: *(Subtly sarcastically)* Yeah, that's a great idea. The Department of Corrections is famous for saving lives.

Caseworker: *(Epiphany)* And this just hit me! Fabric Tech could line the coffins and make the little pillows!

Inmate: *(To audience, stands)* Do you remember that old '50s sci-fi movie where the alien warns us in his robotic monotone, "Resistance is fu-tile?" That alien must have worked for the Intergalactic Department of Universal Corrections. But aliens *are* known for their superior intelligence. So, beam me up, Scotty. I'm gonna ride her crazy UFO.

(Turns to caseworker excitedly) Ms. Simmons, we could even invent a whole new class to make the headstones. People die every day and must be immortalized! You should speak to the vo-tech lady and see if she'd look into offering a "master stone cutting class."

Caseworker: I never thought of that! I bet that's a lucrative career opportunity.

Inmate: *(To caseworker)* Prisoners used to break rocks all the time. Somehow, we've gotten away from tradition. You could lead us back in the right direction.

Caseworker: Let me make some notes. *(Grabs paper and pen)* This is why I called you, Prewitt. I knew you'd see my vision, and we'd be able to brainstorm.

Inmate: *(To caseworker)* And, get this, the cosmo class can style our hair and do the makeup. Hair and makeup on corpses is a *real* career.

Caseworker: Aren't you afraid they'd be kinda squeamish about working on you women after you're dead?

Inmate: *(To caseworker)* Shoot, no. Many of these girls are in here for murder. I certainly won't be the first corpse they've ever seen, and everyone knows all the old lifers.

(To audience) We're collectively lumped as "life-doin'-bitches" while some affectionately call us "toe-taggers."

Caseworker: You have a good point there, Prewitt. I guess it wouldn't have to be mandatory for all the cosmo students to participate. It could be an "extracurricular" option.

Inmate: *(To caseworker)* Yes. Extracurricular option. Perfect.

Caseworker: Thank you, Prewitt. You've been a big help. I'm going to take all these ideas and write up a proposal.

Inmate: *(Rousingly to caseworker)* Don't give up! Don't let them shoot you down. If this administration doesn't go for it, take it to Central Office or to the governor.

(Pause, still brainstorming) Of course, the chaplain would conduct the funerals. He does memorial services all the time for the hapless who croak in here. The only difference for him is that we'll have the dead bodies right here for viewing.

Caseworker: Yes, yes, that's in his job description.

Inmate: *(To caseworker)* Oh, my gosh! Get this: What if we added an embalming class, too. We could take care of the entire process right on these grounds. Our own morgue! We wouldn't even have to transport the cadavers off the prison grounds and back again. We have refrigeration—right in the food warehouse!

Caseworker: *(Scribbling)* Yes, refrigeration. Thanks. Thanks so much. This is great.

Inmate: *(Rising from chair)* Well, Ms. Simmons, glad to be of service. And thank you so much for thinking of us. I feel all warm and fuzzy. We usually feel forgotten, ya know. Let me know how it goes.

Caseworker: *(Scribbling, distracted)* Yes, yes, of course.

(Grabs papers and exits quickly while inmate talks to the audience)

Inmate: *(To audience)* All in all, this was not a bad caseworker experience. I'm not in trouble. No one died. *(Pause)* Yet. She's finally getting the princess wedding she always dreamed about, and she thinks I'm chock full of great ideas. On top of that, I feel a renewed vigor aimed toward my efforts to get free before I *do* die in here.

I'd better warn my old lifers that there's a "plot" against us, and that this is a "grave" situation. *(Laughs)* Get it? Oooo, I gotta stop.

(To herself) Nobody's going to believe this. I haven't got a "ghost" of a chance.

(Exits shaking head and chuckling)

Fin

December 2, 2013

Dear Marsha,

My trial attorney Bob Beaird wrote an op-ed in the *Kansas City Star* about me! The headline reads, "Prewitt Should Be Granted Clemency." He opens by mentioning the vacating of Ryan Ferguson's murder conviction that shows our criminal justice system is not perfect. "As a prosecutor, defense lawyer, and recently retired judge, I have seen our system from all sides and can attest to its strengths and its shortcomings."

The article is lengthy and brings in the fact that investigators, "Failed to collect and, in some cases, simply ignored key evidence." He mentioned that they withheld the fact that the neighbor saw a car watching our house the night Bill was murdered. He wrote that if I'd accepted the plea agreement offered, I would have paroled after seven years. He also went on to give facts about the executive power of commutation used by presidents and governors. He pleaded for Governor Nixon to free me. All in all, he wrote a great argument, and I thank him!

January 6, 2014

Dear Nancy,

When I called home today, Mary could hardly pronounce the words that Daddy is gone. Since he and Momma have been in the same hospital for days, I was able to call and talk to both of them through family. The last thing I assured Daddy was that it's OK to go on, we will take care of Momma. Frank held the phone to Daddy's ear, and I whispered what Daddy already knew—how much he was loved and admired.

When I numbly emerged from the phone room after trying to soothe my sister's heart, Janiece saw my face and rushed over to hug me hard. Over the loudspeaker, we heard them call, "Moore to the rotunda." We both knew she was being called out for hugging.

We are not allowed any physical contact, no matter the reason.

I marched into the rotunda with Janiece, and as soon as they started chastising her, I broke in, "Oh, so you're only going to call out the Black girl? It takes two to hug! I'm guilty, too, but you were only going to make a scene over the Black girl." We both launched in on them, and when we felt we'd made our point, we turned on our heels and waltzed back to the dayroom.

Daddy would have enjoyed our civil disobedience. I'm having trouble coming to the realization that he's no longer with us.

February 17, 2014

Dear Nancy,

No work today. It's Washington's birthday. The state loves Monday holidays, but this whole week will be messed up for me. Tomorrow will be Tuesday, but it will feel like Monday. Plus, holidays don't mean anything in here. We're not traveling or visiting or eating something special—like cherry pie for George. We don't even have recreation on holidays.

Gary came to see me Friday for Valentine's Day. That silly man always uses markers to draw a heart on his chest with our initials (GK+PP) for Valentine's Day and has to sneak his shirt open slightly for me to peek at it. And it's always kinda wonky since he's executing it in a mirror. And scary since he'd get kicked out and I'd get written up if we're caught!

During a serious discussion, his blue eyes bored into me and asked, "Do you honestly think you're never coming home?" The only answer for him that made sense was, "No, I don't think I'll ever be free." If I told him the truth that I can't ever give up hope, he would count on that and keep torturing himself. So, I gave him an answer that would make it easier for him to move on with his life.

It's obvious to me that he's tired of traveling across the state to sit in an uncomfortable plastic chair for hours, eating stale vending machine junk food, and having to obey all the stupid rules—with no end in sight. They've installed cameras in the visiting room to ensure that we don't touch, even ever so slightly, or gaze too long, too lovingly. This place is no place to act naturally. We can't even talk quietly without an officer sidling over to ear hustle. The only visits he truly enjoys are the 4H visits with the kids when he can bring in his guitar and entertain the club.

We Had A Good Run

May 7, 2014

Dear Gary,

Your letter didn't surprise me. When you were here last weekend, you were not only distant, but you were also nervous—not yourself. I felt you had something to tell me, and you did.

This woman sounds like a good match. You may think that I'm angry, but I'm not. Haven't I been urging you to move on? I never wanted to keep you from having a good life. I never wanted you to be saddled with this life-doin' prisoner. My doggone sister started this!

I understand why you didn't tell me in person. You would have bawled like a big baby and caused an embarrassing scene. Relationships in the visiting room are never "normal." There's no privacy. Only toddlers get to have a meltdown with no judgment. "He's sleepy" or "He's teething" are valid excuses for a kid but not for a grown man.

I believe in a clean break, so tomorrow I'll have you removed from my visiting list. I'll no longer call or write. You can't move on if you have a foot in two ponds. Don't write to me, either. Concentrate on your new relationship. It's the only way, Gary.

I truly wish you the best. You've been a kind and fun companion. Take care.

May 24, 2014

Dear Mary,

In this zoo, we never know what craziness might ensue. Last night after recreation, I scored a shower. Getting a shower between 8:00 and 9:00 am, rush hour, is a miracle. As I schlepped my way down the hall, shower shoes flapping, I noticed Hazel sitting on the floor beside her cell door. She was holding all her clothes and shower bag, just like me. I hollered, "Hey, Hazel, what's up? Locked out?"

Hazel is a tiny, young blonde, like a Hummel doll, from Southeast Missouri. Somewhere down near the Bootheel, I believe. She's lived up the hall for a while, but I've never caught her sitting on the not-so-clean hall floor at count time.

Hazel looked like she might cry, so I walked closer. She sensed that I was not moving on until I got an answer, so she whispered, "They locked me out." I peered into the window of her cell door to see three people. "What? They won't let you in?" Sheepishly Hazel explained to me that she didn't pull the door close enough to the jam when she exited the room. Two of her cellmates had previously chewed her out for not closing the door to their liking. As punishment, they shut the door. The cell doors in this prison can only be opened from the outside with a key. Hazel hadn't taken her cell key with her to the shower. I never do either, unless there's no one in my cell—and that rarely occurs.

The whole situation angered me, so I knocked on the door while looking straight at one of them. She just kept staring at her TV. I stomped back to my cell and threw my clothes and shower bag onto my bunk. I needed to have both hands free for this battle.

The loudspeaker boomed, "Count time. Count time. Go to your rooms. Count time."

Hazel sat on the floor while I beat on her door. I yelled at the top of my lungs, "Open this door!" In desperation I screamed, "Open this goddamn door right now!"

(Since I'd cursed with the GD word, I was glad my mother wasn't there to hear me. When we were kids, we got records in the mail from the Columbia Record Club. Momma chose piano concertos, Daddy picked Johnny Cash, and we kids loved rock 'n' roll. Frankie was playing his new Steppenwolf, when the singer sang, "Goddamn! The pusher. Goddamn! Goddamn the pusher. I said Goddamn! Goddamn the pusher man," Momma appeared from the kitchen, ripped that LP off the turntable with no regard for the scratching needle, marched to the screen door, and frisbeed that record out into the yard. "No one will take the Lord's name in vain in *my* house!")

Amy was doing her best to stay out of the mess, but Ashley leaped off her top bunk and joined me. (Ashley is young, beautiful, a tall athlete, and ready to join in on anything crazy.) We kicked and screamed like mad maniacs! Heads poked out of doors, but no one wanted to cross the occupants of Hazel's room. You must pick your battles in prison.

As the officers popped the door of our wing, the main bully opened Hazel's door and lied, "Oh, we didn't hear you." I yelled back that people in Jeff City heard us.

Early the next morning before I'd left for work, Mrs. Wilder, my caseworker, asked me what that was all about last night. She'd already heard. I told her the truth, of course. I was wrong to yell and beat on the door, but I didn't care. No one should be bullied like that. Later that day Hazel was moved into our cell and the bully was moved to another housing unit. Sometimes you just gotta make a stand regardless of the ramifications. And sometimes you come out on top.

July 10, 2014

Dear Janie,

So many of the new kids, the ones who just arrived in general population from Receiving and Orientation, come to aerobic classes. They are bursting to break an honest sweat and have physical fun. I love to see them enthusiastically run into the gym for step aerobics class or "Butts 'n Guts." I carry a plastic file to classes, in which

I keep exercise plans and ideas, my headband, music CDs, and hair ties. Most of these kids have massive amounts of hair and no way to hold it up off their necks. I've been giving out hair ties for many years! They're cheap, but it takes about four to get control of a messy bun for most of these kids.

Tonight, before class, a kid told me that there are guards who stand outside 4-House and confiscate hair ties if the kids don't have canteen receipts proving they bought them. How petty. This is a maximum-security prison. Surely there are more serious infractions than wearing a hair tie that you didn't buy. But there are ways around these guys. I couldn't announce this over the mic, so I walked around and told the ones who had my hair ties to make sure they took them out of their hair before they got to their dorm. "Pull the hair ties out and shove them in your bra or socks." I heard that all the ones who hide them failed to lose their prized hair ties!

Oh, there's another hair tie insanity here, too. If we're not using the hair tie in our hair at the moment, we put the tie on a wrist for safekeeping. Recently it's become an unwritten rule that a hair tie on a wrist is a violation! Yes, guards tell us that the hair tie is not being used for the purpose for which it is intended. Of course, this is just another made-up reason to harass us. Outsiders would never believe this crap. You'll never see a prison movie in which prisoners are chastised for hair tie infractions, but it's a big pain in here!

July 15, 2014

Dear Nancy,

Hello! Hope you are all in great health and spirits! I like to keep you posted on any developments, and Brian emailed me the following last week: "John Ammann is organizing a conference call with about a half dozen lawyers in an effort to create a clemency coalition.

That is precisely what Tom, Jane, and I think is necessary to get the governor to move on the petitions. Tom and Jane will join me on the call. I'll keep you posted."

John Ammann is a law professor at St. Louis University, and he's had success with clemency petitions. He's a friend of lawyer Jane Aiken, who is also mentioned. Tom is Brian's lead counsel at Brian's law firm in DC.

Those lawyers want to form a clemency coalition of lawyers who represent older women and put out a press release and a letter to the governor. They figure that they need to try hard to push him to grant clemencies this year, but if they don't, it won't happen until late in 2016 when his term is up—if at all.

On Monday, I got an email from Brian saying that none of the other lawyers John A. contacted want to join the clemency coalition, but they are going to form it anyway. I emailed Brian that I bet Beaird, Cardarella, Burnett, and O'Brien from KC might join—and they are all well known.

Please hold this latest strategy in your prayers.

Danny Kohl and Elizabeth visited me last Friday, and Danny (who will be eighty-six at the end of the month) and his wife will be on the East Coast and will get to see my play performed at the Kennedy Center on August 30. Brian and Jane Aiken plan to attend, too. It's sponsored by the Safe Streets Foundation.

Elizabeth has been traveling quite a bit, but she's been working on our play, too. She's writing a one-woman play about my plight.

Cierra is fourteen!? Callie turned thirteen at the end of June. They were all in diapers not long ago. In a short four years, Cierra will be going off to college. Callie is in theater camp most of this month. She loves that stuff. Abbey is in a photography class at Longview. It's fun to watch them explore and find their interests. Callie and Leah must have a lot in common. Callie made a killing at a lemonade stand last year. My Drew is still the sweetest kid with a huge smile. Megan is bossy and athletic.

Morgan got to see his three kids over the Fourth of July weekend. His wife remarried and moved to Nevada, but she has family in Grain Valley. Morgan got to have about four hours with them. He couldn't stop talking about Patrick, Alyssa, and Matthew. Poor

Morgan ruptured a disk and will need surgery. I hate that for him.

Thanks for the Summer Solstice Celebration program and readings. Love, love, love.

July 18, 2014

Dear Beth,

I'm really excited about you being in St. Louis for two semesters! Woohoo! I want you to meet Elizabeth Townsend, the actor who's working on the one-woman play about me. Danny found her, and she's so warm and loving. I'm just crazy about her.

Oh, and thanks for the birthday card. You asked about my sixty-fifth birthday. Well, the kids on the dorm worked on it for months, but it didn't go as planned. Nothing in prison ever does...

The day shift officers on our house simply detest those of us who inhabit B-wing. Why? Janiece asked point blank and was told, "You think you are so smart. You get away with everything. You make us sick. Just because you have dogs, you think you can get by with anything."

Janiece retorted, "What are we getting by with? We abide by the rules. We are the only wing on camp that does. We don't smoke inside. We don't fight or shoot drugs. We keep the place clean and quiet, too. And we don't get anything, any privileges, more than any other wing gets. We live under the same rules." They countered with, "You *think* your shit don't stink and that you're better than the rest."

That is *not* true. We *are* better than the rest. We only allow the cream of the crop to live on our wing. I tell you all this to prepare you for the events of July 4, 2014.

The guards found a memo in the file stating that we had permission to celebrate my birthday together on the evening of the holiday. The memo was written and signed by our caseworker. Did I mention that these officers hate her, too? She's well aware of that in case you wondered.

One reason the guards hate us is because we have the service dog training program on our wing. It makes no sense, but they hate that women are being instructed to train dogs to help people who need them. They think we shouldn't have the luxury of having dogs in our midst. I've heard them say that! Most guards seem to be miserable themselves. As soon as they put on a polyester outfit and a tin badge, they think it's their job to make inmates more miserable than they are—and those of us who keep a stiff upper lip and make the most of our plight are disgusting in their book. Sad but true.

At around four on the Fourth, a no-nonsense white shirt (that's what we call officers that rank above COI, like a private in the army, because they sport shirts of white), who's been here for ages and knows us well, burst in and loudly ordered all sixty of us to the dayroom to warn us that we could not have a party. (So much for the surprise aspect of the surprise party.) He said that Warden Mesmer had been called at home and sent down the command that there will be no party. (We didn't believe they really called the warden on a holiday, but we later found out that we were wrong. They did! And she did!)

Janiece stepped up and calmly asked, "Sir, can we sit in the dayroom like usual? Can we bring our food out and eat in the dayroom as usual? Can we play games in the dayroom as usual? Then what is your problem? We won't do anything we don't usually do and won't break any of the housing unit rules."

I honestly think he was a bit embarrassed to be bothered with the task, so he stammered, "Do what you usually do," and he turned on his heel and left us. We burst out laughing before the steel door slammed on our passive-aggressive response. We then meandered back to our cells while yelling to each other, "See you all after count! We'll do exactly what we usually do. *Not* party."

After count, after smoke break, and after med line call, we assembled, ate our finger foods, and played games while the guards glared at us through the glass of the rotunda. Katie, our hostess and party organizer, had checked out a book of word games and emceed. Each table of girls became a team. Katie had also bought a bag of suckers and cheap candy for prizes. Inmates will do most anything for prizes and/or for candy.

Shelley handed me a bag of Rolos, "This is not a birthday gift since this is not a birthday party."

"OK, I won't thank you then!"

Once, when we were laughing a bit loudly, a strange new white shirt wearing a Grim Reaper mask stepped in the door of our wing. I rose and announced, "Ladies, let's bow our heads in prayer." Everyone did, as I continued, "Heavenly Father, thank you for blessing us with a warm, safe dry place to live and for good friends..."

He retreated into the rotunda and closed the door between us. Prayer always scares them. I continued, "And thank you for giving us guards who hate our guts but are too stupid to know when we are actually having a party. Party animals, can I get an amen?"

Everyone joined in with an amen that would have made any Baptist proud. We then went on to the next game, which was to find the best guard imitation. I think we partied longer and harder since we weren't supposed to.

Oh, also, the wild women on D-wing also had a birthday party for an old-timer over there. Their party was a complete surprise to the officers, but it turned out to be a wonderful diversion for us, because they are naturally louder and ruder. The rotunda officers were overwhelmed!

Lord only knows what kind of trouble we'll get into for my seventy-fifth birthday celebration.

Finger foods in prison: All food must be purchased from the canteen or stolen from food service, so all prison parties serve pretty much the same fare.

A couple of girls made "fudge balls" out of peanut butter, sugar, and a Hershey bar all melted together in the microwave and rolled into little bite-size balls. The balls are then rolled in powdered hot chocolate mix. Not everyone can manage the correct consistency, but those ones were perfect.

Another fan favorite is a round corn tortilla chip smeared with plastic squeeze cheese. On top of that is a layer of rehydrated refried beans, then a topping of white rice seasoned with diced and fried summer sausage. Jalapeño rings are optional.

Katie also hardened flour tortillas in the microwave and quartered them into triangles. On those pie shapes she scooped a teaspoon of a mixture of Mrs. Dash seasoning, chopped jalapeño wheels, bagged chicken breast, white rice, finely chopped broccoli and cauliflower (sold frozen in bags as a fundraiser) and ranch dressing as the glue. They also disappeared quickly.

Round tortilla chips layered with plastic cheese, spaghetti sauce (that comes in a plastic bottle and is beyond mild—more like watered-down catsup), and fried pepperonis were also served. Pizza-like.

Snack crackers (Ritz knockoffs) smeared with peanut butter and topped with a dollop of strawberry preserves, grape jelly, or honey are always a hit.

Games: Katie had each table sing a popular song in an odd style. My table had to sing "99 Problems" as an opera, so Lindra and I rose to the occasion and wowed the crowd with our off-key but dramatic rendition. (To give you some idea of how awful it was, I don't even know that song.) Theresa killed it and won with Beyonce's "Put a Ring on it" sung as a Broadway musical. She danced better than Ethel Merman, which was genius. (Of course, no one in here knows Ethel Merman.)

Amy Sherrill drew pictures and had everyone guess who they were. Amy can't draw, so it was not as easy as one might think.

Today our caseworker told Janiece that she'll never write another IOC in regard to a party. They were forewarned, and that will never happen again. We'll just surprise them.

I call Momma daily, and I'm encouraged at how chipper she sounds. She seems to be doing good on her own with the help of my siblings. My son Morgan visited yesterday which made her day, but I know she must look at Daddy's empty chair a lot.

A mutual friend wrote me that he recently ate lunch with Gary and his new woman. Our friend reported that they seem very pleased with each other. I'm happy for him. Honestly.

He deserves a good life.

September 10, 2014

Dearest Janie,

Ever since Gary and I broke it off, girls have been giving me grief. It seems that our love, our relationship had been revered as a fantasy that became real. He was the kind, gentle beau that every inmate in here wished she could find. He came to see me regularly and even brought his family to meet me. He went to all the trouble to transport my family to visit and played music at our 4H family visits. He was never angry or rude. He was perfect in the eyes of these kids who don't know many good men. And Gary is a good man. They got that right.

Even staff members have asked me what happened. Everyone loves Gary. But everyone was not privy to his anguish at the inability to get me home. He came into this struggle late and at first couldn't understand the frustration felt by our family, who have been battling since your daddy was murdered. Now for nearly two decades, he's talked to and argued with lawyers and legislators and better understands that no matter what anyone does or says, no matter how many rallies we have or how many letters or calls are made, the people in power don't care.

Amy looked at Gary as a father figure and misses him with the same hurt she felt when her parents divorced. Our breakup has picked the scab from the wound of her father's suicide. I feel guilty for inadvertently hurting Amy—and you, too.

No one seems to be looking at this from Gary's point of view. He deserves a full life—a full life, *not* a life spent in a mean prison visiting room worrying about me. Unfortunately, you kids can't extract yourselves from this nightmare, but I'm hoping that Gary can.

February 19, 2015

Dear Nancy,

Agnes decided we will perform French playwright Molière's one-act farce, *The Flying Doctor.* I won the double role of Sganarelle and his twin doctor brother. I asked Agnes if I could use a French accent for the doctor, and in all seriousness, she asked, "Do you have a French accent?"

In all seriousness, I replied, "I have Pepé Le Pew." I was thinking he'd fit since Pepe was the epitome of self-delusion.

With a straight face, Agnes asked, "And who is Pepé Le Pew?" I blinked and realized that she was being honest. She had no clue. Sacré bleu!

But she is letting me do it with my lame French skunk accent.

April 29, 2015

Dear Sade,

Today marks twenty-nine years since I've been locked away from you all. And it's the 29th. I wonder if there's some sort of numerology significance. Probably not. I'm so sorry that I haven't been able to get back to you.

A woman who lives on my wing had her first grandbaby a few months ago and is expecting her first visit with her daughter and the baby. (Currently policy is that no one, including newborns, can visit without a Social Security number.) Shirley is scared that the baby won't want her to hold him since she's a stranger. This is a common fear, so I explained to her my theory since my grandbabies had no problem coming to me and nuzzling into my embrace. My daughters look like me, and we share a familial scent. I assured her that this baby would instinctively know he belongs to her.

Today Shirley returned from her visit bursting with joy and pulled me into the laundry room to hug me tight. I was right! Her grandson didn't hesitate and immediately reached out to her with a drooling grin. I hope her daughter can bring this kid to visit Shirley on a regular basis during her prison term. I think she's only serving a seven at 50 percent.

The unnatural separation of family because of imprisonment is rarely discussed inside or outside prison. If I ever get out of this cage, I want to shout out about the extreme heartache endured by both children and inmates.

June 1, 2015

Dear Carrie and Tom,

I'm still in shock. Today the wardens came to my shop and told us that we would no longer be coding for the Department of Corrections. In other words, we are unemployed! They are moving all our work to the men's prison in Jeff City.

In the early '80s, before I entered the polluted world of incarceration, a group of female prisoners filed a gender discrimination suit because the only classes for women were classes involving cooking or hair and nails. Classic women's classes. Because of that suit, our law library was pumped up with the books needed to do actual legal work, like appeals. Vocational classes for skills like automotive, carpentry, and gardening were talked about, and some were instituted. We also got to study to be computer programmers. That's what I fell into. For the other classes, we had to be close to our parole date, but they took lifers for coders. I began studying in 1995 and have been designing and writing tracking systems for twenty years. I'm darned good at it, too. Which really angers me that the men at JCCC now have all the work, and we have been kicked to the curb. Talk about gender discrimination!

I'm digging in my footlocker to find the law agency who won the suit in the '80s. I plan to write them to see what can be done. It seems that we are constantly gaining ground, then losing it a few years later with changes in the administration.

June 10, 2015

Dear Mary,

Get a load of this insanity. When I called Momma today, she was upset. She said that Morgan had called from jail in Florida and needed bond money. I asked if she was sure the voice was Morgan, and she was. She said it was a bad connection though. The voice didn't specifically say it was Morgan, but she said who else would call her "grandma" and need that kind of help?

Momma doesn't have control over her money and was desperately calling Mary. I tried to convince Momma that Morgan wasn't in Florida, but she was adamant that he had called and was in need. I then called Morgan who said, "I wish I were in Florida."

He was working on a kitchen remodel in Lawrence and soaked in sweat. I told him to take a break and call his grandma. I called Momma about an hour later, and she was still confused even when I swore that I'd called Morgan myself.

What a cruel scam to try to pull on a sweet grandma. If I got my hands on this man, there would be hell to pay.

August 13, 2015

Dear Marsha,

Finally, finally! Finally, we know what we have! We have scabies! We've suffered for months! Months! Since last year! We've been miserable! I didn't even know about such a thing. We've been terrorized by microscopic spiders under our skin!

This began with just a couple of girls who complained. The nurse told them they were allergic to their detergent, but that was not it. While those girls tried to find the cause and some relief, the scabies spread. Nearly everyone on our wing was affected. I had itchy scabby skin all over my back. A hot shower made it worse!

After I'd gone to sick call a half a dozen times, I finally got to see the nurse practitioner. I cried on her examining table. Cried! She told me I had eczema and had had it all my life. That's not true. I cried harder. To get me out of her room, she gave me ten days of steroids. I have to say it did help with the pain, but didn't cure me.

After a month or so, Medical put up a sign for sick call that read, "If you're here for itchy skin, we will not see you." Can you imagine a sign like that at a free-person clinic? We caused such a fuss that the doctor came to our wing to tell us that this was either a group hallucination or too hot shower water. We collectively yelled at him. When he entered my room, I whipped off my T-shirt to show him my back. He stumbled back like he'd never seen flesh before and reiterated the hot shower theory. I loudly told him that there's no hot water in prison in the winter!

ShaSha thought it was bed bugs, so she threw her mattress on the floor and slept on the steel bunk. That's how awful the problem has been. We got no help from Medical or from the administration.

Emily's mother decided to fight and started calling the warden and everyone in the Department of Corrections. Bless her! She caused such a fuss that Medical decided to send three inmates out to a dermatologist. Emily, Tessa, and Jean were trussed up and shipped out. They came back with the diagnosis of scabies. Tessa told me that the doctor took one look at her hand and scrapped one of the buggers out easily. We were not "group hallucinating" and it's not because of hot water! It's an infestation! And it easily spreads. Tessa's mom caught scabies from her on a visit.

Once we got the diagnosis, we were culled from the herd. We could not go to work or Rec or church. We went to chow as a group and ate alone. Because we were an added inconvenience for staff, they were short-tempered with us. We had to march single file to the chow hall, and as we fell into step, Amy launched into that march song, "I don't know, but I been told...this damned place is getting old!"

Even the shrinking violets joined in, while our lyrics grew raunchier. It was freeing fun until a big, bellied sergeant bellowed, "Stop that now!"

Medical had to order insecticide for scabies, and we went through a weird treatment. We stood in line while nurses showered us and helped us rub this special scabies killer on our raw skin. I felt like Oliver Twist as I cupped my hands and asked, "More, please."

We had to leave the substance on our skin for hours before we could wash it off. During that time, we were issued no-longer-white jumpsuits, used bras, used drawers, new socks and marched to the gym to wait. Stained panties are disgusting, so as soon as I got to the gym, I dipped into the toilet and discarded them. A bunch of us did. I went "commando" from then on. After the prescribed number of hours, we had to shower the stuff off our skin and put on another set of clothes. That time I simply refused the used panties. Also, our bedding was washed and treated in the institutional laundry. All our personal clothes were washed with some sort of insecticide, so we didn't have anything of our own. We demanded disinfectant and rags, and a group of us washed down the whole wing from top to bottom.

That process had to be done twice! During the second time, after we showered the medicine off, there was no jumpsuit to fit Jean, who is a full-sized woman. (One morning she smuggled two oranges for me from the food warehouse but forgot they were in her bodacious bosom until that night.) Poor Jean stood naked in a shower stall while this tall, thin asshole lieutenant hollered at her to get out of the shower. (If I were making a prison movie, I'd cast him. He's perfect: weak chin, too close eyes, too big nostrils, pathetic attempt at a mustache, Adam's apple the size of a real apple. Perfect.) I could hear her trying to explain, but he is not the kind of man to listen to an inmate. He yelled, "Put a sheet around you!"

That's when I got involved. To defend Jean, I approached him. He snatched my arm and dragged and jerked me down the stairs, hollering that he was taking me to the hole. I thought for sure I would fall face-first since my feet only hit every fifth riser, but he had a very secure hold on my upper arm. Since I had the gall to debate him about anything in this godforsaken prison, he was furious. Once we were hidden in the classification hallway, he slung me into a plastic chair and started in on me.

Why he started with this question, I'll never know. But it is a common guard-like question. "Do you wanna go to the hole?" He wanted crying and begging. I refuse to do either. I replied, "Does anyone *ever* want to go to the hole? Do you expect me to say yes? Has anyone ever said yes? If so, who was it?" What'd I have to lose? He planned on slamming me no matter what I said.

The next ten minutes consisted of him screaming obscenities at me while I calmly talked about choices. Somehow, I got way off-track preaching that we all need to plant trees right now and not wait. We could be Johnny Appleseeds. In exasperation, he grabbed my arm and jerked me to my feet while pushing me to the door into the rotunda. We have big windows from the four wings so that guards can look into our housing unit for security, but windows look both ways. Crowded behind the glass of every wing were hundreds of angry ladies. Word had spread that he was threatening me and that he'd told our beloved Jean to wrap herself in a thin state sheet. This mob delighted me as much as it frightened that "tough guy." He released me and gruffly, but not loudly, ordered me to go to my cell. I didn't. I stopped dead and slowly commanded, "Find a jumpsuit to fit Jean." The mob started chanting that mantra. They found one.

December 25, 2015

Dear Nancy,

Hazel designed a big 3-D Advent calendar complete with gifts behind little doors and hung it on the back of the door on the third, the beginning of Advent. I can't tell you how much Amy has enjoyed it! Every morning she pops up to see what little gift or words of wisdom she'll find. Amy's childlike exuberance is infectious. My heart swells and smiles at the antics of these funny kids. I think many people would be very surprised to know that some of us make the best of a bad situation by simply being kind, creative, and loving. It's easy to do and makes so much difference in our daily lives. Out of scraps of paper and toothpaste as adhesive, Hazel designed and built the best Advent calendar ever, and that creation made our Christmas season exactly what Christmas should be about. I know you worry about me, Nancy, but I am blessed with good kids under my wings.

We also have a tradition on Christmas morning. We make copies of the best-known Christmas songs, like "Joy to the World," and the Christmas story from scripture, and distribute scripts to each of the eight rooms up here. (Amy keeps these copies in her foot-locker from the year before.) When they call "count" at 11:30, we begin singing from our cell doors. Most of the girls love it, because we don't have any church services on Christmas day. This morning, we had nearly 100 percent participation. It feels so good—nearly normal in a far-from-normal prison way.

March 20, 2016

Dear Carrie,

My sweet friend Danny Kohl died a few days ago. I can't believe it. You met him at your grandpa's funeral.

Danny was such a loving and interesting friend. He was eighty-seven and sharp as a tack—a scientist and professor at Washington University for thirty-eight years and still working. Danny was a lifelong political activist involved in antiwar efforts and environmental and civil rights movements. When he'd visit, he'd tell me amazing stories of traveling to the South to fight against segregation and racism. He was part of the advocacy for the people of Times Beach and got those residents evacuated. (Oh, Missouri used to spray a toxic mix of dioxins and waste oil on roads and horse tracks. People and horses died, and eventually the town of Times Beach, just southeast of St. Louis, was evacuated in 1982 after public outcry.)

Besides all the academic achievements, Danny was a kind and generous soul. I loved him so. They don't make them like that anymore.

July 10, 2016

Dear Beth,

On Friday, Brian and Jane Aiken called the prison immediately after their ninety-minute fantastic meeting. Brian mentioned you, and I said, "I had no clue that Beth was part of the team." Brian shot back with, "She didn't either." Then he went on to explain how he used you to "tighten" up his presentation. Thank you so much.

Elizabeth Townsend also talked to Brian. They are coordinating efforts for her play *Count Time* at the Fringe Festival in August in St. Louis.

July 28, 2016

Dearest Nancy,

Got your card and applied for a special visit with you, Tom, and Heather. What a treat to see pretty Heather! It's been a long time. See you on August 26.

For our PPA adaptation of George Orwell's *Animal Farm*, I designed and sewed vests for each actor according to their animal, while Tessa made headdresses to match. The lady I work for at Restorative Justice, Mrs. Stathem, allowed us to use donated fabric. For example, I found a scrap of a black and white "Holstein cow" print for Tessa's cow vest, and she made her own horned cap.

When I was nearly finished, I brought samples over to show Chris, our director, to hopefully get approval. Thank heaven, he loved the collection! I felt like I was a contestant on the *Project Runway* reality show and winning! My Granny Snow taught me how to cut patterns out of newspaper, a skill that has served me well through the years.

My nearly-fifteen-year-old Callie recently wrote a paper on *Animal Farm*, considers herself an expert, and is so excited to see us. She counseled me to *not* take the part of Old Major, because she dies very soon, but I took it anyway. I'm old and the kids need to shine.

August 6, 2016

Dear Bunky,

Today was crazy! We've been performing our adaptation of *Animal Farm* in the gym and moved the set to the visiting room in order to perform two shows for visitors and staff. When Sheena showed up, she "signed" that she had completely lost her voice—and she's Napolean, the head hog!

Chris Limber, our director, declared that since my character pig dies at the beginning of the play, I'll have to stand at the side of the set and recite Sheena's lines. What?! We were all scared this wouldn't work at all, but we did our best. Carrie, Tom, Callie, and Drew attended. The kids love these plays.

After we took our bows, I ran over to our family to see if they thought our *fix* was OK. Tom explained that at first it was weird for my voice to seemingly come from Sheena's mouth, but since we'd rehearsed so much, our timing was nearly perfect. Sheena mimed the lines as I spoke. It worked!

Oh, another actor, Tessa, lost her father to a massive heart attack between shows Thursday. Her mother came into the visiting room to tell her the bad news. We were shocked and selfishly feared Tessa wouldn't be able to make the final show, but she girded her loins and pushed through.

October 15, 2016

Dearest Nancy,

I'm *thrilled* to hear that yoga is rejuvenating you! Yeah! Yoga and Pilates are so smart and body friendly!

Elizabeth is searching for other theater venues—and has some for next year, but we're anxious to get the word out *this year* for Governor Nixon.

I called my sister Mary yesterday. She will start chemo soon but is healing now from the surgery. Frank is a great guide for her since he's blazed the cancer trail. Mary would welcome a call. A couple of weeks ago, she was too ill from the surgery, but now she sounds like herself. This weekend her son Justin and her old friend Sue Nichols are there to put away all her plants—winterize—since she can't lift.

Momma's doing good—just wanting me to come home before she dies. I work on that goal every day and have been forever. It's so frustrating.

I just completed a big, bright, round multicolored afghan for Abbey's fifteenth birthday.

Oh, I nearly forgot to tell you that for the past two weeks, I was part of a PPA workshop with a NYC playwright professor, Stacie Lents, and an LA videographer, Lisa Boyd. It's been amazing! We've been playing all sorts of games as a group while also being interviewed individually. Stacie says she will write a play inspired by us (the cast of *Animal Farm*), and we'll perform it in April. The filmmaker will record the whole process and create a documentary. It was *intense,* but the two women are fascinating.

At first, we were overwhelmingly "fazed" by the camera. We'd get shy when Lisa pointed that camera at us, but I can see how the Kardashians got accustomed to going about their day while being filmed. We morphed into unfazed and brutally honest.

They are coming back in a couple of weeks for more workshops. This PPA *"Mass Meaning—A New Plays Initiative"* includes the development, production, and documentation of three new plays. Those original scripts, by nationally respected playwrights, will illuminate the voices and experiences catalogued in theater workshops for incarcerated individuals in three Missouri state prisons. An independent documentary will follow the development and performance of the new works and enlighten the power of art as a "transformative element of rehabilitation and re-entry"—according to the flyer. It's been a much-needed vacation from incarceration! We "chosen few" are lucky to be involved in the experiment!

January 28, 2017

Dear Carrie and Tom,

What a day! I had a feeling, so I called home to find that
your Aunt Mary had passed on. She fought so hard these past
months, but the cancer had spread too far. When I hung up the
wall phone, I slowly walked back to my cell thinking about my
sweet sister.

You know as well as I do that Mary was a loving character who'd
actually give someone the shirt off her back. You were very young
and may not remember that snowy Christmas Day when she
showed up with a stranger and his young son that she'd picked
up hitchhiking. He was carrying a guitar, so Mary, as a musician,
figured he was safe. Turned out he was indeed a fine guitarist and
knew every Beatles song! We wrapped up gloves and socks as gifts
for them while the father sang for his supper.

When I was shipped off to prison, Mary stood outside of grocery
stores collecting signatures on clip-boarded petitions to persuade
Governor Ashcroft to pardon me. I think you kids were with her.
That was long before the internet.

As soon as I sank into my bunk and told my cellmates that Mary
was gone, a hateful guard cop-knocked (banged needlessly hard)
and yelled for us all to go to the dayroom. He was going to search
our cell. And that he did.

He spent hours in there, tearing everything apart. We six victims
huddled around a table while scouts periodically reported which
locker he was ransacking. It may sound like an awful thing to
happen when I'm mourning, but anger is a healthier emotion
than sadness in prison. Collectively, we of room 208 were beyond
pissed at that ass of a redneck idiot. Everyone on our wing was
also disgusted since major crimes were being committed all over
the housing unit while he terrorized the room occupied by the
most lawful. All six of us received conduct violations for piddly

items, such as three pencils. Policy states that inmates cannot own more than two.

I did my best to ruin that guy's Saturday by producing receipts for nearly everything he tried to confiscate. Amy always laughed at my obsession with hanging on to receipts, but that is exactly why. He did get me for having vegetables stored in my six-pack ice chest. As a fundraiser for the Long Timer's Organization, they sell two-pound bags of frozen vegetables on Fridays. Years ago, I asked a sensible white shirt if storing veggies in recycled plastic peanut butter jars was kosher. He determined that it was fine, especially since the jars are clear and officers can see exactly what's in them. I've reused those jars since, but that guy stated that the actual rule is that everything must remain in the original package. There was no debating.

As we were laboring over the monumental mess in our cell, a nice officer stopped by and told us that the "searcher" guard saw my face as I left the phone room and stated, "Something bad just happened to Prewitt, but I have something worse in mind."

Donna used to say that we never know if something is a blessing or a curse. That ass thought he cursed me, but he actually helped me get through the pain of losing my sweet little sister. White-hot anger cleansed my soul.

February 10, 2017

Dearest Nancy,

Did you see it on the news? We won the Super Bowl! We haven't done that since Len Dawson, I believe. I know you don't care about football even though your sons-in-law are Vikings fans, but we Chiefs fans have waited so, so long for a big win! This new quarterback is unique! We love Patrick Mahomes!

Amy wanted to throw a super Super Bowl party. We always have a Super Bowl celebration, but Amy wanted to include everyone, so we made decorations and lots of food. We invited every person who lives on our floor, about forty-eight (eight cells with usually six in a cell), and especially the girls who have nothing. Amy designed room invitations and slipped them under the door about a week before. Nearly all were surprised and grateful. I say nearly because no matter where you are, there's a party pooper in every crowd.

We have a fairly large TV in the dayroom upstairs, and both Amy and Aimee brought out and hooked up their little personal TVs. They wanted to create a "total sensory experience." Their words, not mine.

We popped a lot of corn. Some girls are good at making bite-size desserts and really showed off with Arrowhead logos on top of brownie bites and decorated cookies. I slathered fake cream cheese on little round fake Ritz crackers and added a squirt of strawberry jam on top. (Made hundreds, and they disappeared!) I filled my biggest plastic bowl full of my famous beans and rice to go over tortilla chips. Another girl made a big bowl of chili and cheese for the same purpose. We also stirred up generic Kool-Aid in all the water pitchers we could get our hands on.

As far as Super Bowl parties go, it was pathetic—but no one in prison or in the free world had more fun than we. Lady Gaga entertained us with her halftime show. (We use a lot of her music in our aerobics classes, so we sang and danced along with her!)

Since the game was so close and we won, the celebration was wild! At first guards tried to squelch our enthusiasm and complained about us sharing food, which is against the rules, but as the game progressed, some guards joined us in watching and cheering.

It was a great game, but it also was a loving, sharing time of community in hell.

June 25, 2017

Dear Mary,

I'm just now recovering from last week's play. We performed a very emotional piece all week. Last year, playwright Stacie Lents from New Jersey spent a few weeks here at the prison with the PPA cast of *Animal Farm*. From her interactions with us, she wrote *Run-On Sentence*, set in a prison. She was nervous when she brought the script in for a table read. Since it's about female prisoners, I told Stacie it would be like having a dozen cowboys critique a western. But she had nothing to worry about. Even though it hits on hard subjects, we love it. She captured our language and lives. It's painfully authentic.

Our director, Chris Limber, got permission to use steel prison "furniture" for our set. We used a bunk bed, a standup locker, and a footlocker. The bedding was what we inmates all use. Before and after the performances, I invited audience members to sit on the bottom bunk. Everyone who did was visibly appalled at the hardness of the steel bunk and thin plastic mattress. They also got to see that there's no room to sit up on the bottom bunk. I hammered in the point that we are confined thusly, day in and day out.

Tessa and I created a big, one-of-a-kind quilt for Stacie, and I urged all the cast members to personalize sections. When we presented it to her, she looked like she might explode with a combination of amazement (we are really good at art quilts), appreciation, surprise, and love. Her sweet face made all the stitches and hours of labor worthwhile.

Stacie skillfully wove in the daily difficulty prisoners have dealing with women guilty and not guilty of murder, sex crimes involving children, drug crimes, plus the pain of lifers who will never leave, restricting prison policies, and the effect on our families. Her play turned into a tapestry of understanding.

Although we didn't write it, we actors are proud of the production and the lessons taught. I wish that every man, woman, and child in the world could bear witness to our collaboration.

August 21, 2017

Dear Jane,

This place is just nuts! Today was the big total solar eclipse day! I know you guys traveled north to a great place to see it clearly. Well, in here, nothing is simple. Last week the prison canteen sold us solar glasses that were guaranteed to keep us from going blind while we watch the spectacle. Today as the time approached, we were ordered to leave our job details and all sent to our housing units. No inmates were allowed outside. No one in charge seemed to realize that we have windows, big windows, on the housing units. Especially in the phone rooms.

We had our special glasses, so we thought we were set. Sack lunches were wheeled in. We love sack lunches because we can freely trade stuff and even add cheese, jalapeños, pickles, and other condiments to make a dry sandwich edible. Can't do any of that in the chow hall. As she gave me her apple, Sheila commented, "I love a *snack* lunch."

Then the loudspeaker squawked that our eclipse sunglasses were not "approved." What? Approved by who? We were ordered to line up and turn in our cardboard glasses. Keeping glasses would result in a conduct violation. Those cardboard spectacles were now deemed to be contraband. We unruly loudmouths hollered that we had paid for them! We were told to shut up or get cuffed up.

Where there's a will, there's a way! I poked a small hole in a piece of notebook paper and projected the eclipse onto a wall. The most innovative method was the saltine cracker method. Yes, a bunch of kids watched the eclipse through the holes of crackers. During the whole beautiful eclipse, guards hollered at us over the loudspeaker. Some even ventured onto the wings to tell us to get away from the windows. We just migrated to other windows until the staff gave up. It all turned into the kind of event that can only happen in a stupid prison, but we had fun. The best part is that no one went blind!

August 29, 2017

Dear Janie,

Our Agnes is gone. I never imagined death could catch Agnes. The news is still not believable or real. I just found out this morning. My name was called over the loudspeaker to go to Rec and see Ms. Baskett. Of course, I figured I'd said or done something wrong or inappropriate while teaching aerobics. Not long ago, one of Misty's class participants had whined that her yoga class was difficult. Misty had innocently commented on the mic, "Yoga's not for pussies." For saying the dirty word "pussies," she was restricted from teaching for six months.

I met Loren on the sidewalk coming toward me from the Rec, looking concerned. She asked me if I was OK. I replied, "Am I?"

She knew. I could see it in her eyes. Loren responded, "I know you were close to her." Before I could open my mouth to question that statement, she blurted out, "Agnes is dead."

I couldn't hear the rest of the words. I pushed past her and hurried to the gym. When I arrived at Rec, Ms. B handed me a *St. Louis Post* article that I tried to read. I couldn't focus. How could Agnes be gone? I'd just received a letter from her—fat and full of hopes, dreams, adventures, and plans.

My head and heart were reeling while Ms. B was all about business. She wanted a list of inmates who worked with Agnes so they could film a tribute video, but I left her abruptly in mid-sentence to run and tell Tessa, Lawanda, and Amy. We all sobbed, then we marched back to Rec to read the article. Agnes had floated luminously like an elfin angel into this gray prison desert. In death, she floated—slipping away like a mermaid in Lake Erie, away on another adventure, leaving a black hole in our fragile world. We will always love Agnes.

October 22, 2017

Dear Marsha,

You like language, so you might enjoy this little nugget. This morning Byrd was telling a story about how she was nearly taken to the hole over a misunderstanding. She ended her tale with this sentence: "I almost had a *culinary*, you know, a heart attack!"

One of the four upstairs toilets is not functioning. As I walked down the hall on my way to work, I heard one of the inmate plumbers declare, "It's just minimal *problage*."

Last night RaRa asked if I'd play a *scramble* game with her.

Amy tells me that the real definition of *wing nut* is a crazy person who terrorizes your housing unit wing.

When I entered the phone room earlier, a kid there was up in the window hollering that a huge vulture was flying over the soybean field across the razor wire, "Oh, Miss Patty, I wish I had a *binoculator*!"

November 26, 2017

Dear Beth,

Glad you like your early Christmas gift. We are allowed to have only one craft project in progress and one completed at a time. I break that rule all the time, but I couldn't hold onto him until closer to Christmas. I'm sure it's the only Trump you will embrace. They are a big hit. My grandkids asked for them, and now I've made hundreds of Trump dolls. Everyone loves them, no matter what side of the aisle you are on.

Thank you so much for the $25. For a fundraiser, one of the organizations is selling a container of assorted Dove chocolates for $15. That's a big deal in here! I told my cellmate Amy that we'd hide them. The three other kids in our cell will only get cheaper Hershey chocolate.

Hazel wrote that she's pregnant with a girl! Yes, she married that guard she was kicking it with. He was stationed in the visiting room, and her prison job was to clean it. I could see the chemistry between them, but these flirtations don't always end up in marriage.

I'm enclosing the playbill for *A Christmas Carol,* which we are performing next week. I get to play Jacob Marley as a zombie ghost with eight backup zombies, and we dance to "Thriller," which will be a crowd pleaser. Janiece plays Ebenezer Scrooge.

These Recreation plays are crazy, with huge casts, great costumes, and music. In 2006, after three successful years of Prison Performing Arts productions, our Recreation officer, Jim Lingua, had the bright idea to stage a recreation play. In all honesty, he asked Agnes to produce *The Wizard of Oz*, his favorite movie, but she politely told him that he could do it. And he did with our help. The Emerald City and the Yellow Brick Road were constructed from paper, cardboard, and paint. With that production, a tradition was born.

Since then, we have banded together to create a big musical hoopla in December as a Christmas gift to our inmates and staff. We tackled *Grease* in 2008 and have just kept on going.

This is Jim's final production because he's retiring. His loving wife brings in homemade treats for the cast and crew, too—and these musicals use hundreds of actors, dancers, and artists. We're going to miss Jim. I can't tell you how many city girls he has patiently taught to play softball. Jim's a good person and a gentleman. I think he has mostly worked here so he'd have state health insurance; his family business is their truck farm that sells produce and literally tons of pumpkins.

December 20, 2017

Dear Nancy,

I was in the upstairs dayroom eating a sandwich with some friends when Sherry Mitchell came running out and blurted, "Turn on the TV! Judy's free!"

Someone flipped the dayroom TV to the news, and there was

footage of Judy and her family walking out of the prison in Chillicothe. Turns out that Governor Greitens had traveled to CCC to give Judy Henderson the news in person that he'd commuted her life with no parole for fifty years prison sentence to life and time served! By now, she's home in Grain Valley with her daughter, Angel, and planning a huge Christmas celebration!

Immediately, I called Janie, who was crying with both joy and jealousy. My kids and you want that so much for me, too.

January 7, 2018

Dear Marsha,

Tonight, the Oxygen channel aired the first installment of the *Final Appeal* show about me. They researched a bunch to prove that I didn't kill Bill. The whole dorm watched, and at every commercial, a group of kids ran into my cell and jabbered about what they'd seen. When the show restarted, I hollered, "It's back on!" They'd then run back to their bunks. It was weird watching it with a group of strangers, but there's no privacy in prison. At least those kids were on my side. I just pray the exposure does some good.

January 18, 2018

Dear Mary,

Today, my mother was laid to rest at the Wallace Funeral Home in Pleasant Hill. You were probably there. I miss out on all the important family events. She died on the seventh, the same day that the *Final Appeal* show aired on Oxygen.

This may sound weird, but it's really a blessing that she didn't live to see that show. Bill's murder and my conviction and incarceration were always too painful for her to stand. She suffered greatly from the injustice of it all.

Now she's with Daddy. The girls told me that she talked as if he were in the room with her. I think he was. I think he was trying to coax her into coming with him, crossing over, assuring her like he always did. Daddy's the only one who could talk her into crossing that hanging bridge when we took that big camping trip out West. When they took that train trip for their anniversary, he coaxed her into crossing to the dining car. I also think Momma didn't want to leave the family. She felt responsible for all the kids, but those lovers are together now like they always were in life.

When I'd come back from work for the noon count, I'd always stop at the wall phone in the dayroom upstairs and call Momma. Just check in. Habits die hard. I'm still pulling over to the phone before it hits me that I no longer have her number. I miss her. She was a character!

Today also marks my halfway point. Bill was murdered thirty-four years ago, when I was thirty-four. For the first thirty-four years of my life, I was joyful and free. These last thirty-four have been a nightmare. Every day of these last thirty-four years, I have awakened with the hope and prayer that this would be the day I'd receive the news that my husband's killer had been found or come forward and confessed or that I'd be called out and informed that I was being released from prison. Every minute of every day of every week of every month of all thirty-four years, I have hoped and waited, while growing old, feeble, and gray.

But I'm never ever any closer to going home to my loved ones. They're all waiting with me. Matt yearned for my return to be his mother again, but he died. All Daddy wanted was for me to come home, until he died. Mary prayed for that every day, until she died. Momma cried for it every day until she died.

January 22, 2018

Dear Mary,

Just saw on the news that Governor Greitens was indicted for felony invasion of privacy for a 2015 incident in which there is a three-year statute of limitations. This is crazy!

Today, while teaching bridges during beginners' yoga class, I instructed, "Squeeze your butt cheeks." I heard a little voice in the corner of the room ask, "With my hands?" The entire class giggled. I didn't want to embarrass the kid, so I explained it was a glute exercise not a hand exercise. Keeping a straight face was difficult.

When the girls ask me how to lose weight, I usually inquire as to how much of the white bread served at meals they consume. We are fed six big slices a day, two for each meal, which is like half a loaf. Today, after yoga, a kid stopped me, "Miss Patty, I don't know about this no-bread thing. It's *really* hard."

I asked, "Are you seeing any results?"

She looked puzzled, "What? Oh, no, I haven't *tried* it yet."

February 27, 2018

Dear Beth,

Last week, Missouri Governor Greitens was indicted over some sex photo/blackmail fiasco. Lawmakers are demanding he step down. His fate and mine hang in the balance...Amy Sherrill remarked, "You have the worst fucking luck!" Ya think?

Brian is flying to KC on the 14th to attend the DNA hearing in Sedalia with the Midwest Innocence Project lawyer, but he must fly right back. He does have a real job besides trying to help me.

So sorry about your friend in jail. She won't be the first fish out of water in prison. She'll learn quickly. I had great teachers. My first cellmate told me, "You're the stupidest fucking woman in the world. Quit being 'Friendly Bob' with your Waltons country ass. This ain't no place for civility."

June 1, 2018

Dear Janie,

I don't know if you saw the news, but today is Governor
Greitens's last day. He issued pardons for Stacey Lannert, Judy
Henderson, Mark Whittle, Gary Thomas, and Betty Coleman.
He commuted the sentences of Verdia Miller and some men.
I'm so happy for Verdia. It's a real blessing for her, since she's
elderly and in poor health. She might have died in prison from
lack of medical care.

A few years ago, a young girl named Jennifer, who lived in the cell
next to Amy and me, died. She was only like, twenty-six. It all
started with a toothache that turned into sepsis. The day before
she died, I saw her in the bathroom. She was gray, not the color
of a human. Amy and I got her down the stairs and made such
a fuss that the officers allowed us to use a wheelchair to take her
to medical. The nurses, a doctor, and officers did *nothing* to help
her. Amy and I were furious. Jennifer could hardly hold her head
up. She was dying!

We were forced to take her back to her bunk. I barely slept that
night, thinking about that poor kid. The next morning at the 5:00
count, the guard started hollering in her cell, "Get up! I said get
up or I'm taking you to the hole!"

I jumped up, and Amy grabbed me, "Don't get involved. You'll
get in trouble." I shook her off.

When I saw Jennifer's face, I screamed, "She's dead! You
killed her!"

Amy and my other cellmates wrestled me back to our cell. A
few hours later, Amy and some other girls were recruited (read:
ordered) to carry her lifeless body strapped to a stretcher down
the stairs.

July 3, 2018

Dear Marsha,

Since I turned sixty-nine today, the kids upstairs went all out, with happy birthday signs on the walls, stall doors, and even the microwave. But they weren't just the run-of-the-mill happy birthday signs. They were, as Amy described them, nasty. Have you heard of MILF? They used GILF: Grandmother I'd Like to…Amy was worried that we'd get in trouble, so right before the 11:30 am count was announced over the loudspeaker, she ran around like the Tasmanian devil and pulled all the "naughty" signs down. But as soon as the guards counted, the kids put up more signs. Only in prison!

April 23, 2019

Dear Mary,

Reporter Angie Ricono from KCTV-5 news interviewed me this morning here in the visiting room. She and her photographer were so kind and interested in my story. They plan to film Janie tomorrow at her home. The story is slated to air on May 8 in KC, St. Louis, and Springfield.

We are doing everything we can think of to get the governor's attention. If you have any ideas, don't keep them to yourself!

September 20, 2019

Dear Janie,

I tried to call you tonight. I need to process this. I'll have to sort this out on paper.

After supper, Chris from PPA showed up unannounced and called all the PPA actors to the Nutrition room. As soon as we walked in, we realized he had bad news. He didn't say one word until nearly all of us were in the little room. Chris could barely say the words. Laura Hulsey is dead.

Yesterday she was in a car crash. Shorty raced out of the room, I assume to call Laura's sister. The room fell silent. A few left the room quietly to grieve alone. I stayed with Chris. He's heartbroken. Since she was paroled, she's gone to schools and spoken to students about how she came to prison—assault with a knife. Chris helped her schedule those events. He thought the world of her. I'm still in a numb place. I can't believe it's true.

Laura was so utterly full of life, multitalented as well as beautiful. She sang, danced, and acted. I'm making myself sick just writing this. You've seen her in our plays. When she played the tortured sex offender in *Run-On Sentence*, she stunned audiences. Those complicated dances that we hyenas performed in *The Lion King* were choreographed by her and Shorty. During one rehearsal, I commented, "I'm not sure I'm the person for this move."

She smiled that thousand-watt smile, "I wouldn't ask you to do it if I didn't know you could." How could I argue with that?

When I first met her, she and Autumn sat near me on the bleachers at a softball game. She had never played softball, which seems to be a country sport, not a city one. I explained the rudiments of the game, and in a week, she joined a team and proved to be a fierce competitor.

She joined the CHAMP service-dog training program and PPA. She became a highly proficient dog trainer, but she was always a very talented performer. I heard she had the chance to attend Juilliard, but I don't know if that's true. But why not? She had the chops.

I'm sick for her loving family, too. She left us before she could fully demonstrate her artistic potential. Too soon. Too soon.

Janie, I've run out of words. Tears are all that feels right.

Love,

Mom

Janie, I can't sleep. I've been thinking about Mickie's death, too. When she was paroled this last time, she landed a good job as a computer programmer. That St. Louis company sent her to Chicago for training. She was a bundle of mixed feelings: anxious, proud, scared. She was nearly frozen by impostor syndrome as I tried to convince her she was a proficient coder and would be an asset to the company.

I don't know what happened, but I fear she fell back into her heroin addiction. All I truly know is that her body was found in a rat-infested alley. Mickie was a generous, loving, compassionate, loyal sister-friend and didn't deserve that kind of end. Laura didn't either.

September 27, 2019

Dear Nancy,

You'll never guess who came to see me today—with no warning! State legislators! Tracy McCreery, Shamed Dogan, and Donna Baringer showed up and called me to the Classification conference room to talk about prison and clemency! Two of the wardens hovered around outside the door. We talked for a long time around the big table, then they decided they needed to eat lunch in the staff dining room.

As we walked through the rotunda, Donna noticed dogs on my wing. I explained that we train service dogs for an organization out of St. Louis called CHAMP. I invited them onto my wing to see the dogs and trainers. After we had been in the downstairs dayroom for a while, I asked, "Do you want to go upstairs and see my cell?"

Of course they did. Staff rarely allow outsiders that far into the prison, so we jogged up the stairs while I gave the tour. "On the left, you see the laundry room, then the four showers, then the bathroom, and here's my cell. We four crowded into the walk-in-closet-sized room while they took in the lack of floor space left after six beds (two stacked as bunk beds and two singles), six stand-up lockers, six footlockers, plus a table and six plastic chairs were stuffed into it.

Since he saw yarn on my bunk, Rep. Dogan asked what I was making. I've been crocheting little cartoony, orange-faced Trump dolls like crazy. Initially, my politically astute grandkids asked for them, but everyone loves them—no matter which side of the aisle they stand on. You can use them as voodoo dolls or revere them, so I've probably created a hundred by now.

After they left me, they toured the prison. Amy saw them in the canteen. She said the man had asked what he could do to make prison better, and she blurted, "Free Patty Prewitt." She didn't know that he was a supporter and had been in our room until she came home after work.

October 2, 2019

Dear Carrie,

I was called to the investigator's office today and grilled like a hotdog! On a JPay email, I had mentioned how devastated Chris Limber, the PPA director, was over Laura Hulsey's death. From those innocent words, the investigator insinuated that Chris and Laura were sexually involved, because he has no concept of caring about someone of the opposite sex without sex being involved. He did his best to twist my words around. What a perv! I pray I did a good job of dissuading the idea.

I'm spitting mad! That guy said as much that no grown man could be anywhere around a beautiful woman without having inter-course as a goal. Speak for yourself, perv! Chris is old enough to be Laura's father, and he never ever acts like anything but a gentleman. We know the perverts a mile away, and Chris is not one of them.

Shoot, now you're probably worried that I'm in trouble, but don't fret. Some staff hate anyone who comes in to help us. I've been dealing with these warped individuals for all these years. I'm fine.

December 11, 2019

Dear Nancy,

A writer named J. Malcolm Garcia contacted Brian about writing
a story about me. From what I gather, UMKC law professor Sean
O'Brien told Garcia about my case. Sean was counsel for Faye Copeland while she was on death row, and since she was nearly illiter-
ate, I'd read Sean's legal letters, translate for her, and respond on
her behalf. Brian says Garcia used to be a reporter for the *Kansas
City Star.* I guess everyone in KC knows him, and he has a stellar
reputation, so I agreed. As I assured Brian, it can't hurt.

December 14, 2019

Dear Janie,

Amy walked out of prison today, and we were not totally prepared—
emotionally or any other way. All last spring, I tried to tell her that
a bill was making its way through the legislative session that would
change the percentage of the time that she'd be required to spend
in prison, but she refused to listen to me. In fact, she'd grow cross
with me when I attempted to explain it. Her plan was to labor at
the local nursing home when she became eligible for work release
to save up a nest egg. She knew from experience how awful it is to
parole with nothing. Whenever I broached the subject of the bill
and the possibility of an early parole, she flatly told me she was
having a "sound-sensitive day" and didn't want to talk.

Another of her ploys was to fall asleep. If the goon squad busted
in like rabid Nazis or if a tornado threatened, Amy would be over-
come with drowsiness. When other inmates are running around
like chickens with their heads cut off, Amy would nap. Since prison
is one anxiety-producing occurrence after another, I mercilessly
teased her that she suffered from some form of stress-induced
narcolepsy.

Sweet Tina, the best catcher on our Triple Threat softball team, paroled to a place around Hannibal. When Amy found out from her IPO (Institutional Parole Officer) that she would be leaving shortly after seeing the parole board, Tina spoke to her pastor about finding a place for Amy to parole. There's a house in Hannibal for women who need a place to stay, but it has not been open to women coming out of prison. Tina convinced the man that Amy would be a good bet. That pastor picked her up today.

Your hasty GoFundMe has raised enough to buy a laptop so she can continue her college classes at Ashland. Didn't you tell me that Emily volunteered to use those funds to purchase one and transport it to Amy? In Amy's case, it takes a village.

Her bunk has been stripped, her worn, naked mattress is folded in half, her stand-up locker and footlocker echo the same emptiness as my heart. Sending someone you love out into the cruel world hurts. It's not that I'm not happy for her, because I'm ecstatic about her freedom, but Amy Sherrill has become family, another daughter. I can't help but worry that she's being kicked out of the nest too soon. At the same time, I have great faith that Amy has learned the skills needed to live a good life in the free world. Regardless of what the future holds, I will stand forever in her corner—while I miss her terribly.

A Panic-Demic For Everyone

March 7, 2020

Dear Sarah,

We're still reeling from the news. Visits have been suspended because of COVID-19. I hear this mandate is for all the prisons in the state. For thirty days, they say, but I have a bad feeling that this won't be over in a month. The warden says they sent out blanket emails to our visitors, but I don't trust them. That's why I'm sending postcards to everyone. There will be no 4H visit this month. I really hate this, but CNN reporter Anderson Cooper has been warning us about this pandemic for a while now. I'm scared that no one in charge in this prison will have a clue as to how to protect us. They couldn't even diagnose scabies.

A girl up the hall is on the phone, yelling. Her mother is on a plane from San Francisco to visit her. She's trying to stop the family, but from what I'm getting from my end, it's too late. People make plans!

We've been informed that the telephone provider is offering prisoners a free weekly ten-minute call. That's nice, but it hardly takes the place of a face-to-face visit.

Sade, I hope you're all staying as safe as possible. There's so much about this that we don't know. It's scary.

When I was a kid, Grandma Slaughter told me about the Spanish flu pandemic that occurred when she was a coed at Mizzou in 1918. Young people died by the thousands. Girls in her dorm died so quickly that they had no place to store their bodies. Grandma told me she walked past bodies swaddled in blankets, stacked up on the sidewalks like cordwood. I honestly thought she was exaggerating until I happened upon an old *National Geographic* and read that more soldiers died of that pandemic during World War I than from the actual fighting. You're a smart cookie. You'll research and figure out how to protect the kids.

I'll leave you with a stupid prison story. Yesterday afternoon, my footie, Mel, and I both heard a loud accusation that ended a lengthy argument right outside our open door. We both laughed so long and hard that Boots ran down to the rotunda to complain about us making fun of her and became so agitated that the officer cuffed her and dragged her, kicking and screaming, to the hole. The inhabitants of our wing thanked us profusely with wild applause for removing her, but that was not our intent. We just couldn't help howling at the most "prison" sentence either of us had ever heard.

This is what Boots screamed at Laci while emphasizing each syllable with a finger point to the nose, "You smoked crack out my puss-ay!" (I guess you woulda had to be there...)

March 26, 2020

Dear Janie,

Janiece paroled today. Just in time for this COVID-19 mess! I'm happy for her, though I can't help but worry, too. She's been in here way too long for the minor role she had in that crime, but no one cares what I think. The sweet lady who runs the CHAMP dog training program is generously allowing her to stay with them until she gets on her feet.

I already miss her. We've worked and played together for many years. She called me her white momma unless she was angry with me. Not everyone wants a mother hanging around in every situation. You should know. (Recall your teenage years!) She says she'll find you on Facebook when she can. Katie will take over as director of our Recreation plays.

I do worry because the pandemic seems to be in full swing. We lose something every few days. Church services and visits have been suspended. Chris Limber from PPA can't come into the prison even though we've already started rehearsals for an adaptation of *A Midsummer Night's Dream*. Rumor has it that Recreation will shut down entirely, including our BLAST exercise classes.

I send good wishes to Janiece as she fights to make her way in the free world with the stigma of being a felon as a cumbersome ball and chain.

April 15, 2020

Dear Carrie,

Today we were all issued a mask made of thin, state-sheet cotton. We are to wear them when we leave the housing unit. It seems that we lose more and more each day. First, visits were canceled, then PPA rehearsals were canceled, and then all the CHAMP dogs were taken out of the prison. On March 23, we were given two free ten-minute phone calls to make up for the ban on visits. That same day, we Restorative Justice workers began making masks for a hospital in Ohio. I have no idea how that came about, but we set up an assembly line.

The next day, I was told I could no longer meet with the new inmates as I had for many years. For decades, I've met weekly with a group of new prison arrivals and talked to them about what to expect. I started this mission with Janet, who liked us to do a "I'm Hans, and I'm Franz, and we're here to pump you up" routine from *Saturday Night Live* to break the ice. When she paroled, I brought Amy in as my partner, and after she paroled, I sometimes talked alone. We told the kids what to expect. We mixed humor with good advice on how to keep their noses clean. I'd tell them how they can get a loaner lock from the canteen, because locking up our possessions is paramount.

Since I look like everyone's third-grade teacher, I'd shock and amuse the "fresh meat" with this statement regarding bad hygiene: "Don't be a triflin' ho!" I also explained that mercy flushing can cause a painful bacterial infection in the hoo-ha that is not easy to cure. (Mercy flushing is flushing the toilet while sitting on it in an attempt to dispel the embarrassing odor of a bowel movement in a communal bathroom. It's not uncommon for an inmate to enter the toilet area and holler, "Jesus! Which one of you bitches is blowing up the bathroom?" This can cause the person sitting to fear reprisal and mercy flush, but a flushing state toilet fountains the contents of the bowel upwards, and fiercely. Don't do it.) My main objective in these meetings was to assure the kids they would survive.

On March 31, our aerobics classes were cancelled, Recreation was restricted, and we were sent to the chow hall two wings at a time to allow us to sit farther apart. It seemed the prison was trying to keep us socially distanced, but that was a futile endeavor in an overcrowded prison.

On April Fool's Day, my dear parolees, Amy and Janiece, were on TV to complain about the lack of help for prisoners. I'm proud to see them standing up for those they left behind!

I worry about you kids out there in the thick of it. And older family members.

June 15, 2020

Dear Marsha,

Today, we were locked down because the nurses were tasked with testing everyone for the coronavirus. I don't know if you've had a test yet, but it's gruesome! The nurse sticks a long Q-tip up your nose, *way* up into the sinus cavity, and swabs the snot *way* up there to test! The test hurts and burns like crazy! Lord! Who invented this test?

According to an email from our warden, we have confirmed cases for both inmates and staff. People are being quarantined everywhere, but what's the use? We're on top of each other! We did get a second mask, but it's exactly like the first one. Pretty useless.

July 10, 2020

Dear Nancy,

I can't get to a phone easily and don't know if the kids told you, but I'm now at the prison in Chillicothe. I was transported yesterday and have just received my belongings. These sweet kids were so kind to carry my heavy stuff upstairs. This has been a "trip" for sure.

Thursday night I was up all friggin' night packing with a guard. He had to write down every single thing I own. Before breakfast on Thursday morning, I loaded my boxes on a cart and pulled it around the sidewalk to the Property Department to check in. Then the herd of us was marched across camp to a room in Receiving, a room about the size of a master bedroom in an average house. We all had to be strip-searched, but there are only two rooms, a toilet, and a curtained changing area, for that purpose. The Chillicothe sergeant decided it was taking too long, so she started strip-searching us in the middle of the crowded room—in front of everyone. I was the only long timer in the group. All the rest were new arrivals and horrified.

That mean-spirited sergeant had no sympathy for anyone. When she pointed to a young pale redhead and ordered her to strip, the kid, who held her head down in submission, whispered that she was on her period. That didn't matter to this bitch. (I don't throw that term around much, but there is no other description for her. She was a royal bitch.) She demanded that the kid strip right there in front of everyone, including the male officers. After she had removed all her clothing, including the sanitary napkin, our male sergeant from Vandalia stumbled in and realized what was happening. He took over and rearranged the place to allow for private stripping. That made the bitch spitting mad, but he firmly explained that this was *his* prison.

Once strip-searched, we were leg-shackled and belly-chained to a piece of metal box that holds the handcuffs in place. That added torture device holds our wrists parallel to each other with no wiggle room. It is incredibly uncomfortable, but we all get it used on us when we go beyond the gates. After we were loaded into several vans, we hit the road northwest for Chillicothe. I amused myself by taking in the countryside, fields, lakes, animals, and farmhouses.

The trip took hours, and when we arrived at our new prison, we were unloaded, unshackled, and unchained, strip-searched once again, and funneled into another room, we were lectured that we were to line up in the hall and wait our turn to see a case-worker who would give us our new rules, housing unit, cell, and bed number. My caseworker told me that they had sixty confirmed cases of COVID-19. I exclaimed, "We had none at Vandalia! You took me from zero to sixty? For what reason?"

Of course, there are no answers. He certainly didn't know. He was just doing his job.

This prison looks like an honest-to-god prison camp. It's ugly with no trees or bushes. The only plants I can see are over by a greenhouse. Everything is battleship gray. Since I've been locked up so long, I know so many of the women. As I walked to my new residence, I heard lots of shouts of greeting. One of the kids walking with me said, "You're a celebrity—I'd heard about you before I even came to prison."

Today we were called to Property to get our possessions. Strong youngsters helped me carry my stuff upstairs. I'm on a top bunk. There are two double bunks (four women) in each cell. We have lockers and a table. They use mushroom-shaped stools as chairs. They call these stools *buddies*. Each cell has two small, barred windows with nothing to see outside.

Don't worry about me. The kids here have been friendly. They feel as lost as I do.

July 20, 2020

Dear Mary,

A few days ago, my wing, 6C, was locked down. We all had to stay in our cells. Nurses came and took our temperatures, then our wing was tested for COVID again! The painful Q-tip up the nose! Ugh! When the vans from Vandalia arrived, they were taken to 7C. Guards are nervous. We heard there was a death.

Today, test results started coming in, and we weren't allowed to use the phones on the wall downstairs. We had to stay in our cells. Dinner was delivered in Styrofoam. (I hate to think about our landfill!)

I sneaked into the shower. My room is the last one upstairs, and a shower is next door. I took my chance and slid along the wall, then popped in. The showers here are the worst! It's the floor and the door that are the problems. The floor is uneven, as if someone tried to jackhammer it all over. I've been to cheap campgrounds with better showers. The doors are skimpy. People downstairs can see right up into the upstairs showers. Also, the door is short for a tall woman. The faucets all over camp are the kind where you have to keep punching the button to get water, and you can't change the temperature. It's going to take some getting used to, but I managed to take an illegal shower without getting caught. I claim my victories when and where I can!

Yesterday, we had to use toilet paper to clean with since we were ordered not to use rags. Crazy. A guard told us there are 195 COVID cases in the prison now. That's over 20 percent of the camp.

I got to call Janie. She reported on Malcolm's story about me and told me that *St. Louis Post* reporter Aisha Sultan won an award in St. Louis for her documentary about me.

September 12, 2020

Dear Nancy,

This has been a rough summer. From what I hear, it's been rough for everyone, no matter where you are. My wing spent the entire summer inside. From my cell, there is only a short window of opportunity at sunrise for me to feel a bit of sun on my face. The square bars are close together, so I can't squeeze my face far enough in to get much. You take what you can get.

I've been cleaning the wing to get out of my cell. Jennifer and I start early before anyone's up. We both like to take the trash out, even though the receptacle is right outside the door in the shade. The outside air is precious.

All summer, we've been given fifteen minutes twice a day to leave our rooms and use the phone, the microwave, and the shower. I make sure to call at least one of my kids every day, so they know I'm not sick or dead. I'm also still sneaking to the shower every day instead of wasting my fifteen minutes.

They let us make a library run, and I'm reading a fascinating book about Missouri's history and the terrorists Jesse James and the Younger brothers. When I was a kid, it seemed that those men were revered as heroes. I know that Missouri was a slave state and is still very racist, but to laud those murderers? Only in America!

October 10, 2020

Dear Nancy,

A couple of days ago, I was removed from the dorm cleaning team and reassigned to food service! I was not happy. I'd done my food service time when I was an R&O in '86! I was assigned to pots and pans and complained to everyone. My feet can't take those horrid, hard, state boots—especially when you're on your feet for more than twelve hours. A bunch of the kids in food service complained on my behalf, and Judy Henderson and Janie called the warden. Yesterday, when I showed up to work, they told me I no longer worked there. That broke my heart. Not!

Yesterday, a vanload of my friends from Vandalia were transported here. Last night I was walking the yard and spied them outside Property getting their stuff. We talked across the fence until I was kicked out of the yard. A guard hollered, "Are you talking to them?" I nodded in the affirmative. She chewed me out for talking across the fence in *her* yard and banished me back into my wing.

January 6, 2021

Dearest Sade,

At mail call yesterday, I was surprised with a letter from the daughter of Dr. Bridgens, written December 6. (Prison mail is beyond slow.) She came across an article in *The Marshall Project* about her father and how he concocted junk science in my trial. She also mentioned how evil he was to her and everyone. Her words hurt my heart, because I was always a daddy's girl and couldn't imagine being happy that my father died. Anyway, I called Brian only to find out that she had already reached out to him and Tracy McCreery last month. She wants to help, but none of us know how. I saw the invasion and insurrection at the Capitol live on TV today. I'm stunned. I'm appalled. How could that happen? What is going on out there?

January 20, 2021

Dear Marsha,

The governor denied clemency to my old friend Sandy Hemme. I'm so sorry for her; at the same time, I have not been denied yet. Sandy says she has an Innocence Project working on her case, so she's OK. Sandy told me about the denial at a carnival on Monday in the gym, which I consider a "super spreader" event.

Instead of showing mercy to Sandy, the governor signed a proclamation allowing prisoners to have video games on our Securus tablets. I'm sure the e-company lobbied for that one. Years ago, Governor Blunt signed a proclamation preventing prisoners from access to video games. He considered them akin to gambling and therefore sinful. Times change.

Medical staff came to our wing and asked the elderly and infirm (including me) whether we wanted the COVID-19 vaccination. I shot my hand up, "Me! Give me the shot! Now!" They shook their heads. They just want a headcount, so they know how much to order. Half refused because of supposed "side effects." One old heroin addict said, "I'm not putting anything into my body if I don't know what's in it?" I rolled my eyes so violently that I almost fell over. I commented, "What? We don't know what's in Tylenol or Coca-Cola, but we put them both in our bodies without a second thought!"

Then the nurse told us the vaccinations aren't FDA-approved, and she's not going to get one. That caused others to step over to the no line. By the time she finished, there were only three of us left in the yes line—and two are mentally impaired. (I won't tell you if I'm one of those two or not! Ha!)

Mercy Begging

May 10, 2021

Dear Governor Mike Parson,

Because I refused to take the Alford plea agreement offered to me during my 1985 trial, I've served thirty-five years in prison, away from my family, for a crime I did not commit. I did not murder my husband. I can't state that truth any plainer.

The courts have blocked DNA testing, so you, sir, are our only hope. Your mercy in the form of executive clemency is our constant prayer. My children and I want so badly for you to meet with us. It is in your power alone to right this wrong. Please hear us out.

May 16, 2021

Dear Governor Mike Parson,

I grew up on a three-generation family farm just west of Lone Jack in Jackson County. After years of lobbying my Daddy for a pony, he finally gave me Chiquita, my beloved pinto, in 1959 when I was ten.

Since lobbying worked on Daddy, I plan to pester you until you talk to my children or me. Sir, I have served thirty-five long years for a crime I did not commit. More than 12,792 days. Can you imagine what that's like?

Please meet with me or my grown children. They will travel to you. I'm not nearly as mobile. The bottom line is that I didn't murder my husband. Courts make mistakes. That fact has been proven.

May 23, 2021

Dear Governor Mike Parson,

Grandchildren are a tremendous blessing, and I've heard that you're a doting grandfather. Well, I'm proudly called Granny by thirteen talented, amazing people, ages thirty-two to eight. Unfortunately, not one has seen me outside of a stark prison visiting area. I've never baked cookies with them, never hiked the woods with them, and never attended any of their birthday parties, ballgames, choir performances, or graduation ceremonies. Both Megan and Drew graduated from high school this very month. My grandkids, my kids, and I all mourn my absence from their lives.

I beg your mercy, sir. Your mercy is my only hope of ever cuddling with any of those precious grandchildren. Your mercy can be the ultimate blessing and gift for our whole family.

May 31, 2021

Dear Governor Mike Parson,

A few days ago, on the national news, I caught a story about Eric Riddick, who served twenty-nine years in a Pennsylvania prison for a murder he did not commit. A so-called eyewitness recanted, so the prosecutor offered Riddick a lesser sentence, which allowed him to be paroled, although he stated that he will never quit working to clear his name.

The TV commentator reported that there are thousands of innocent men and women in prisons across the country. When asked why it took until now for Riddick to be freed, he simply said, "Justice is in season."

I am among the thousands of wrongly convicted prisoners. You possess the power to make justice in season in Missouri. Please exercise that power.

June 6, 2021

Dear Governor Mike Parson,

Yesterday, my oldest daughter, Janie, and her husband, John, came to see me. Janie has regularly travelled to prison since she was sixteen. She'll be fifty-two this summer. Because of the COVID lockdown and because there are no video visits in this facility, we haven't had the opportunity to lay eyes on each other for eighteen long months.

When I emerged through the strip search door, tears blinded us as we fell into each other's arms. Prison hugs can last no more than three seconds, so we reluctantly stepped apart, wishing we could spend the day embraced. That wish has been our lament for more than thirty-five years.

June 13, 2021

Dear Governor Parson,

I've been writing to you weekly so you can get to know me a bit. This week, I want to brag about a grassroots rehabilitation program I'm very proud of: BLAST (Better Living Awareness Support Team).

About twenty-two years ago, a group of us were presented with the rare opportunity to train to become certified fitness professionals through AFAA (Athletics and Fitness Association of America). Since then, we have continually trained new members and taught fitness. If you feel good about yourself, and exercise helps you feel that way, you're less likely to act badly. With hands-on training, our members are prepared for an excellent career in a growing field. Those success stories are what I'm most proud of. A primary reason parolees don't make it is a lack of viable employment. Our members leave prison job-ready with the paperwork to prove it.

June 20, 2021

Dearest Sade,

You're going to laugh when you hear that I love chihuahuas. As you know, I joined the Puppies for Parole training group. My cellmate, Kelli, loves chihuahuas, but I've never been around that breed. We had collies on the farm, and they are still my favorite. They herded you toddlers away from the road and were great help.

A few months ago, we were told we were getting a chihuahua-terrier mix. I plainly told everyone I do not like that yippy, shaky breed. I like big dogs, but I fell in love with Jed. Everyone fell in love with Jed, and he was adopted by an officer's over-the-road truck driver son. She proudly showed us a picture of Jed wearing a tiny Carhartt jacket on the way to California.

Then we got another one, Chalupa. He's so funny. We think he must have belonged to a Black woman in a wheelchair because when he passes one, he jumps up on her lap as if he belongs there.

Millie has a beagle mix who is scared to death of men in ball caps. We're using friendly guards to help us desensitize Albert. So many of our dogs have been abused, and we use observations and guesses to figure out how to help them rehabilitate. We're quickly finding out which guards not to approach for help. Surprisingly sweet Albert loves to smell flowers! I walk him over by the greenhouse so he can stick his nose into every bloom. He returns to our wing smiling with yellow pollen riding on his black nose.

June 27, 2021

Dear Governor Mike Parson,

I recently saw Eric Strickland on TV explaining that he has nowhere to go after being pardoned. He said he would find a cardboard box and live under a bridge. I don't know if he was kidding, but I've had a solid home plan since the day I was walked into Renz Correctional Center over thirty-five years ago.

When my children were young, my sister, Mary, dedicated a beautifully decorated room to me in the hopes that I'd return to the family. Everyone close to me knows I did not murder Bill Prewitt. When Mary died of cancer a few years ago, my grown daughters took over. Janie has a bedroom ready for me right now, but Sarah and Carrie have space as well.

A safe and welcoming home plan is a considerable hurdle many paroling inmates struggle to secure. I, on the other hand, am blessed with three stable, loving homes in good communities.

July 5, 2021

Dear Governor Mike Parson,

If you believed that your sister-in-law went crazy and murdered your brother, would you allow your nieces and nephews to remain under her roof? I wouldn't, but my in-laws left their son's young children with me alone on our farm for more than two years with no concern for their welfare. When the trial verdict was read, my husband's family cheered and applauded as the heartbroken children screamed in anguish. A year later, when I went to prison, those people did not attempt to help the kids. My dear parents and siblings took in five half-grown traumatized orphans and ensured they were safe, loved, and cared for.

The children are the actual victims. They endured the shock and horror of their father's murder, police interrogations, testifying at trial, becoming orphans, plus the harsh abandonment of their father's whole family. And those children continue to be victimized by this family of strangers who refuse to cease protesting, proving that they still have no Christian love for them.

Victims of crime carry a significant impact, but you, sir, are listening to the wrong victims. Please talk to the children who have lost everything and continue to be directly and adversely impacted.

July 11, 2021

Dear Governor Mike Parson,

You've heard stories about stupid criminals and probably have some of your own from your years as sheriff. Well, this is the tale of a stupid noncriminal. A month or so before we went to trial in April 1985, my lawyer called me to his office, leaned across his desk, and gravely stated, "The prosecutor doesn't believe you murdered your husband, so he had Bill's body exhumed. His pathologist then decided that Bill committed suicide and that you made up a different story to spare the children and collect the insurance."

My mouth flew open in disbelief and sadness that Bill's grave had been disturbed. I then asked, "What caused the doctor to say suicide?"

Mr. Beaird answered, "Bill shot himself in the mouth and knocked out his front tooth."

"What? A wild elbow knocked out Bill's front tooth in a high school basketball game. He wore a temporary cap. He did not kill himself!"

If I had murdered my husband, I would have jumped at that opportunity. In fact, if I had any criminal tendencies at all I would have agreed to the suicide theory and returned home to my children. But I am not a criminal, and I was still naïve enough to believe the murderer would be apprehended. A month later, as the kids and I headed to Sedalia for the trial, in our rural mailbox, we found a bill for the exhumation.

I'm relaying this so you have another piece of the puzzle regarding Johnson County's major crimes investigation. Sir, I'm seventy-two years old and have been in prison for more than half my life. Please commute my sentence before I die.

July 12, 2021

Dear Nancy,

It's so hot! I miss watermelon. I have such fond memories involving watermelon. When I was little, my Grandpa Snow grew a field of watermelon. He got such a kick out of treating his grandkids to all the melon they could eat. He had so many that he'd cut one open, and we'd dig in with no utensils. Fingers and mouths. While we tore into one, he'd cut open another. We'd eat the hearts out (the sweetest middle) and move on to the next one. Eventually, we'd get so full that we lay down among the vines in a melon stupor. Once I was grown, I always carved a watermelon bowl for the Slaughter family reunion and mixed in Bing cherries, grapes, and cantaloupe balls with the watermelon balls. That took hours, plus I had to eat all the melon pieces that didn't ball—and that the kids couldn't eat. Then I'd be up all night running to the bathroom.

Decades later, during an Independence Day family party in '83, I put a watermelon in the garage freezer for a quick cool. When I retrieved it, it was so cold and slippery that I dropped it on the patio tiles, and it exploded. We only had to clean up the green rinds because our kids and all the nieces and nephews jumped on it like a horde of locusts.

In the early '90s, when I was housed in the Renz prison, the men prisoners at the Algoa Correctional Center grew acres of melons. Several times during the summer, they would send a two-ton truckload of melons to us. Besides their juicy gift, some inmates carved their names, prison numbers, and certain data on them. For example, there might be a melon with "Jack Smith B3948494, 6'2", 190#, buff."

I always jumped up in the truck to help distribute, and I'd holler, "I have a guy here who's 6'2" and buff!"

Someone would yell, "What's his name?"

"Jack Smith!"

"I know him! He's 5'2" and scrawny."

"Yeah, I have two kids by that son of a bitch!"

"What are you talking about? That's my husband!"

Silly stuff like that, but some did gain penpals from those watermelon ads. I miss watermelons.

July 18, 2021

Dear Governor Mike Parson,

Before my husband's murder, I'd never met any known criminals, so I was clueless as to the reputation of the investigator who headed the Johnson County Major Case Squad. Not until I settled into prison life did the inmates at the old Chillicothe Correctional Center fill me in on the history of that particular investigator's underhanded drug dealings. As the revelation of his true character sank in, I saw his actions in a completely different light. I'd figured he'd failed to take any fingerprints at the crime scene because he was inept. But that omission, and the real reason why he switched off the tape recorder during my initial interrogation, became clear to me.

He never looked for my husband's killer. He was busy pointing guilt at me and away from the truth. By the way, he's no longer an officer of the law. Years ago, in another state, his dirty dealings caught up with him.

I firmly believe that he had a hand in my husband's murder because Bill was nosing around our community in an attempt to discover who was supplying drugs to high school kids. We were naive to the ruthlessness of those involved, and we paid an awful price for it.

July 25, 2021

Dear Governor Michael Parson,

On June 22, a group of state legislators toured this prison and met with Puppies for Parole dog trainers and our rescue dogs. Many of those good folks didn't know about this worthwhile program that was created by former MDOC Director George Lombardi. You may not either.

Unwanted dogs from local shelters are delivered to our prison so we can groom them and teach them the skills needed to pass the Canine Good Citizen training and meet the testing criteria. Only then can the pups be adopted to forever homes. The CCC Puppies for Parole is a special program that not only heals broken, abused dogs but also heals broken, abused, incarcerated women. In other words, we not only change lives, we also save lives.

Because of my advanced age in this prison and my long prison sentence, there are few rehabilitative opportunities for me, so I'm proud to be a part of this inspirational community helping other animals. My prayer is that you find it in your heart to return me to my loved ones, but until that day, I continue to do all the good I can from behind razor-wired fences.

August 1, 2021

Dear Governor Michael Parson,

In the pre-dawn of February 18, 1984, after Bill Prewitt was shot and I was attacked, I was determined to get our children to safety. As I pulled jackets on two sleepy little boys, twelve-year-old Sarah and eight-year-old Carrie saw a flashlight shine and heard noises from under the closed basement door. Later that same horrid day, while I was grilled by an investigator, our small, traumatized children were separated and interrogated mercilessly by strange policemen. Nearly a year passed before our lawyer received the prosecutor's file, and he and I discovered what the girls had witnessed in the basement.

At trial, those shy, scared country kids were forced to testify in open court. They were once again tortured for their truth. When the jury foreman pronounced, "Guilty," Sarah screamed while racing out of the courthouse and down the street. No one will ever forget the soul-piercing sound of her raw anguish as she attempted to flee from that wrongful verdict.

To this very day over thirty-six years after trial, Sarah and Carrie continue to be burdened by excruciating emotional pain because twelve jurors think they lied. But the truth is theirs. They know their father's killer was in the basement when they left. They know I did not murder their father, and we all know they adored their sweet daddy.

August 8, 2021

Dear Governor Parson,

Out of the blue, around Christmas, I received a letter from the daughter of Dr. James Bridgens, the pathologist who testified for the prosecution at my trial. She wrote that she'd found an article about my flawed trial on *The Marshall Project* website. (That group, named for Justice Thurgood Marshall, collects information concerning criminal court injustices.)

Ms. Bridgens was jolted, but not surprised, to read the words "controversial pathologist" attached to her father's name. She wrote, "My father was an evil man, hellbent on creating misery for many people, you and me among them. I was so happy when he died, but these many years later, I see that his influence continues long after his death. I can't undo the damage my father did throughout his life, but I can write to a sister who was harmed by him."

In 1984, my trial attorney described Bridgens as a "prosecutor's whore." After my conviction, jurors admitted his seemingly scientific testimony convinced them of my guilt, but a few years ago an FBI criminologist debunked his theory when NBC put together a two-hour TV program about my husband's murder for their series *Final Appeal.*

Dr. Bridgens lied on the stand. His own daughter knows that. His lies convicted me of a murder I did not commit.

August 15, 2021

Dear Governor Parson,

The day after my trial and conviction in April 1985, I was released on bond to my five children and our farm. The kids returned to school while I reopened the lumberyard, our sole source of income. I labored diligently to maintain a safe, loving home and was even given a community softball team to coach.

On the school bus, a neighbor girl asked my daughter Janie why her mother hadn't been called to testify about the strange man in a white sedan she'd seen watching our house the stormy night of her father's murder. (Country folk know every person and every vehicle for miles around.) Turns out, Juanita Stephens had reported that suspicious phenomenon directly to the sheriff that morning, but he failed to investigate or even document the tip.

We returned to court asking for a retrial since pertinent evidence had been withheld, but the judge quickly decreed that a stranger stalking our house on the very night of Bill's murder would have made no difference in the verdict. Jaws dropped. Even the prosecutor sat silently in disbelief at the unjust ruling.

Governor Parson, the jurors never heard about this strange stalker. I'm sure you agree that such eyewitness testimony would have prompted a much different deliberation and verdict.

August 22, 2021

Dear Governor Parson,

Last week, I wrote you about the lone man in an unfamiliar white sedan who stalked our house during the stormy night of my husband's murder. After the trial, when our neighbor told us about him, we realized we'd caught him at our farm on two other occasions.

A few months before Bill's murder, twelve-year-old Sarah stayed home from school alone, sick and cuddled in our bed. She was awakened by the crunching of gravel in our long driveway and peered out to see a man exit a white car and rush to the front door. He pushed his way in and sprinted straight up the stairs to our master bedroom. Terrified, Sarah rolled off and under the bed. She watched his boots walk into our closet where the rifles were stored, then back around the bed to her father's dresser. He exited as quickly as he entered. The police thought the intruder was a neighbor boy, but Sarah knew it wasn't.

The evening prior to trial, the kids and I huddled in the family room of our dark house when we heard a vehicle slowly crawling up our driveway. I looked out to see a strange white sedan. Seven-year-old Morgan flipped on the yard light, and the car immediately backed away. We knew every vehicle in our neck of the woods, so all three events are odd, but when added together, they are quite significant.

September 1, 2021

Dear Governor Parson,

When I hear a politician quoted as saying that an innocent prisoner must remain incarcerated simply because a jury convicted him or her, I long to rebut loudly. Most jurors already believe the defendant before them to be guilty simply because she was arrested and charged. Even with thousands of wrongful convictions unearthed each year, a defendant is presumed guilty until proven innocent. Most jurors never hear the truth, the whole truth, and nothing but the truth, so help them God. Truth can come to light long after the verdict—information that would have changed their minds—facts that they may never know.

The jurors who convicted me had no clue that a stranger stalked us and was there the very night of my husband's murder. They weren't aware that the pathologist lied for a living. They didn't know I was offered plea deal after plea deal. Their verdict was not based on truth. The foundation of ignorance is not justice.

I know from inmates themselves that guilty women nearly always take a plea, as do many frightened innocent ones. But many innocent souls like me make the tragic mistake of believing in a jury trial, not realizing they are taking a huge, costly gamble. Executive clemency was created as a safety valve to correct errors of the judicial branch. Please use your executive power to free other innocent prisoners and me.

September 12, 2021

Dear Governor Parson,

I wish you could see executive clemency from the other side—through the eyes of my children who have endured this torturous process for over thirty-five years, since they were little. When a clemency application is submitted, we receive no confirmation that it has been filed. Inquiries as to the status of the application are either ignored or answered with form letters. There's a lack of transparency from the administration, but an abundance of frustration for my friends and families, who are all good citizens.

Since Governor Ashcroft, every Missouri governor except for Mel Carnahan has basically ignored my family. Before Christmas, my oldest daughter handwrote to you begging to meet with you. Jane's a taxpaying voter in Missouri. For her heartfelt outreach, she received another form letter. Governor Carnahan actually met with my kids and was gracious enough to explain that he planned to commute my sentence before the end of that year. Tragically for everyone, he perished before he could make good on his promise.

We realize you're doing your best to reduce the number of applications you inherited, but in the meantime, can you please schedule a brief meeting with my family?

September 26, 2021

Dear Governor Parson,

The women I know who were freed from prison through executive clemency embrace that amazing gift from their governors and are exemplary, law-abiding citizens. All were serving the extreme, unforgiving sentences of life with no parole for fifty years or life with no parole at all. (Both are simply slow death sentences.) The governors realized the injustice and cruelty of keeping those ladies incarcerated forever, until they died, and generously bestowed mercy. Rightly so, their governors believed they were worth saving—worth a second chance—worth the political gamble.

Governor Ashcroft freed Helen Martin and Rebecca Hughes. Governor Carnahan planned to free Judy Henderson, Roberta Carlene Borden, and me. Governor Holden freed Lynda Branch. Governor Blunt freed Stacey Lannert, who is now an attorney. Governor Greitens freed both Verdia Miller and Judy Henderson. As you well know, Judy hit the ground running and has appealed to you personally to save the deserving women she left behind in prison.

I venture to guess all those former governors are proud they were able to use their executive power for good—to save lives. We pray you join their ranks and free good women like me who will otherwise die behind bars.

October 3, 2021

Dear Governor Michael Parson,

Do you know about Prison Performing Arts, an amazing organization in our very own state? About twenty-five years ago, the dynamo Agnes Wilcox traveled from St. Louis to our prison in Vandalia to teach us how to read, understand, and perform Shakespeare. *Macbeth* was our first endeavor, which you may think is too deep for lowly prisoners, but Agnes was an energetic, creative director. We related to Macbeth's tale of deceit and murder because, in many ways, we are tragic Shakespearean characters ourselves.

Agnes guided us through two plays a year and prompted our tradition of producing an annual Christmas musical through the Recreation Department. Our cast members improved their reading and artistic skills while gaining confidence in public speaking. Agnes even brought in a Spoken Word curriculum, complete with guest poets. Many of our plays and poems are available online.

Unfortunately, the pandemic has squelched PPA in prison along with all outside programs, but PPA is still alive and well due to our enthusiastic ex-con alumni. I'm very proud of all the good I accomplished prior to COVID and, with your mercy, hope to join the ranks of the PPA alumni company in the free world.

October 10, 2021

Dear Governor Parson,

Due to the influence of Prison Performing Arts, I have entered and won several literary contests. For example, I won First Prize for Non-Fiction/Essay in the 2006 Prison Writing Awards for "Contraband." In 2014, Bleak Publishing House in New York presented me with the Tacenda Literary Award "Best Play" for *The Dayroom Club*, a play I wrote about women in prison. That same year, through Prison Performing Arts, we produced *The Dayroom Club* on stage to rave reviews.

In 2017, the same year Governor Greitens commuted Judy Henderson's prison sentence, we PPA members at WERDCC recorded an audio podcast of *The Dayroom Club*. DJ Jeff Humfeld from KKFI Community Radio in Kansas City aired it along with interviews with our audio tech and me. PPA Director Chris Limber was the only nonprisoner involved in creating this professional production. You can find the podcast on the KKFI website, PPA website, and pattyprewitt.com. Nowhere will you find a more accurate glimpse into a woman's prison.

I relay all this to praise Prison Performing Arts and to toot my own horn. I never waste time in or out of prison.

October 17, 2021

Dear Governor Michael Parson,

Because of your background in law enforcement, I'm sure you realize the importance of the science associated with a gunpowder residue test, also known as a nitrate test. Within a few hours of my husband's murder, I voluntarily travelled to the Holden Police Department to report to a Johnson County Sheriff Patrol investigator. As traumatized as I was, it was my duty to help the police find my husband's murderer.

I met privately with Officer Hughes, who warned me that our discussion would be recorded. I figured that it was standard operating procedure, but a few minutes into his interrogation, he switched off the recorder. He then asked if I would allow him to swab my hands to test if I'd recently fired a gun. Although I lived in the country where every pickup has a gun rack in the back window, I'd never heard of such a test. Of course, I agreed because I knew I hadn't fired a weapon. Hughes carefully swabbed both my hands and wrists. Later, I was told the residue test indicated that I had not fired a gun. There was no gunpowder on me.

The fact that science proved I did not shoot my husband is important. Please weigh that information along with all the other evidence proving I did not murder my husband.

October 24, 2021

Dear Governor Parson,

Like all country folk, I owned a pair of rubber boots for chores. Mine were short with white fleece lining. Those boots were dramatically presented at the preliminary hearing, ridiculously caked with thick dried mud that a deputy had to hold in place. That shocked us all because mud does not stick to slippery rubber boots. On top of that, our friend handled those boots shortly after Bill's murder. The shoes were lined up with other boots outside the door under the eave, clean and dry, not wet, muddy, or stained. Our friend considered bringing them to me but decided I had no need for chore boots at the moment and set them back down.

The prosecutor's story was that I ran to a shallow pond to discard the murder weapon. But even if that were true, which it's not, mud would never stick to slick rubber that tramped across a fescue pasture and gravel driveway.

Governor Parson, you possess common country sense and know mud will not adhere to rubber boots. That's why we wear them in sloppy barn lots. I did not murder my husband.

October 31, 2021

Dear Governor Parson,

Last week, I wrote to you about my rubber barn boots that the deputies plastered with mud. They claimed that I shot my husband, then traversed to the muddy pond in the middle of a thunderstorm to hide the gun. The rifle was quickly found in that mudhole they called a pond, but I would never have disposed of anything in that puddle. Either the man who killed my husband didn't realize there was a deep spring-fed lake on the southeast corner of our forty acres, just over the rise from the house, or he wanted the rifle to be discovered.

My pajamas were neither muddy nor wet. There were no wet

clothes in our house. No one could have been out in that downpour and remained dry.

Governor Parson, I did not kill my husband. I did not run across the pasture in the pouring rain, with lightning flashing and thunder crashing. I did not attempt to hide a rifle in mud. I did not murder Bill Prewitt.

November 7, 2021

Dear Governor Michael Parson,

In last month's *Missouri Lawyers Weekly*, your lawyers emphasized that you grant clemency to those who have been rehabilitated and displayed positive behavior since their conviction. Your lawyers also stated that they don't believe clemency is appropriate for innocence claims, since courts should handle those.

In a perfect world, there would be no wrongful convictions, but there are. Also, courts are not open to handling all post-conviction claims of innocence. My case is a prime example. After the trial, a witness, who said a stranger was stalking us the night of my husband's murder, came forward. The court refused to consider that. The pajamas I wore when attacked were finally found, but no court will allow DNA testing. Clemency is our only recourse.

Your online pages headed "Executive Clemency Process" list criteria for "Eligibility for Confined Applicants." "Claims of Innocence" is number one. On top of that, no prisoner has shown more positive behavior after conviction than I have.

November 14, 2021

Dear Governor Parson,

After my 1985 conviction, while free on appeal bond, I enrolled at CMSU in Warrensburg because I was the children's sole provider and needed to finish earning my teaching degree. I completed one semester, but in my second semester, my appeal was denied, and I was forced to abandon my children.

As soon as I arrived in prison, I enrolled in every college program and class available to a lifer—for myself and in order to be a good example for my young children. Lincoln University awarded me an Associate of Arts degree in 1994, when Pell grants were taken away from prisoners. I then trained as a computer programmer for the Department of Corrections on the IBM AS/400 and designed software for twenty years—saving the state millions. Through Prison Performing Arts, I have won writing contests and had two of my plays performed at the Kennedy Center.

I wrote a parenting curriculum for PATCH (Parents and Their Children) and helped launch 4H in Missouri prisons. I've been a nationally certified fitness instructor for over twenty-five years, and I'm currently a trainer with Puppies for Parole. Those are only the highlights of over thirty-five years assisting the Department of Corrections, staff, and inmates while displaying rehabilitation and positive behavior.

November 21, 2021

Dear Governor Parson,

Brian Banks was a young NFL hopeful in California when he was convicted of rape. After he served his prison time, the woman who accused him recanted—told the truth. Banks received a monetary settlement from the state after his exoneration and decided to reach out to identify and assist other innocent prisoners. That's when he heard about me.

Banks and a former prosecutor came to the prison in Vandalia and interviewed me for hours on several occasions. NBC hired an FBI criminologist to test the prosecutor's theory put forward by disgraced pathologist Bridgens, and the agent quickly debunked it. NBC also finally found my pajamas in the evidence box. The

Johnson County Sheriff's Department told various lawyers, over thirty years, false stories about their whereabouts.

On January 7, 2018, a two-hour special about me for Banks's TV show *Final Appeal* aired on the Oxygen network. Banks and NBC worked diligently to prove my innocence. Please view that show and realize that the jury did not hear the truth. If they had the facts, then they would not have returned a guilty verdict. I am not guilty.

November 28, 2021

Dear Governor Parson,

Last week, I wrote about Brian Banks's TV show, *Final Appeal,* and the two-hour special about me. This week I want to point out the segment of that show with the Johnson County deputy who relayed on camera that when he stopped my inebriated eighteen-year-old son, he told the deputy that he knew who killed his father, and it wasn't his mother. Then the deputy said he sent Matthew home to return the next day. What law enforcement officer would put a drunk teenager back in his vehicle to drive thirty miles home unescorted in the middle of the night?

But that's not the strangest part of his tale. My son was arrested in Jackson County, the county in which he resided. Those events in Jackson County are on record. The Johnson County deputy fabricated the entire story and even agreed to tell it to a film crew. But why? Did the deputy feel guilty about how his department railroaded me? Was that a feeble attempt to right his wrong?

We may never know, Governor Parson, but you must agree that this story makes no logical sense, along with other events surrounding my husband's murder.

December 5, 2021

Dear Governor Parson,

The morning after my son Matthew was arrested in Jackson County, my father and young son Morgan, while doing farm chores, discovered what appeared to be a body. Daddy ordered Morgan to remain on the tractor while he investigated. Finding his beloved grandson dead was the worst shock imaginable for my gentle father.

Matthew's slim body was wrapped tightly in a blanket, a .38 on his chest firmly gripped in his left hand, his blonde head blown apart. Daddy raced to the house to call 911, but Johnson County deputies arrived even though the farm was in Jackson County, west of Lone Jack, nowhere near the county line. Those deputies pronounced the death a suicide, but there's no possible way for a person to shoot himself dead, then wrap up. The kick of a .38 is powerful. The gun should not have still been in Matthew's hand, not to mention that he was right-handed. Nothing about his death ever added up.

My son Matthew had just graduated from high school, had enrolled in college, had already tested out of several classes, and was embarking on a bright future. He would not kill himself. His death is yet another tragic mystery connected to the Johnson County Sheriff's Department.

December 12, 2021

Dear Governor Parson,

I am not guilty of murdering my husband, but I do hold gut-wrenching guilt over my eighteen-year-old son's death thirty years ago. If I had accepted the prosecutor's plea offer, I would have served only a few years in prison and been back home years before Matthew graduated from high school. If I were home with my five children, I could have protected them. My decision to refuse the plea offer and go to a jury trial is my most monumental regret as a mother.

Matthew's birthday is November 17, 1973, and every year his brother, sisters, and I imagine what his life would be like if he were still with us. I would literally give a limb to go back in time and accept the plea agreement offered. I would be an innocent mother who served prison time but was free to raise her children. Instead, I'm an innocent mother who has served decades separated from her remaining four children after the horrid loss of her older son, with no end in sight.

Prison Education Project a.k.a. Back to Vandalia

December 14, 2021

Dear Nancy,

What a day! A group of us who are enrolling at the new Prison Education Project with Washington University were transferred back to Vandalia today. Each prison has its own routine, so at Chillicothe we packed up all our belongings yesterday. This morning, before breakfast, at the ass-crack of dawn (according to Dallas), we were told to report to Receiving.

Evidently, not everyone was prepared, because it took about two hours to assemble. I only know the girls from my wing, the Puppies for Parole wing, but several more were stripped, searched, shackled, and chained, and pushed into a van. We could have taken two vans, but instead we were packed in, four across, in seats made for three small or two large women. I didn't think we'd ever get on the road.

The trip was kinda funny. The officers stopped at a Hardee's and left us in the van, salivating as we smelled French fries and hamburgers. Of course, we were only provided with the usual prison-issued sack lunches, which we helped each other eat since we were handcuffed to our belly chains and could not reach our own mouths. Jazz must be a contortionist because somehow she could drink from her own water bottle.

By the time we reached the gates of Vandalia Hell, we had all become friends. Foxhole buddies. It took a torturously long while to get us free from the steel restraints and to the toilet. That's a long trip across the state.

A Chillicothe officer had us strip out of the Chillicothe uniforms, and we stood naked and crowded in a small space. Girls new to prison were naked and being deloused within inches of us. I felt sorry for those who were uncomfortable in close quarters, without the benefit of clothing around strangers. I remember those days. Long ago.

The Clothing Issue worker who handed us uniforms, underwear, tube socks, state boots, and bedding was visibly angry—I don't know why—and took it out on us. She made sure we received the most badly used of each item. Certain prison jobs are rife with criminal activity, so there's heavy turnover among the inmate staff in the department that houses state merchandise. I've been gone for a year and a half. That kid didn't know me. She'll give good stuff to her friends and inmates who pay a tariff. I'm neither.

Once we were all dressed in Vandalia uniforms (which are exactly like Chillicothe uniforms, manufactured in the same prison, except for the font on the name labels), we were given the addresses of our new bunks. Some had to go to Medical to get their meds first, while some of us trudged down the sidewalk to see where we would land. That is always a stressful journey. You hope your new cellmates are clean and halfway easy to cohabitate with. You also hope you don't get put in the cell with a known crazy or sworn enemy. Tasha from our herd and I ended up as footies and are getting to know each other.

We'd all been housed at the camp before, so we thought we knew exactly what we were walking into. No. Since we were gone, the place has fallen apart! Seriously. It's filthy and rusty and smells of sweat, urine, and menstrual blood. The handful of old-timers who couldn't be shipped to CCC during COVID told us that no one cleans or repairs anything. Morale is at an all-time low. The place needs some livening up!

I did see a caseworker on the walk, and he observed, "Prewitt, I knew you'd be back for school. Dammit! It's been easy with these kids who don't know policy and are too scared to file papers. Dammit! I suppose you'll be filing grievances by tomorrow."

I laughed, "I could file one right now if you have the form on you."

But not everyone is sorry to see me. Kids keep yelling at me across the yard that they don't have aerobics classes anymore since COVID. They want me to teach again. I'll have to check out the new post-COVID landscape at Recreation.

My new caseworker called me back and said my job is Food Service. Sheesh! We were told that Wash U would be our job, but we've been told lots of things that never came to pass. I will start in the kitchen tomorrow. I'll let you know how that works out. The old-timers say it's awful. Sigh.

On the bright side, you know how this visiting room is run and will not be a fish out of water when you come down to visit.

December 22, 2021

Dear Nancy,

The old-timers were right. The kitchen is filthy. Roaches and mice are running the place. But the good news is that the Food Service supervisor is sweet as sugar and has assigned me to the PDR (personnel dining room). She also is not forcing me to wear those awful stiff state boots that weigh about ten pounds each. I changed my shift, too. I asked for the 3:00 am shift so I'll be off work between 10:30 and 11:00.

I'm running the PDR as if it were my own diner in a small town. I've scrubbed it shiny and serve breakfast and small talk to staff who wander in, then later I make up lunch trays for the kids in the hole and staff who work details in which they can't leave their posts, like Medical, Control Center, and Visitation. I stay through lunch if no replacement worker shows. The Maintenance men are big on lunch.

When a girl is on suicide watch in the hole, we can't give her bread or anything she might use to off herself. (Bread is not allowed because we had a woman who hid her allotment of bread for days and killed herself by stuffing it down her own throat.) As I slung oatmeal in a flour tortilla shell with gravy, I commented, "This meal would make *me* kill myself."

If no one is looking, I'll peel a banana or break a soft cookie and hide it in the bottom of the brown paper bag. It must be soft or that one cook finds it. She detests me.

We heard that when Wash U starts sometime next month, we must also have a part-time job. I'm loathe to stay in this kitchen, so I asked the kind chaplain if he needs help. He seems to be open to me working the evening shift in the chapel, which is when we have all the church services except for the Sunday morning one. Chap comes in every weekday morning for milk and bananas, if we have them. I'll keep on him. I gotta get outta the kitchen.

Oh, funny story. One of the cooks swears that I was set free and have come back to prison. She says she saw me on TV when a governor pardoned me. I can't convince her otherwise. I guess it doesn't really matter.

December 26, 2021

Dear Governor Parson,

On December 14, I was shackled, chained, and transported along with a dozen others from the prison in Chillicothe to the prison in Vandalia in order to attend the Washington University Prison Education Program offered here starting next month. All of us, except two medically compromised ladies, are full-time food service workers. That's where I discovered that many inmates and staff were under the impression that you freed me last year. My supervisor argued that she had seen on the news that I had been pardoned. I wasn't sure how to delicately debate with her.

Yesterday marked the thirty-sixth consecutive Christmas my

dear children and I were apart. Every Christmas card I've received over the past thirty-six years has carried the sentiment: "Praying you're home next year."

January 2, 2022

Dear Governor Parson,

On the morning of my husband's murder, immediately upon their arrival, deputies retrieved life insurance policies from our file cabinet. How do I know? That morning, the deputy who interrogated me and tested my hands for gunpowder residue told me as he accused me of murdering my husband for money.

The error in that theory is that we were in debt more than the policies were worth. In 1976, with bank loans, we bought a lumberyard, a Sentry hardware store, and a forty-acre farm. It never occurred to us that Bill, who was only thirty-four, would die, so we dropped a policy on him and took out policies on our five children and me. The kids' policies would grow into their college funds.

Hindsight is 20/20, but I wish my lawyer had used a presentation easel to lay out the actual math clearly and show that we owed the bank more than life insurance would pay out. There was no monetary gain for me in my husband's death.

January 9, 2022

Dear Governor Parson,

A few days before Christmas, your office issued a press release announcing that eighteen citizens had been pardoned and that one prison sentence had been commuted, but added that, in the interest of privacy, the names were not provided. That press release caused an enormous heartache for my family, especially my oldest daughter Jane, who was forced to field tons of calls and messages.

She had to proclaim on Facebook that she and no one she knew had received a call from your office. Her many Facebook friends commented that your staff is cruel for putting her in that heartbreaking situation. My other daughters refuse to subscribe to social media for that very reason.

Every month, my loved ones and stalwart supporters hold out high hopes that you will act on your Christian mercy. Please, Governor Parson, commute my sentence to life and allow me the opportunity to interview with members of the Board of Probation and Parole, like most prisoners.

January 29, 2022

Dear Governor Parson,

Recently, one of my daughters unearthed the police report that the Johnson County Sheriff's Department compiled concerning me. Jane described it as a long, rambling collection that demonstrates how they were determined from the start to point their sexist fingers only at me.

One strange entry concerned the condition of towels in my home. The deputy noted that I had towels the average housewife would have thrown out, implying that owning less-than-pristine towels indicates murderous tendencies. First, I was not a housewife. I worked right alongside my husband at our business and on our farm. Second, we were raising five active country children who played every sport. Many of our towels were used for birthing puppies, muddy volleyball clean-up, and every other messy activity.

But why were deputies investigating the linen closet instead of investigating Bill's murder? They were too occupied digging through terry cloth to dust for fingerprints, check tire tracks, or dig for leads. Gender shaming was alive and well in 1984. Have we not matured in thirty-eight years?

March 9, 2022

Dear Janie,

I'm devastated. Ms. Baskett at Recreation gave me the horrible news. Amy died yesterday. She was doing so well. She was in love—in love with a good man. She loved her job as activities coordinator at the nursing home. She loved the people who were incarcerated there. (Yes, nursing homes are prisons for people whose crime was growing old.) She finally felt good about herself. My heart is broken. Several of the addicts here told me that she must have overdosed. She did not! Amy was *not* using. I know that for a fact. She would have confessed to me if she had backslid. I feel so bad for her daughters and grandkids. I hate this!

I know you were jealous of Amy because she spent so much time with me, but you then befriended her and realized the truth. We mothers don't divide our love; we multiply it. I adopted Amy as my own because she needed a mother. You are my firstborn baby girl, and nothing can change that. Thanks for helping Amy so much. You were a good "sister" to her.

March 13, 2022

Dear Governor Parson,

A week ago, my sweet prison daughter Amy Sherrill passed away suddenly. I'm still reeling from the loss. Amy and I shared a cell for ten years, and I witnessed her grow into the woman she was always meant to be—full of humor, wit, kindness, generosity, and resilience. For the past few years, she had been creating a good and honest life in Hannibal, but as my pragmatic Grandma pointed out, death finds us all.

When a loved one dies, especially one a generation younger, it is a grim reminder of our own mortality. Decades behind bars are hard on the body, mind, and spirit, and I'm no spring chicken. Please commute my prison sentence to allow me to die surrounded by loved ones.

April 24, 2022

Dear Governor Parson,

Have you noticed that the current defamation trial between Johnny Depp and his ex-wife, Amber Heard, is taking place over weeks? I just heard that it may take longer than six weeks. There is no crime. The problem is that Heard wrote something derogatory about Depp, and they are Hollywood fools.

The trial that took me away from my children lasted less than four days. In under four days, my fate was decided by people who were friends with the judge, the bailiff, the police, and the prosecutors. That's what we call justice in Missouri.

I did not murder my husband. During my short jury trial, no actual evidence that I killed Bill Prewitt was brought in, but regardless, I've been imprisoned for thirty-six years, a lifetime, with no end in sight.

June 19, 2022

Dear Governor Parson,

Elder abuse in prison comes in many forms. Medical care is a big one. In the free world, cataracts are easily and completely treatable. No one needs to live with obscured vision due to cataracts in this day and age—unless you are incarcerated.

A few years ago, during an eye exam, the optometrist told me that cataracts were forming. As I began to ask what he planned to do about the condition, he explained that if I can see a little bit, the Department of Corrections medical provider will not remove the cataracts. I then remembered Henrietta, a cellmate I had years ago who was eighty-five, blind in one eye, and nearly blind in the other. But she could distinguish shadows, so she was denied simple laser surgery. I'm heading down the same road.

July 24, 2022

Dear Governor Parson,

I've been a member of the advisory board for Missouri CURE (Citizens United for Rehabilitation of Errants) for decades. In this winter's newsletter, vice chair Keith Brown El wrote an article entitled, "Citizens Want Missouri to Stop Opposing Release of Innocent People." He pointed out that over 3,700 innocent and otherwise wrongfully convicted individuals are incarcerated in Missouri prisons. Research by the Department of Justice proves that more than 10 percent of the incarcerated in the US are innocent.

A recent law in Missouri allows innocent claims to be reviewed by a court if the prosecutor agrees, but thus far Kevin Strickland has been the only one afforded that opportunity. No other prosecutors have stepped up. In my case, the Johnson County prosecutor denied our request to simply test DNA, so there is no chance he will allow a review of my innocence.

August 21, 2022

Dear Governor Parson,

Because I'm categorized as "chronic care" due to hypertension, I see a prison doctor for a few minutes every six months. On Tuesday, the doctor commented that I have a heart murmur. Every five years or so, a nurse or doctor mentions my heart murmur, but that's all. No action. A nurse practitioner noticed my tremor and asked if I have Parkinson's. I've never been tested and have been incarcerated since I was young and strong, so how would I know? Neither the NP nor the doctor plans to investigate.

October 3, 2022

Dear Nancy,

Sometimes I must vent a little about this place—even though it does little good. When you sociably ask guards, "Hello. How are you today?" most respond, "Can't complain—won't do any good."

Well, I am getting ready to complain, even though it won't do any good. Yesterday, I walked to medical because "med-line" was called. When I got there, the officer jumped up and hollered, "I didn't call med-line for two-house!"

I attempted to explain quietly that I had heard his voice on the radio and that COI Smith, in the rotunda, had announced "med-line" over the loudspeaker. He didn't listen and screamed, "Get out and tell anyone you see from two-house to go back. I only called one-house."

He threatened to write me up. I turned around and exited the building just in time to run into others from two-house. I told them that Munson said he hadn't called two-house, but they argued that he had and tried to go into medical. Munson kept hollering. Some prisoners hollered back. It climaxed into a loud, angry crowd outside the door, with Munson blocking it.

No one was on the walk from one-house. If he were right, we'd have had inmates from one-house here. We made him so angry that he refused to call our housing unit at all that morning.

One of the many problems with prisons is that control is entrusted to people who don't know how to wield it properly.

October 9, 2022

Dear Governor Parson,

Recently, I read about the large number of pardons you've granted, which led me to a great idea to save you time and effort. Other states have enacted laws stating that after ten years with no problems under the law, a felon's conviction "drops off." In other words, a decade after probation or parole ends and is satisfied, that conviction is no longer on the person's record. In that way, people who have learned their lesson, served their time, and proven they will live as honest citizens for ten whole years do not have to apply for a pardon to have their conviction removed. Clean slate. That would save Missouri governors from thousands of pardon requests and thousands of hours of state staff time.

October 16, 2022

Dear Governor Parson,

Your executive clemency website lists certain criteria to be eligible for a commutation, but thus far, none of the prisoners you've granted clemency to have met them:

Claims of innocence; or

Served 25+ years; or

Age 70+ and has served 12+ years; and

All judicial remedies have been exhausted.

I, on the other hand, meet every single one of those conditions. So, my question to you is: why have you not granted me clemency?

November 13, 2022

Dear Nancy,

I've been a terrible letter writer, but the end of the semester is approaching! This is crunch time. I've told you how much I love my Critical Research Writing class with Meredith Kelling, even if it's been challenging. Research is not easy in prison without internet access, but we are allowed to file requests for information. It's

just not as fast or as convenient as having Google at your finger-
tips. Meredith gave us a little break and asked for a "nonfiction
essay," which is right up my alley. No researching that. I'm living
it! Enclosed is a copy.

One Woman's History of Sexual Abuse in Prison

In May '86, twenty days after I first came to the prison near Jefferson City, I was shackled, chained, cuffed, and shoved on a state
bus to the prison in Chillicothe. Upon arrival, a male corrections
officer caught me alone in my cell and strongly suggested, threatened, that I would be his sex slave with no choice in the matter.
His words and manner were horrifying to this newbie, but his
prediction did not come to fruition because my new guardian
angel cellmate, Theresa, made it her business to protect me. She
was a large, no-nonsense, heroin-addict biker chick who had done
serious time in Florida, where she acquired absolutely no love for
prison staff. She also teased me about being a scrawny country girl,
a rube, but we both agreed that the perv was not going to get his
hands on me, so help us, God.

In August of that year, after Theresa was paroled, word wound
down the prison grapevine that a federal court had declared that
male and female corrections officers were to be treated equally
with the same duties and rights. That sounded only fair until we
realized that it meant that all guards could frisk and strip-search
us. A bit of panic ensued, but the officers I spoke with swore they
didn't plan to jump into that trick bag fraught with unforeseen
and seen problems. But it only takes one.

As Carol and I exited the chow hall, this particular guard, a stout,
big-bellied, greasy man, motioned for Carol to turn around and
assume the position with feet apart, arms outstretched. Prior to
that, we'd only been patted down by females. To our shock and
surprise, that man stepped close to Carol's backside with his face
buried in her hair, then reached around to cup and squeeze her
breasts. I stood frozen—the next in line. The color drained from
her face as he roughly moved his beefy hands over her buttocks,

then reached between her legs to feel her pubic mound. Color came back to her visage with a scarlet vengeance, while he retraced his steps from buttocks to breasts. I couldn't stay to witness the rest because fear kicked my rabbit legs into gear, and I found myself running, racing up the stairs to hide in my cell.

After I calmed down, felt safe to come out since he hadn't come after me, and shift change was over, I found poor Carol, a tall, handsome lady with considerable intellect and two teenage daughters who adored her. But her husband was abusive. During one violent event, as she attempted to leave, he chased after her like the maniac he was. He yanked open the car door but slipped while grabbing at her. She inadvertently ran over him. To ensure he wouldn't kill her and the girls as he had promised, she slammed it in reverse and backed over him, which earned her twenty-five years for second-degree murder. After twenty years of horror at her husband's hand, she did not deserve that guard's sexual assault in the name of penal security. From that day on, if that guard were on post, we'd miss a meal. Sometimes the chow hall would be nearly empty except for a handful of masculine inmates whom he never bothered.

A few months later, on December 14, I was called to the visiting room to see my parents and five kids. To my dismay, the guard stepped aside and moved in front of the female officer as he motioned for me to assume the position. (In those days, we weren't strip-searched before a visit, just frisked. They rightly reasoned that we wouldn't be bringing drugs out of prison to our visitors.) I quietly appealed to his inner gentleman, "Please, sir, I'm a rape victim. I beg you. Please allow the female officer to search me." Trembling in trepidation, I saw and felt his rage explode like atom bombs within his gray eyes.

My five young children and parents watched this exchange while trying to figure out exactly what the holdup was. The pat search before a visit had always been quick, so to them this was suspect foot-dragging, but my protective father got the picture, narrowed his eyes and set his jaw. Attempting to sound like a grown-up who's in charge, I sternly advised the officers, "If you're not going to allow me to visit, give my family the big box of Christmas gifts I made for them." Both stared blankly at me, so I bravely added, "Do you understand?"

By that time, every husband in the visiting area was asking his wife if that particular greasy-headed fat man had run his hands over her. I was not alone in my indignation and could feel the energy shift. The guards exchanged looks and silently decided that the female could frisk me and that I could visit. But the moment all the visitors left the area, I was escorted to the hole for "creating a disturbance and disobeying a direct order."

In May '87, that same man sent me to the hole again for the same transgression—refusing to submit to his sweaty hands on my body while huffing his sour breath on my neck. That was the last straw. A group of us dug around in the law library and successfully sued the Missouri Department of Corrections in federal court. On September 30 of that year, seven of us rabble-rousers found ourselves shackled, chained, and sitting in court testifying to not only the abuse of officers, but for some, the years of abuse by husbands and boyfriends. The kindly older federal judge was visibly shaken to hear a lady tearfully explain that a male guard had felt her sanitary napkin and interrogated her about it. Another lady had a double mastectomy, the result of cancer, and was torturously embarrassed when a man made fun of her "flat-as-a-pancake" chest. The officers and we also explained that the searches were targeted to find cookies—cookies that were served to us on our trays at chow.

That particular guard stumbled through his testimony as to why he must thoroughly search our breasts, buttocks, and inner thighs to keep America safe, all while his fuming wife glared from the gallery. Because of the fuss we caused, the Missouri Department of Corrections was mandated by the federal court to create a method for officers to cross-gender pat search without fondling and grabbing certain body parts, but of course no one can make rules by which everyone abides. I've had issues since with both male and female guards who can't help but take liberties.

In December '89, a large group of us troublemakers were shipped back to the prison north of Jefferson City. While there I ran into several minor sexual skirmishes and wrestling matches, but nothing I couldn't handle, until a new education supervisor was hired. Unfortunately, I was his clerk. This persistent little man thought it was his duty and right to have sex with me, so he literally chased me around his desk. Our warden got wind of this problem and asked me if it were true. I explained, "If I tell you he is inappropriate, I will go to the hole under investigation. Right? Well, I will not do that and miss visits with my kids."

And I didn't. But I had another plan. My lecherous boss was friends with an officer. I let it be known to that officer that my brother would do bodily harm if I told him about the man's unwanted advances. Everyone had seen my big brother visit, and evidently, my boss believed my lie, because he nearly ignored me after that. The truth is, my sweet brother was a peaceful preacher and never fought anyone in his life, but those people didn't know that.

The Great Flood of '93 ruined our prison and sent us packing to a men's prison called Church Farm. I was so accustomed to unsolicited, unwanted sexual encounters that those years seemed pretty mild—nearly peaceful. For example, one maintenance man quickly lost interest in me when I harshly kneed his groin. Then in January '98, we were transferred to a brand-new prison in Vandalia with all new guards. During a count time, one COI, who resembled a bloated Elvis impersonator, knelt at my chair in front of my other three cellmates and sincerely inquired, "What do I have to do to get you to suck my big old dick?" My friends inhaled in shock, but after he disappeared, Donna remarked that he had jumped up and left so quickly because of the lightning-quick, drop-dead look I shot him. As if!

During the next couple of years, several staff members were caught with their pants down and lost their jobs. One sergeant had a type: petite, pretty, young, white. One of his targets, a lovely twenty-year-old with a soft Bootheel accent, asked me for advice as to what to do. I counseled her that if she tells what he's up to, she will go to the hole. Her only safe recourse is to never get caught

alone around him. But that panicked kid confided to a grand-
ma-like officer who slammed her in the hole just as I predicted.
The girl rotted down there for months until she "admitted" that
she'd lied, then was transferred to another prison. Standard operating procedure.

Years of that sergeant's terrorism passed by until he met his
match. His final victim, who was beautiful in a mean way, spat his
semen on her sheets and called her lawyer, who called the cops. I
never found out what became of the sergeant, but that gal sued
and settled for millions and freedom. I thanked her, saying we'd
been trying to get rid of him for years. With her hands on her slim
hips, she leaned back, cocked her head and plainly told me, "Ya
weren't tryin' too hard." With a chuckle, I had to agree.

For years, we were terrorized by a guard who loved to grope us
and call it a routine pat search. Not only did he pull up close to a
butt, but he'd also then grind his hard little penis on you and whis-
per nasty words in your ear. If you protested in the slightest, he
cuffed you and hauled you to the hole, the original walk of shame.
Everyone, including the staff, knew about him, but they turned
a blind eye. Every hour he was on shift was torture. My friends
and I were repeatedly in trouble over him, and he took down too
many good women. He would still be employed here, except he
was arrested for a pervert-related crime in the free world.

In 2010 I heard about a federal law called the Prison Rape
Elimination Act, which was designed to prevent vulnerable prisoners from being sexually assaulted by either staff or inmates. A
few years later, as I exited the chow hall, a male lieutenant called
me over to assume the position for a pat search. In my smartass
way, I casually commented, "So much for PREA."

PREA must have been a sore subject, because he yelled at me
in a long tirade about how they don't have to follow the law and
can do anything they want with us and to us. After all, we have no
rights, and nobody knows what goes on in there because we are
hidden, and nobody cares about whores. He was so angry that he
didn't even see that a crowd had gathered around us. That's how
crazed he was with neck veins bulging and snot and spittle flying.

He finally noticed his audience and gruffly ordered us to disperse. A few more years passed before our prison was forced to abide by PREA and stop cross-gender pat searches, but by that time, I had grown old and gray, so guards and other staff ignored me as an object of desirability.

I may be the only woman ever who was thankful for wrinkles and white hair. Prison staff still yell at me and treat me like a stupid slave, but no one wants to have sex with my bony old body. Praise the Lord.

November 13, 2022

Dear Governor Parson,

On Monday, the seventh, my daughter Jane, my old friend Mary, and I were featured on an episode of the Dr. Phil show, along with two wrongful conviction experts, two Missouri state representatives, and our attorney Brian Reichart. Dr. Phil's excellent staff researched like crazy, and Dr. Phil came to the firm conclusion that I'm innocent. There is not one shred of evidence to convict me, but I was unfairly and wrongly found guilty. Dr. Phil has worked with lawyers and juries for decades, and he's asking you, Governor Parson, to grant me clemency.

November 20, 2022

Dear Governor Parson,

This morning, while I moved laundry to the dryer, I chatted with a young Black girl who was waiting for the washer. She'd heard that I'd been incarcerated for thirty-six years, but she couldn't believe I was locked up sixteen years before she was born. With tears in her big brown eyes, she told me she'd like to pack me up and take me home with her. I'm in this prison full of kids serving short drug sentences who can't imagine how long I've been incarcerated and how long I have left to serve—if I live that long.

December 4, 2022

Dear Governor Parson,

I just discovered that actor Jamie Lee Curtis posted on Instagram in support of me. She wrote, "After a trial riddled with sexism, slut shaming, and faulty forensics, Patty Prewitt was sentenced to life in prison for the murder of her husband—a crime she had nothing to do with. To the state, she is a murderer and an adulteress, but to those who know her, Patty is a mother, grandmother, and mentor. And she is innocent. Listen to Patty's incredible story on *Wrongful Conviction* with Maggie Freleng to learn more and get involved."

December 11, 2022

Dear Governor Parson,

The most frequently asked question by inmates and staff is, "Why don't you have the evidence DNA tested?" After I explain that the prosecutor and two courts refused to allow DNA testing, the next question is, "Why don't you take the evidence to an independent lab to be tested?" When I explain that the Johnson County Sheriff's Department has sole possession of the evidence, they are undoubtedly dumbfounded. The usual response is, "Don't the powers-that-be want justice?" I never have to answer that question. The answer hangs in the air. Justice is not part of the system.

February 12, 2023

Dear Governor Parson,

After my husband was murdered and I was brutally raped thirty-nine years ago this month, I couldn't explain what had happened. The words would form in my head and couldn't escape my mouth. I have felt shame and guilt all these years for this inadequacy.

In one of my Washington University classes, I learned that trauma can block a region of the brain called Broca's area. Without a functioning Broca's area, you cannot put your thoughts and feelings into words. Even years later, remembering trauma can cause our bodies to re-experience the terror and helplessness, but those feelings are nearly impossible to articulate.

I can't tell you what a relief it has been to have scientific knowledge. All victims of trauma and those who deal with them need that information.

January 8, 2023

Dear Governor Parson,

Please, sir, something needs to be done about Margerie. She resides in the cell next to mine, but she's not doing well at all. Margery is eighty-one, is in a wheelchair, has Alzheimer's, falls frequently, and wears a diaper because she's lost control of her bowels and bladder. She suffers from other geriatric medical conditions, but the ones I mention are at the top of the list. She should be in a residential care center and not lost and confused in this crowded prison full of loud, rude kids.

Prison is punitive, but Margerie is being tortured. Is this what the state of Missouri is about? I'm appalled that this treatment of an elderly citizen is state-sanctioned. You all should be ashamed of yourselves.

January 8, 2023

Dear Bunky,

You like these crazy stories, so I've got another for you. I work in the chapel, which means I set up and clean up several services a week. This morning, a girl walked into the room, picked a seat, then wrapped her face mask (made from a white cotton state sheet) around her eyes. During the service, she stood and loudly announced that she was blind, "I want to thank you for being kind to me and not excluding me because I can't see."

After the service, the lovely church ladies, who hadn't noticed her wrapping the fabric around her head, asked me about her. I asked, "Did you notice that she took her blindfold off as she left the chapel to walk back to her housing unit?" This place sometimes doubles as an insane asylum.

January 29, 2023

Dear Governor Parson,

A couple of weeks ago, I reported to you about Margerie, the eighty-one-year-old with Alzheimer's who lived down the hall. About a week later, she fell and hit her head on the tray that's welded to her bunk and was taken to the Transitional Care Unit on a backboard. I didn't see her until last week when an officer wheeled her through Medical. She looks awful, pale, with greasy hair matted to her head, tilted at an odd angle on her shoulders. A nurse told me that Margerie fell in TCU and broke her neck. This prison is not set up for adequate care of anyone in Margerie's feeble condition, and I fear for her life.

My letters to you are merely messages in bottles, but if anyone reads this, please help Margerie. Prison is for punishment, not life-threatening torture. Please have mercy on the helpless elderly in Missouri prisons.

February 12, 2023

Dear Marsha,

Since you're in Colorado and not a sports fan, I feel it necessary for me to shout to the rooftops that we won the Super Bowl! Who might you ask? The Kansas City Chiefs won the Super Bowl! I used to call my Daddy during the games. The dayroom TV would be on, and the upstairs phone is only a few feet away. Daddy and I would talk about the players and strategy. Momma couldn't care less, so that was our time. He would be so excited! I'd call Uncle Ivan, Daddy's brother, but he's so deaf now that phone calls are useless and frustrating. Anyway, we won the Super Bowl!

February 18, 2023

Dear Governor Parson,

Bill Prewitt's young life was tragically ended thirty-nine years ago today, and the coward who murdered him was never apprehended or even sought after. Bill should be enjoying his children and their children, but that opportunity was stolen from him.

He left a legacy of wonderful children, and I pray that from heaven, he sees them thriving. This anniversary of his death is difficult for everyone, but we will never ever forget Bill Prewitt.

March 26, 2023

Dear Governor Parson,

Do you ever wonder why I refused the generous plea agreement offered by the desperate-for-a-win prosecutor? At first, the lawyers tried to talk me into the deal, but I kept repeating, "I didn't murder Bill. I won't say that I did."

They explained that with an Alford plea, I wouldn't have to lie.

On the final day of trial, my lawyers agreed that the jury couldn't possibly find me guilty, since there was not one shred of evidence against me. The nitrate test proved I never fired a gun. The insurance motive was shot down since we didn't have enough to cover our debt. There was no reason for me to murder my husband. Also, I didn't accept the plea offer, even though I would have been home before 1990 if I had, because I couldn't fathom abandoning my children.

Honest people think that justice is served by a trial. They don't know that the guilty make deals and tell on others to get them. The jurors who sat on my trial made a huge mistake, but so did I. I shouldn't have trusted them. I should have taken the deal, spent a few years in prison, and returned to raise my children.

April 2, 2023

Dear Governor Parson,

After decades of mandatory sentencing laws and reductions in parole, the number of aging inmates in our prisons has increased dramatically. Is death by incarceration the new normal for aging prisoners? I and thousands of older people occupy bed space in maximum security prisons, even though the recidivism rate for people over sixty-five is nearly zero. The prison population of people fifty-five and older has tripled since 2000. According to the ACLU, the average annual health care cost for one incarcerated person is $34,135, but the average annual health care cost for a prisoner over fifty is $64,270. That figure increases exponentially each year.

I have been shackled to a massive prison sentence for a crime I didn't commit, and I'm costing unaware taxpayers millions to keep me in this human warehouse. Is my confinement worth the cost to the state when right this minute children are hungry?

May 14, 2023

Dear Governor Parson,

My beautiful mother, as a farm wife with no A/C or running water, put three hot and hearty meals on the table every day; carried two five-gallon buckets of water from the well near the barn many trips a day; did laundry with a wringer washer on the back porch, hung it on a line to dry, then ironed it all; carried in firewood to keep the kitchen stove going all winter; planted, weeded, harvested, and canned vegetables and fruit all summer; grabbed two hens out of the yard every Sunday, dressed and fried them; was our nurse, doctor, and veterinarian; could drive a five-speed two-ton truck; put on fresh lipstick when Daddy was due home; and joyfully, by ear, played the upright piano at every opportunity.

When I was taken to prison, she and Daddy stepped up to take in my five orphans. They don't make them like my Momma anymore. I come from honest people.

June 15, 2023

Dear Nancy,

Prisons buzz with rumors, many false, but when I heard that the state had contracted our food to a for-profit company, I fervently hoped it wasn't true.

Back in the '80s when I first came to prison, our kitchen was run by country cooks who cared about the meals they produced and the cleanliness of the food prep areas. They even used fresh produce from our prison gardens. But as time went on, the quality of our food deteriorated. When we were getting geared up to leave Church Farm in late '97, we were told there would be no seconds served at the new prison and that the "line" would be closed.

Up until that point the kitchen was open, visible from the dining area. We picked up a tray at the beginning of the line and pushed it along while looking at the food selections just a foot away in big stainless steel serving pans. We could skip an item. For example, if you hate beets, just push your tray past the girl serving beets. Even in my free world life, that was the way cafeterias were arranged.

At that prison, after everyone in camp was served, the head cook called "seconds" and we raced to get more. Marshall, the head cook at Church Farm, who blasted his music on the way to work, loved calling seconds to watch us beggars scurry. (Our prison was deep in the hilly country near the Missouri River, and the bass of that guy's stereo thudded, boomed, and echoed for miles. We smiled to hear him arriving.)

When we were transported to the new prison in the little town of Vandalia, we found that our trays were filled behind a wall and pushed out one-by-one. We had no say in what we got. We didn't even have the opportunity to examine the empty tray for lingering old food. I can't tell you how many times I've found dried oatmeal stuck on my tray under the rice served at dinner. And oatmeal hadn't been served for breakfast for three days.

Not long after we opened the new prison, our food service personnel decided to participate in a program called "cook chill." Our food was cooked somewhere in Jefferson City, bagged, refrigerated, and delivered to our prison. Those boil-in-bag meals of gruel were pretty disgusting, although I did like the basil tomato soup. What's funny is that we thought those meals couldn't get any worse.

I asked my free people to Google Aramark, the company taking over our meals. As I feared, other states had cancelled their contract because of filth, maggots, rotten food, and food poisoning. Why would Missouri pay tons of money to a company that even a little research can prove is awful?

As soon as Aramark took over completely, the quality and amount of food changed dramatically. Fresh fruit was no more, except for knotty little hard apples that can be requested instead of the cookie or cake. We used to get grapefruit, oranges, peaches (in season), melon, and kiwi on special occasions. Bananas came in on Tuesdays and were usually served only for breakfast on Wednesdays. I never missed Wednesday breakfast. Aramark doesn't even serve canned fruit. Veggies are frozen and only corn, diced tasteless carrots, or slimy green beans. Often no vegetables are served at all. Potato soup is just watered-down instant potatoes with a random real potato chunk now and then. In the noisy chow hall, you can sometimes hear an excited, "Oh, look! A piece of potato in the potato soup!"

But the quality of the food served is not the worst part. Mice and roaches abound in the part of the kitchen where food is served. I've lived with many girls who have jobs back there, and they come back telling of cooks stomping mice with their boots and cooks pulling roaches out of the beans. Maggots eat more of the food than we do. Bags marked "not for human consumption" are opened for our hot cereal.

I know that there have been many complaints voiced, but apparently to deaf ears. Prisoners and staff complain in prison, and our families complain outside of prison to legislators and to anyone who will listen, but the state cares not about the health or satisfaction of their prisoners. As long as police and judges send citizens to prison, the state will continue nurturing this cash cow of incarceration.

June 18, 2023

Dear Governor Parson,

Do you remember Margerie, the elderly inmate about whom I've written? She has dementia, along with a host of other ailments, and is now in solitary in the Transitional Care Unit because she falls so often. A friend obtained permission to wheel her out to Recreation a few days ago for fresh air, and we entertained her as we rehearsed our upcoming PPA play. Margerie is not much older than I am, and I see my future in her sweet visage. Although her confinement is pointless, Missouri will pay to keep her, and others like her, until death. Aging lifers are a problem throughout the country, although some states mercifully release the elderly to save tax dollars. Missouri does not. Meanwhile Margerie and I are slowly and expensively decaying. Please use your power to free the elderly. It's a fiscally sound practice.

June 25, 2023

Dear Governor Parson,

The news reported that a female prisoner who's been incarcerated since 1980 has been granted a court hearing next month. Every woman who was convicted in the '80s should get a hearing. In 1984, when my husband was murdered, the many hours of interrogations were not recorded. The officers were able to invent lines that I didn't say and never would have said. Interrogations are now recorded on video.

The female jailer, who strip-searched me prior to booking and just hours after the murder, was horrified by my bruised body but did not report that observation because it didn't fit their story. Physical proof of violence would not go undocumented today. Country officers were untrained in the art of fingerprinting and DNA in the '80s. If I were guilty, there would be physical evidence, but there was none.

Is our justice system designed to find truth and dole out justice or only to convict?

July 16, 2023

Dear Governor Parson,

All this week staff have pulled me aside to rant and rave about your recent list of pardons. These solid employees, who interact with me daily, some for decades, are terribly upset that you failed yet again to pardon me. I don't know how to respond since I have no clue as to your methodology in granting executive clemency. These Republican taxpayers are disillusioned by your political blindness.

Some have gone so far as to swear they will switch parties and elect a Democratic governor.

These are good people who work hard for your government. They are upset because you never consult us, the experts, about prisoners—me, in particular. I don't know what else to do but warn you of their frustration.

August 6, 2023

Dear Governor Parson,

Shakespeare wrote a beautiful speech for Portia in *The Merchant of Venice*. "The quality of mercy is not strained; / It droppeth as the gentle rain from heaven / Upon the place beneath. It is twice blest; / It blesseth him that gives and him that takes. / 'Tis mightiest in the mightiest; it becomes / The thronéd monarch better than his crown…And earthly power doth show likest God's / When mercy seasons justice."

August 13, 2023

Dear Governor Parson,

Today my daughter turns fifty-four. She was fourteen when her father was murdered and this family nightmare began. She and her brother and sisters have spent most of their lives praying, wishing, wanting their mother to return to them. They have tried to set up a meeting with you, but you refuse to talk to them. My question is why. Have you forgotten that you are a public servant?

August 27, 2023

Dear Governor Parson,

It's a hard fact that incarceration shortens a prisoner's life by twenty-one years. With that in mind, I'm constantly reminded that I'm in a race against time. Begging you for mercy seems futile since you've shown neither compassion nor courage in your choices for commutation, but what am I to do? Give up?

I cannot die without knowing that I've given my best effort in my quest to return to my loving family.

September 3, 2023

Dear Governor Parson,

The new policy denying loved ones from sending prisoners reading materials of any kind was spelled out in the latest DOC Family Newsletter. The ban includes all books, magazines, newspapers, correspondence courses, and religious materials, such as Bible studies and daily meditations. Thus far our wardens remain silent. Do they hope we won't notice? Will they simply discard our mail?

In my weekly letters, I usually ask you for mercy, but that is no longer enough. I am not only denied physical freedom, but I'm now denied freedom of information. This ban leaves us with only the right to remain silent, a right I refuse to employ.

September 6, 2023

Dear Mary,

I've crocheted small teddy bears for so many years that now and then a young kid approaches me to tell me that she has a bear I made for her mom to send to her when her mom was in prison. Yes, I've been locked up so long that I'm into generations!

A few days ago, a girl showed me a picture of herself when she was five holding a teddy bear that I'd crocheted for her imprisoned mom two decades ago. Lexie's now twenty-five and still has that bear back home. In fact, today she showed me a picture she just received on her tablet of her toddler daughter holding that very teddy. Since that bear appears very worn, I promised I'd make her a new one.

Helping mothers used to be simple. I'd just crochet a little teddy (like four inches high), and the mother could shove it in a big envelope bought at canteen, put a few stamps on it, and drop it in the mailbox. Now we can't do that. The sergeant that runs Property demands that we show a receipt for the yarn (that specific color) and crochet hooks in order to legally mail out any craft item. So now I am forced to take the teddy gift to Property, show my receipts, and mail the bear myself. They make these petty rules, but we still get around them. Mothers ache to send their children tokens of love, and I will do what must be done to help them.

September 10, 2023

Dear Governor Parson,

Last week I wrote to you about the reading material ban slated to go into effect on the 25th, and I told you the wardens haven't told us a thing. That fact hasn't changed. We only know about the ban from outside sources. The story has been on TV news, but we prisoners at WERDCC have not been provided one piece of information. We don't know if our magazines, daily meditations, and Bible studies will be discarded on the 25th.

Your clemency application process is the same. My application was filed in 2010, but neither I nor my people have ever been given any indication of the process, if there is a process. A democracy is not supposed to run like an oligarchy. The government should not be shrouded in secrecy, but it is.

September 17, 2023

Dear Governor Parson,

Budget concerns weigh heavy on you and the legislature, but if you were honestly concerned about the state budget, you would investigate and release the vast number of frail, elderly, and harmless prisoners in your correctional facilities. The recidivism rate for those over fifty-five is less than 1 percent. The recidivism rate for prisoners over sixty-five is zero. This solution is a no-risk economic bonus for the entire state. Use the millions saved to help children in impoverished areas of the state and be remembered as a benevolent hero.

October 8, 2023

Dear Governor Parson,

I'm torn about the topic of this letter. Should I mention that this prison was without water and toilets for most of the week due to ill planning, or should I write about the new mail policy that is forcing prison mailrooms to reject nearly all paper mail? My free AARP newsletter was rejected, and my case manager told me that I must write AARP and ask that they send me a form proving that their mail is free. I explained that their corporate office will not acknowledge a pathetic request from a prisoner. AARP is a huge business, not a mom-and-pop candy store.

Not one prison staff believes that publications are gifting free drugs. Is this policy enacted to fool the general public into believing that our prisons are safe and effective? You and the public should have seen our toilets piled high with feces to know that the MDOC knows nothing of safety or effectiveness.

October 9, 2023

Dear Nancy,

On Friday, UMKC School of Law Professor Sean O'Brien and his daughter Quinn came here to see me and talk about our options. They are convinced that I'm innocent and should be free. They can't give me a time frame, but they impressed upon me that this process will take a long time. No less than five years. Quinn is an excellent investigator, but this is an old case. I'm thrilled for their assistance. I just hope I live to see outside the gate.

October 13, 2023

Dear Carrie,

My buddy Jasmine got to parole yesterday. She's a beautiful young woman who was a college student in Columbia when she got crosswise with the law. We were in the Puppies for Parole program at Chillicothe right after COVID and then we both transferred to Vandalia for Wash U. We sat together in class and side-eyed each other when something stupid was said. I really like her. Her son, Carmello, is a doll and a character. Jazz gave birth to him in prison, but her family has been taking good care of him. She is a fantastic hairdresser, can braid like crazy, and has big dreams of owning her own studio, and I have great faith that she will!

October 15, 2023

Dear Governor Parson,

This is just a reminder that your office has had my clemency application for more than thirteen years with not one peep from you or any of your staff. If you were researching or investigating, surely, you'd have one question to ask someone. You have but a year left in this office. Please don't pass the buck to the next governor. Have the courage to free an elderly innocent woman who's been incarcerated over thirty-seven years.

November 3, 2023

Dear Janie,

I wish you could have seen Sammy and me dancing tonight. Recreation sponsored a so-called TikTok challenge. So-called, because it's not on TikTok. I don't even know what TikTok looks like. We just pretend. Sammy, who's from north of the river, a former social worker, and a great, gorgeous person, asked if I'd team up with her. I'm always game. We chose Bruno Mars's *Uptown Funk* because I like the beat. I made up some dance moves, and then we put our heads together to form our routine. Kim, our Recreation officer from Thailand, allowed us to rehearse in a back room. Tonight was the show in the crowded gym, and we did great. I was so pleased to see girls who don't usually participate in craziness like this out there! I think we won second place. Why don't I know for sure? Because I was talking when it was announced! Imagine that!

Sade, Megan, and Abbey plan to visit tomorrow. Can't wait! Then the Chiefs play the Dolphins on Sunday—a home game! Oh, Brian Reichart and Caitlin had their baby girl Thursday. They named her Elodie Pearl. What a pretty name. Of course they don't know our Aunt Pearl, but I love that the name is still out there.

Sean O'Brien talked to me this morning on the phone about their plans to take my case to court. The Midwest Innocence Project is humming along. Feels good.

November 12, 2023

Dear Governor Parson,

Missouri citizens are aware that there needs to be a mechanism for asserting a freestanding claim of innocence as a deterrent to wrongful convictions. Reevaluating and reviewing the evidence through the lens of constantly evolving technology is key.

Legislation is being proposed for that purpose, but you already possess the power to right wrongful convictions. Many governors before you employed this executive power for exactly that purpose.

November 15, 2023

Dear Marsha,

Since you've never had the opportunity to visit me, you don't know about state soap. You're thinking, "Why should I care about state soap?" It's on my mind right now, because it's ruining our dorm washing machines. The canteen sells laundry detergent that is manufactured by prisoners for a multi-billion-dollar company named Missouri Vocational Enterprises. This same company makes most everything inmates use, including bars of state soap. Most inmates make the base pay of $8.50 a month and can't afford to purchase detergent, but state soap is free.

Many inmates break down bars of state soap to use in the washing machines, but that soap is not made for that. State soap is oily and gums up the machines—it also gums up the shower and lavatory drains. We inmates do our best to stop the use of state soap in our washers, but it's impossible. If I have a cellmate who needs to wash, I offer detergent. Not because I'm so nice. Only because I'm trying to keep the washer working.

You are probably thinking this can't be that big a problem. You're wrong. When a washer or dryer stops working, the laundry room is locked up until maintenance fixes the appliance. That can take weeks or months. If we have no way to clean our clothes, we have to wash them in a trash can in the bucket room or shower. Where do we hang wet laundry when it's against the rules to hang laundry in our cells? In our cells. If the person is not an excellent wringer, the laundry drips all over the floor and the laundry sours because it dries too slowly. If the wrong officer sees the laundry, trouble ensues. Getting laundry clean and dry is a constant problem in prison.

In the prison at Chillicothe, each load costs fifty cents for the wash and at least fifty cents for drying (usually more because the timer stops before the laundry is dry). One load of laundry usually costs $1.50. The machines are large, so I always washed with a buddy to defray the cost. The kids that have no money at all can send their dirty clothes to the prison laundry once a week, but it's a crap shoot as to whether you get your stuff back. At Vandalia, it's almost a guarantee that you won't.

In the '80s, state soap was old-fashioned lye soap. When I was at Renz, I recall helping Jane smuggle a few bars into her diaper bag, because it was perfect for scrubbing dirty diapers. I can't recall when the recipe changed, but it's not nearly as good now, although the kids tell me it still helps in removing pit stains.

I have a theory that free people, if they think about prisoners at all, think of us languishing on bunks, not responsible for anything. But in reality, keeping ourselves, our living quarters, our toilets, showers, bedding, towels, and clothing clean is a constant struggle.

November 19, 2023

Dear Governor Parson,

Yesterday my youngest daughter, her husband, and their two grown children visited me from Illinois for our Thanksgiving visit. They are lovely people. Staff tell me all the time what a wonderful and supportive family I have. These same people tell me that they hope and pray they are here at work to cheer me on the day I walk out of here into the anxious arms of my loving family.

Have a great Thanksgiving surrounded by family. I long for the day when I can do the same.

January 16, 2024

Dear Sade,

Since we have a new medical provider, a bunch of us long timers were called over to Medical, and a nurse explained to our group that none of us would be issued any vitamins or probiotics or anything that wasn't absolutely necessary—anymore. We grumbled, but the policy is not this nurse's fault. It's a corporate decision. Making money off prisoners means worse health care. The same thing has happened with our meals. Aramark, a big corporation, has been contracted by the Department of Corrections, and we are given less food of worse quality. A kid in the chow line ahead of me complained to the cook who was pushing out trays, "This food sucks, and there's not enough of it!"

The cook retorted, "If you don't like it, don't eat it!"

The kid replied, "If I don't eat, I'll die! You're the only person keeping me alive, ma'am!"

Everyone in line hollered, "Yeah!"

And the cook disappeared into the back.

January 27, 2024

Dearest Mary,

I don't even know how to start this letter. I called Morgan this morning around seven for our usual Saturday morning visit, but he could hardly speak. When he cried that Patrick, his older son, had died yesterday, I, too, was speechless. I didn't get any details. Morgan couldn't explain, but I gather that Patrick died on the highway in a motorcycle accident. Morgan is making plans to fly to

South Carolina right now. Patrick was so young and left a baby boy.

The events around losing my Matthew have rushed into my head and heart. Both young men, so young. Tragic.

Tomorrow marks seven years since my sister Mary passed on. This is a blue and gray winter weekend.

March 5, 2024

Dear Sade,

I received a letter today from lawyer Nicole Gorden who works with Sean and Quinn O'Brien. She told me about herself, which is so thoughtful. At UMKC Law School, she became passionate about innocence work. She also sent a bunch of research about Dr. Bridgens's controversial career. She suggested that I read the articles before we talk about how to proceed. I like the sound of that. Proceed. It's been a while since we've even thought there may be progress.

Most likely you can look up these articles. One is from the *Kansas City Star*, dated July 8, 1990, by Martin Connelly and John North called "Pathologists' Findings Trigger a Range of Criticism." See if you can find it, Sade.

We're in the middle of the semester. Crazy busy, but most of the first Wash U Prison Education Project cohort will graduate in May with our Associate of Arts degrees. In 1993, I already earned an AA through Lincoln University, so it's not that meaningful to me, but the rest of the students are extremely excited! Most of them are the first college students in their families, so their families are over the moon, too.

May 16, 2024

Dear Marsha,

Washington University and Professor Kevin Windhauser hosted the most amazing Associate of Arts graduation ceremony today for their first cohort here with the WU Prison Education Program. They dragged in a big stage with built-in stairs and fancy chairs plus a huge carved walnut podium. We were all issued green and red caps and gowns, the school colors. The professors all wore special caps, gowns, and academic sashes. A three-piece band played, heads of the university spoke, and we all walked across the stage in front of families and friends who could make it. Janie and John were here and loved it all.

After the ceremony, they served us a variety of good food, including delicious vegetarian options, fruit, and cake. We sat around and visited while stuffing ourselves. Janie, John, and I sat with Rachel and John from PPA and Meredith from WU. It was a celebration.

The best part for me was watching my friends receive the royal treatment. Some had never graduated from high school. Instead, they had taken their high school equivalency—usually in prison. It was a huge deal for them and their people! Wash U did it right. They know how important this milestone is. I'm thrilled to be a part of it.

I plan to earn my bachelor's degree at Wash U. Either I'll finish in prison, or the governor will take notice and grant me mercy. In that case, I'll finish my degree in the free world. I've been trying to graduate with you, Nancy, and Lynn since 1967. I'm the only one who failed, but I haven't given up!

March 15, 2024

Dear Carrie and Tom,

This week, we performed *Britches,* a play by Courtney Bailey, who came to our Spoken Word classes and got to know our group. She then created this experience. The play is about a real nineteenth-century Shakespearean actress who famously played male roles.

She also wove in our prison experience when she saw that our prison theater troupe is no different than an outside-world troupe. It's a great play, and the audiences, both in the gym for inmates and in the visiting room for family and friends, loved every minute of it.

July 7, 2024

Dear Nancy,

Just a few minutes ago, I was at the microwave in the dayroom nuking coffee water and overheard the following statement. I had to turn to the wall to keep from laughing. These are the kinds of conversation snippets that I ear hustle here in prison: "When I get out, I'm gonna find a moral street pharmacist [drug dealer] who will only sell me meth on Friday nights."

My friend Deb paroled last week. I met her when we were in the Puppies for Parole program at Chillicothe after the COVID shutdown. We ended up in the same cell and then discovered we were both from Eastern Jackson County. She's from Blue Springs and went back there to live with her parents until she can scrape enough together to get her own place. Deb came to Vandalia with me to attend Wash U, even though she had been a teacher before entering real estate. She's around Jane's age, thin, and blonde. Why was she here? DUIs or DWIs. It's statistically proven that men receive less punishment for the same crime as women.

August 25, 2024

Dear Governor Parson,

Last week I read a comment by the attorney general that an innocent person wouldn't take an Alford plea. During my 1985 trial, I
was offered and refused an Alford plea that would have freed me
prior to 1990. Hindsight is 20/20, and I wish I'd accepted the deal.
I am an innocent person who didn't accept an Alford plea. Please
commute my sentence and allow the parole board to decide my fate.

October 20, 2024

Dear Governor Parson,

If you look up the story "Pathologists' findings trigger a range
of criticism" in the July 8, 1990 edition of the *Kansas City Star,*
you will be shocked at the unethical "junk science" Dr. Bridgens
employed as an expert trial witness. He's deceased, but his outra-
geous theories live on with prisoners like me who were convicted
due to his testimonies that were contrary to forensic facts. In other
words, I was convicted because Bridgens lied.

December 1, 2024

Dear Governor Parson,

When my grandson Drew visited me on Saturday, we discovered
that we both will earn our bachelor's degrees next year. When that
sweet baby was born, I never dreamt we'd both graduate from
college together. I pray you grant me a merciful commutation so
I can attend Drew's graduation, and he can attend mine.

December 8, 2024

Dear Governor Parson,

A few days ago, I discovered that my daughter Jane, due to decades of ladder climbing, will soon have surgery on her ankle, an ankle replacement. She'll need someone to care for her and her home. I pray that you will see it in your heart to commute my sentence so I can be of much-needed assistance to my daughter and her husband. Thank you.

December 15, 2024

Dear Governor Parson,

I've written you nearly two hundred heartfelt letters begging for mercy and will write only a few more before you pack up and return to your grandkids. Please, I beg you for my children and grandchildren, please grant me a merciful commutation.

Our Miracle Story

December 21, 2024

Yesterday began as a pretty normal prison day. I knew Janie was coming to visit, so I only got a short thirty-minute workout at 8:00 am when Rec opened. The officers were late calling me to my visit, after ten. When I got to the strip search room, I found out they were short-staffed as usual.

The visiting room was nearly empty, with only three visitors. Kylie was there with her husband and cute toddler Oliver, whom we all love to see. For only a few minutes, Janie and I discussed the fact that we didn't think the governor would grant clemency before Christmas. We then moved on to talk about family Christmas plans.

About ninety minutes later, a tall officer (unknown to me) in plain clothes, except for the huge badge hanging from his neck, interrupted Janie and me, "Patty?"

Staff are not supposed to call us by our first names, so I sat still, not at all sure of what was happening. Before I could ponder long, he turned to my daughter, "Jane?" She nodded.

"Follow me, please."

We both froze, but then he added, "You're not in trouble."

I quipped, "That's what they always say."

We got up. What else could we do? Stage a mini-sit-in in the middle of the prison visiting room? I knew we hadn't broken any rules. We didn't touch, share food or drink, or laugh too loudly— our usual transgressions.

This stranger led us to a small room across the hall from the strip search room, where we found both Warden Mesmer and Deputy Warden Francis, both of whom I'd known for decades. The warden instructed us to sit. We did. The deputy warden, who could not stop grinning, pushed a button on his phone, and several voices introduced themselves as bigwigs in the Department of Corrections. One went on to say, "We're working on your commutation paperwork."

What? What did that mean? We've been working on commutation papers for the past forty years. No one said that the governor had granted me clemency. I was stuck in What Land. What? What's happening?

Then the warden asked Janie, "Can you stick around?"

Quietly, with uncertainty in her quivering voice, Jane answered, "I can spend the night if you need me to."

What? What are we talking about? It still had not hit me that I was leaving the prison that day. Then the warden said, "Since you've been here a long time, I'll allow you to name two offenders to come over here to say goodbye."

Goodbye? This is real. I'm going home.

Jane asked, "Is my face red?" Her face couldn't have been redder. I worried about her blood pressure. She also said her heart felt like it was a foot away from her chest. Janie was experiencing a huge visceral reaction to the fact that I was coming home with her. That day!

We were then escorted to a conference room. Janie and I kept touching each other to make sure it was real. Tessa and Dylan arrived. Tessa bawled when she understood I was leaving. Dylan, who is more stoic, sat quietly, and took it all in.

I noticed a big carved seal of the State of Missouri on a wall and asked the officer, "Is that seal made of wood?"

"Yes, they make them at a prison."

With a straight face, I asked, "Can I have it? As a parting gift?"

Dylan and Tessa giggled. The officer did not. He had no idea how warped my sense of humor is. He was very sober throughout. In fact, he soberly explained where I can purchase one. As if.

Janie worried that her husband would think the worst, since he knew from the location of her phone (inside her vehicle) that she was still at the prison long after visiting hours had ended. She noticed an old desk phone on the console and asked the warden for an outside line. The warden asked for the number and dialed John right after she told us we couldn't tell anyone about my coming home until the press release went out.

We sat dumb, thinking about what Janie could possibly tell John. When he answered, she said, "This is Angela Mesmer, the warden, and your wife has something to tell you."

Janie's a terrible liar. With a weak and wobbly voice, she said something about how the prison was letting her stay longer and how they were being so, so nice. I'm telling you—she sounded like a hostage. Dylan and I shook our heads. There's no way John was buying this, but what could he do?

Eventually, a parole officer ran in with forms for me to sign. I asked, "My clothes? I don't have my clothes. My shoes, coat, and a T-shirt are in the strip search room."

Someone retrieved them. To everyone's amazement, I stripped off my khaki uniform shirt and the visiting room white tee before I pulled on my own navy-blue tee. I flipped off the khaki-colored slides worn on visits, shoved my feet into my own shoes, donned my extremely old pink winter coat that had been grandfathered in twenty-five years ago, and stood up. I was on my way.

When we got to the airlock, I balked. Inmates of high security like me are never allowed anywhere near the airlock. Someone shoved me through, and we landed at the front doors of the prison. No inmate in the annals of history has ever left this prison on parole through the front gates. Another area is designated for both inmate entrances and exits to the prison. Not the front door.

We hugged the wardens, joined hands, and walked out to the parking lot. I was dressed just like the inmate I'd been forever, walking across the parking lot holding hands with my oldest child on the way to her truck. It was insane. The warden described it as unprecedented. No shit, Sherlock! Unprecedented.

We climbed into her tall four-wheel drive pickup and grinned at each other like we'd just escaped. I suggested we leave the prison grounds as soon as possible, but since it was extremely cold, Janie insisted on warming up the motor. Then Janie said that we had to call Brian, our attorney, who's been with us since he was a law student. He was in Kosovo, but because of the magic of satellites, he answered.

I had no idea where his voice was coming from. It seemed to me that Jane was talking to him through the windshield, so I did, too. Jane told the windshield that I was in her truck. The windshield with Brian's voice said he had heard nothing and laugh-cried from relief, joy, and the same craziness we were feeling. He stuttered, "Let, let me confirm…"

I cut him off and hollered to the windshield, "Confirm what?! Brian, I'm in the truck!"

I kept looking at the front door of the prison, expecting cops to spill out in hot pursuit, and again suggested that we leave the prison grounds. Janie pulled into gear, and, just like that, we exited the premises. I mentioned that I needed to use the restroom, but that we could leave town first. Janie informed me that there was nothing outside of town. We were in the middle of nowhere, so we pulled into a gas station that she was familiar with and knew that the restrooms were clean. It turns out that gas stations have become much more than just places to get gas. They are coffee and gift shops and more.

The toilet was a surprise. It flushed without any assistance from me. I stood up, it flushed, and I said, "I didn't do that."

Janie assured me that automatic flushes are normal. Then I couldn't get any water from the handle-less faucet. Janie told me to wave my hand below the spout, so I did, and magically water poured forth. Of course, I then ran into a recently retired prison officer, but she happily hugged me and sent me on my way.

Once on the highway, we decided to call the kids by birth order.

Sarah didn't answer. Carrie didn't answer, but Morgan picked up on the first ring. Janie asked, "Guess who I have in my truck."

With no hesitation, Morgan answered, "Mom."

Janie and I looked at each other in shock. I hollered, "How'd you know?"

Morgan then switched gears and angrily told us not to play tricks with some kind of three-way call. We both yelled to convince him. The first coherent words he spoke were, "Mom, I have a car for you. I bought a car to flip. You can have it."

That was such a "man" thing to say. He promised that he'd be right on his way from Lawrence, Kansas, to Jane's.

Then we called Sarah again. Once given the news, Sarah exclaimed, "Oh! I'm going to throw up. I'm going to pee my pants. I need to vacuum!" She has two cats, and that was a very "woman" response.

The last child was Carrie. She and her husband both squealed in delight. While we were talking to Sarah, she'd texted Carrie three words: truck, mom, Jane. Carrie decided it all made sense when we called.

So, Morgan and his girlfriend, Allison, hopped in his Bronco, Sarah grabbed some clothes for me, gathered her two grown kids who live locally, and drove over. Her daughter, who lives in Houston, raced to the airport and flew to KCI. Carrie and Tom drove up from Gulf Shores, Alabama, and their two grown kids drove straight here from Bloomington, Illinois. The whole family turned into homing pigeons.

When the press release came out a couple of hours after we left the prison, I saw, in real time, what the phrase "my phone blew up" means. The phone wouldn't stop ringing. Word blazed like a firestorm, but traffic on the interstate crawled at less than five miles per hour. We decided to cut through back roads while fending off calls that weren't family, except most were. We drove toward a spectacular sunset, excitedly relaying our miraculous escape story over and over. Nearly every house along our route was decorated with Christmas lights. Such a treat. Prisons are usually built away from civilization, so prisoners don't see Christmas lights. The realization that I was free to spend Christmas with my loved ones seeped into my broken heart. I hadn't spent a Christmas at home since 1985.

Every vehicle that came from a side road worried me. For no reason at all, I pictured someone ramming into us, killing us before we could reach home. I've seen too many *Final Destination* movies.

On a good day, the trip would take about three and a half hours, but because of Christmas traffic, it took us nearly five hours! As we pulled into the driveway, the front door flew open, and Morgan, Sarah, and Abbey ran out first. Morgan wrapped his arms around me and picked me up. Janie hollered, "Don't squeeze her too hard. She has to pee."

But Morgan ignored her just like he did when they were little. We all laugh-cried like children lost and found in a forest.

That night was crazy! When I sat in a lounge chair, twenty-two-year-old Abbey crawled up on me, and we cuddled—just taking in the miracle that I was finally home. None of my grandchildren had ever seen me outside a prison visiting room. Jane's home became mayhem! Crowds came and went while yelling and eating. I hardly recall how it all happened.

Finally, everyone departed, and I dressed in the pajamas Sarah had brought and crawled into bed with Jane in their guest room. We didn't sleep. We would grow quiet, then say something inane like, "Can you believe it?"

Toward morning, I thought Jane had drifted off, until she reached over to feel my head to see if I was truly there. And I am here. In the free world, surrounded by loved ones. I never gave up on my children, and my children never gave up on me.

Postscript

December 20, 2025

What have I been up to since I left prison a year ago? The easy answer is almost everything. The truer answer is that freedom isn't simple. Its joy tangled with many challenges.

My first free Christmas was a lovefest of unrestrained hugs and kisses. My kids and most of my grandkids became homing pigeons, converging on Jane's house. Also, a flurry of friends and family stopped by with clothes, toiletries, food, and put money in a GoFundMe account to help me out. Jane's friend, Russ, brought me his mother's laptop because she didn't like it, then Miracle of Innocence, an organization for the wrongly convicted, bought me an iPhone. Hallelujah! (Those electronics came with a steep learning curve, but I was up for the challenge!)

I'd been instructed by the prison parole officer to check in with my parole officer on Monday the 23rd. Jane and I were giddy idiots to be out in the world together, but the officer was clearly unmoved by our unrestrained joy. We just couldn't contain our glee, even when we were told that I could not leave Jackson County without a "travel permit."

As we drove away, we saw a Gremlin at an intersection, the same kind of economy car my husband and I had owned in the early '70s. I gasped then yelled, "Bill!" We waved at the confused occupant of the car like happy lunatics. Grief and joy collided in my chest. Memory does that sometimes—rises uninvited and demands to be felt.

During January, my friend Sam from prison, who had also been released, drove out to our house and cut my hair. We hopped around like little kids to see each other in the free world. Jane and I also attended an extravagant Chinese New Year celebration at the Nelson-Atkins Museum of Art, appeared on *Dr. Phil* via Zoom, and got a Kansas City Chiefs manicure. Sarah took me to her daughter Abbey's apartment, and on another day, I had lunch with Abbey—just the two of us. Ordinary moments—once impossible—feel sacred.

In February, I jumped through all the government hoops to get my state ID, and then my driver's license. The DMV hasn't changed much over the decades, but the written driver's test is now on a computer. Since I'm old, the DMV lady asked kindly, "Did you let your license lapse?"

I replied, "That's one way to put it," then explained my nearly forty years in prison.

It turned out her son had served twenty. The next day, I bought a car with the GoFundMe money. I told John, my son-in-law, that I wanted a fun color, so he found a velocity blue Ford Escape. Yes! That's a perfect name for me—Escape! (I practiced driving John's truck around a church parking lot, then graduated to highway driving in Sarah's car. One of my former cellmates asked if I was scared. She was when she started driving again. I'm a farm girl who drove anything with wheels growing up. Rusty? Yes. Afraid? No.) (Roundabouts are still a bit suspicious.) The next day, our Kansas City Chiefs lost the Super Bowl, but I couldn't sulk. Life was too good.

I also worked on editing my first book while starting the enrollment process for Washington University. I was too late to get into the spring semester, and the classes I needed weren't offered in the summer, so I enrolled for the fall term. I also began taking weekly Zoom classes with Prison Performing Arts (PPA) as an alumnus. Toward the end of February, my beloved sister-friend Nancy rented a house nearby, and her whole family came down from Minnesota to celebrate my release.

I was surprised to learn that a couple of my professor friends had spoken to Some People Press about publishing my letters. I'd been collecting them for that purpose, but I must admit I was a bit apprehensive about actually sharing such personal moments. Still, I believe the truth about prisons should no longer remain a secret. The response to the first book was incredible. Former inmates supported me, and those unfamiliar with the justice system said they gained new perspectives. I hope this second book has the same impact.

Back in November, during a prison phone call with Jane, she told me about the possibility of needing serious ankle surgery because of end-stage arthritis. I tried not to say things like this while still incarcerated, but blurted out, "I'm coming home to take care of you."

Turned out I was telling the truth. Jane had subtalar ankle fusion surgery on March 7, and I had the privilege of caring for her. Jane needed her mother. Caring for her—feeding her, sitting beside her pain—stitched something back together in me. After decades of separation, being needed felt like coming back into my own skin.

The next week, after gaining approval from the Board of Probation and Parole, we borrowed a knee scooter for Jane and drove to the prison in Vandalia to attend a PPA play. I hadn't had the chance to say goodbye to everyone when I'd hastily left the prison. My visit surprised the heck out of my "prisoner kids," who screamed, cried, and hugged the stuffing out of me when I showed up. I carry them with me everywhere. Freedom has not erased the sound of prison doors or the knowledge of who remains behind. Some nights, guilt keeps me awake. I eat well and sleep in a soft bed, while the women I love endure noise, fear, and scarcity. Survivor's guilt is sharp and faithful; it never lets me forget.

While Jane was healing on the couch, we began the complex process of applying for Medicare, Medicaid, and SNAP. We were on hold for hours, days slipping away. I qualify for SSI, but not Social Security. Medicare remains elusive. How in the world do parolees get all this done without a phone, a computer, a ride, and help? The system is designed for failure.

Sam, Jane, and I ventured to the Capitol to thank all the legislators who'd helped me find freedom. We met with my savior, State Senator Tracy McCreery, and others. I was honored to be introduced on the floor of the House and the Senate. On the drive back home, Sam and I decided we wanted to skydive, and not long after that we did. Jane's bestie, Maureen, has jumped tons of times and knew a good place. I've discovered that there are two kinds of people when it comes to leaping out of a perfectly good airplane: either you want to or have done it, or you would never, ever take such a foolish action. My body hurtled through open air, and for a moment, there were no walls, no rules, no past—just wind, gravity, and trust.

Because we planned to attend a kite festival, we decided not to host an Easter celebration, but Morgan had other ideas. He whined like a little kid, "But Momma, this is our first Easter together!" At our Easter dinner, I presented Morgan with a bucket full of little-boy things, even Hot Wheels Band-Aids. Morgan was eight when I went to prison, and is forty-eight now, but I happily *Eastered* him as if he were still my little Bunky.

Dental care in prison is so awful that I've practically moved in with a benevolent dentist who does some pro bono work through After Innocence, an organization that helps the newly freed wrongfully convicted. But not everything has been free of charge. My generous Nancy paid some, and we're currently on a payment plan for the rest. I also had laser eye surgery for "narrow canals" and will have more as time goes on for cataracts and macular degeneration. After all, I'm seventy-six. Chiropractic and skin cancer care have also been part of this year. It's amazing to me how kind and helpful the medical staff are out in the free world! It also seems that I have chronic obstructive pulmonary disease (COPD) from living in smoke-filled dorms and ancient asbestos-built buildings for so long. No one leaves prison unscathed.

With friends Elizabeth and Mary, I attended my first No Kings Protest at the Country Club Plaza in Kansas City. I hadn't been part of a protest since the '60s, and it felt great! My niece Betsy burst into tears when she happened upon me at an Aldi grocery store. My second cousin Josh bellowed when he spotted me in St. Luke's Hospital. The first time I drove to Sarah's, she was so excited she ran out into the yard squealing while jumping. Morgan calls me often and always mentions how great it is to be able to do that. While I was in prison, no one could call me, and no one was going to stumble upon me out in the wild. This newfound freedom is such a thrill and relief after decades of limited contact.

Tracy McCreery organized a dinner with special people who helped free me, so Jane and I headed to St. Louis on my first train trip since being released. I was able to see sweet Brian Reichart, who'd stuck with me since he was a law student. Also, there were former State Representative Shamed Dogan, Jane Aiken, John Amman and his wife, PPA's Rachel Tibbetts, Alec Rosenblum, and Brian's brother John and his wife. While taking loads of pictures, someone asked who had the big Pooh Bear sticker on their phone. Brian claimed it with no apologies. It turns out a decade ago, Jane paid for a psychic reading at a fair. The lady asked Jane if Winnie the Pooh meant anything to her because that's who was going to free her mother. Jane laughed about the wacky prediction with her friends. We had breakfast with Brian the next morning after the dinner, and you should have seen his face when Jane revealed that story—Pooh is Brian's totem!

In the fall, I went sailing and even got to steer! I also began my final semester at Washington University. Sarah took me on a road trip to Gulf Shores, Alabama, where Carrie and Tom have a house on stilts right on the beach. I'd never seen an ocean before, and wow. We even took a side trip to New Orleans, where the Garden District was decked out for Halloween. I took pictures for John because he decorates like crazy for Halloween, his favorite holiday. While walking around the French Quarter, I was also dazzled by the daytime debauchery. The best part was just being with my kids. Speaking of kids, my son Morgan and his sweetie bought a place near Warsaw and are enjoying the Ozarks. When we have time, we happily drive down there to see what new things they've done to their home.

I wrote a children's book while I was still in prison, and we're getting that published soon, too. With it, I hope to soothe children who have an incarcerated mother. I've spoken at a dozen or so events, and I will never stop drawing attention to prisons and prisoners. Just call me, and I'll speak at your affair. I hope to obtain a pardon so I can travel out of state without a travel permit. I live fifteen minutes from Kansas, but I can't cross the line without two weeks' notice and a trip to Kansas City to get the paperwork. I'm fortunate to be elderly because I'm not required to work. It's not easy for parolees to find required employment, especially those convicted of violent crimes.

This book includes a shortened version of my capstone essay, which I wrote to complete my bachelor's degree. I focused on incarcerated women because I'm knowledgeable in that field and want to raise awareness about how we ended up imprisoning thousands of mothers. My professor recommended I include it here.

I must admit that I sometimes succumb to fear during a restless night. Fear that Bill's murderer might come back to finish the job. This might be irrational, but it feels real. Around Christmas, a large plastic snowman on the porch blew over with a boom. I startled awake, lay frozen for minutes, then slowly mustered enough shaky courage to creep down the stairs and check. I probably should seek therapy, but I'm too busy right now.

People ask how I stay upbeat after all I've been through. Prison taught me that attitude is the last human freedom. When sorrow comes—and it does—I acknowledge it, but I choose not to live there. I've lost too much to surrender the days I have left. Since I am surrounded by love and blessings, gratitude uplifts me. And still, I remember.

(ran out f' room) enth
the gym for step aer
'n Guts." I carr
in which I keep ex
my headboard, muse.
Most of these kids
hair and no way
necks. I've been g
many years! They're
about four to get c
for most of these girls
Tonight, before clas
there are guards whe
and confiscate hai
have canteen receip
them. HOW PETTY!
security prison. Su
infractions than wea

astically run into
s class or "Butts
plastic file to classes,
e plans and ideas,
DS, and hair ties.
e massive amounts of
hold it up off their
g out hair ties for
p, but it takes
ol of a messy bun

kid told me that
tard outside 4-Hour
is if the kids don't
roving they bought
This is a Maximum
there are more serious
g a hair tie you didn't

Women in Prison: The Past Sixty Years

When I was driven to prison by sheriff's deputies in April 1986, I was deposited in a small, ancient coed prison on the Missouri River near Jefferson City. By the next month, all of us women were cuffed, shackled, chained, and shoved onto buses, then transported to the women's prison in northern Missouri. That facility had been constructed in 1888 as an industrial home for girls. Its mission was to remove girls from "vicious associates and evil influences" so they could receive moral training and be reformed into "good domestic women, cleanly industrious and capable housekeepers." This sexist vision, remarkably, still echoes in modern women's prisons.

In the summer of 1986, most female prisoners in Missouri were housed in that single facility. I remember the day the count exceeded one hundred; the number was announced over the radio, and we stared at one another in disbelief. From behind the razor wire, I watched as that small prison rapidly grew beyond capacity over the remaining years of the 1980s.

At the time, the population was overwhelmingly Black women from St. Louis and Kansas City, incarcerated largely for crimes related to crack cocaine. Most white women were serving life sentences for killing abusive partners, since Missouri offered no meaningful defense for domestic violence. As the War on Drugs expanded and methamphetamine production spread through rural regions like the Ozarks, the prison population grew poorer and whiter. Rich people do not go to state prison. Never forget that.

Indiana opened the first women's prison in the United States in the 1870s. It took over a century for every state to follow. That expansion occurred before mass incarceration fully took hold. According to the Prison Policy Initiative, from 1980 to 2013 the incarcerated population rose from about 500,000 to more than two million. Women—who are more likely than men to be primary caregivers—were especially impacted. Sixty-two percent of incarcerated women are mothers of children under eighteen, and their imprisonment often leads to family disruption, loss of parental rights, and permanent separation.

The United States holds 5 percent of the world's population but 25 percent of its prisoners. Prison and jail spending rose from $7 billion in 1980 to $57 billion in 2000 and has exceeded $70 billion annually since 2007. From 1978 to 2007, women's incarceration rates rose by 560 percent, compared to 240 percent for men.

Women make up roughly one-tenth of the prison population and are mostly incarcerated for nonviolent crimes. "In a 2005 study, more than half of the men's prison population had charges involving violence, compared to about a third of those in women's facilities. Women were, however, about 10 percent more likely to face drug charges." Women in drug economies are rarely kingpins; they are easy targets, pressured to become informants and punished harshly when they refuse.

Drug use among women is deeply tied to poverty, single motherhood, trauma, and isolation. Research consistently shows that economic insecurity and lack of support increase vulnerability to addiction. Impoverished women who use or sell drugs face heightened risks of violence, arrest, overdose, and infection. Drug policy criminalizes survival rather than addressing the conditions that make survival so precarious.

"Today almost two-thirds of incarcerated women in state prisons and 80 percent of those in jails are mothers, and most of them are primary caregivers." Yet most research and policy continue to focus on incarcerated fathers, despite the fact that maternal incarceration is far more disruptive. "Notably, 88 percent of fathers in state prisons reported the other parent as their child's caregiver, compared to only 37 percent of mothers. Between 70 and 90 percent of incarcerated women are single parents." Children of incarcerated mothers are far more likely to enter foster care or be shuffled between households.

These statistics reflect what I witnessed over decades in prison. Nearly every woman I knew was a mother. Some, like me, had family support that allowed for visits, letters, and phone calls—though even these connections were costly. Stamps, phone calls, art supplies, gas money, vending-machine food: none of it was free.

Many women had no contact information for their children. Some fathers withheld access. Foster parents could not afford visits. Under the law, children in foster care for a set number of months can be adopted. I have held women as they collapsed in grief after receiving letters informing them that their children no longer legally belonged to them.

Others existed in a painful in-between—knowing where their children were, but dependent on hostile or indifferent caregivers for any contact at all. These mothers walked a tightrope, clinging to fragile promises of connection.

Beginning in the 1970s, women's incarceration rose faster than men's, driven less by violence than by social abandonment. Poverty, addiction, domestic violence, and mental illness were increasingly managed through punishment. As James Kilgore writes, the prison system became "a machine that processes human struggle into human warehousing." For women, that processing disproportionately targeted those already living at the margins: single mothers, survivors of violence, Indigenous women, Black women, Latinas, poor white women in rural communities, and women navigating the fragile intersections of poverty and caregiving.

One of the most devastating consequences of this expansion has been maternal separation. Joyce Arditti writes that incarceration "fractures the maternal identity at its core," replacing caregiving with distance, surveillance, and enforced detachment. For pregnant women, separation often begins at birth. Abbott, Scott, and Thomas describe carceral childbirth as "a form of reproductive trauma carried out at the hands of the state." The grief produced by this severing is visceral and enduring.

After release, the barriers persist. Erica Breuer's research shows how housing restrictions, probation rules, child-welfare mandates, and employment discrimination extend incarceration's reach long after prison. For many women, incarceration does not end at the gate. Its consequences extend across every domain of life, shaping not only their futures but also those of their children.

This is not merely a story of victimization. It is a story of survival—and of how survival itself became criminalized. Women are punished for coping: using drugs to dull trauma, fighting back against abuse, forging documents to survive, stealing food for children. These are not moral failures; they are acts born of impossible trade-offs demanded by poverty, racism, and patriarchal violence. As Vanessa Alleyne writes, "Women become locked out long before they are locked up." In other words, prison is not the beginning of the story but its institutional crystallization.

The human cost of carceral expansion cannot be measured only in numbers. It lives in the birthdays missed, the children placed with strangers, the shame of giving birth in restraints, the years lost to mandatory minimums, the letters returned because a mother's rights were terminated, the funerals women were not permitted to attend, the quiet grief of mothers who had no photos of their children, and the trauma of strip searches before and after visitation. Arditti writes that maternal incarceration produces "a chronic form of anticipatory grief," in which women mourn children they cannot fully lose but cannot fully reach.

The Violent Crime Control and Law Enforcement Act of 1994 accelerated women's imprisonment by expanding mandatory minimum sentences, increasing funding for prison construction, incentivizing states to adopt harsher sentencing regimes, and strengthening drug policing and prosecution. Although not explicitly written about women, its impact on them was profound. Women were more likely to be convicted of nonviolent offenses that suddenly carried long sentences. Many were swept into "three-strikes" sentencing for property crimes or minor drug offenses accumulated over years of poverty and addiction. Heimer, Malone, and DeCoster note that the 1990s marked "the steepest period of growth for women's incarceration in US history."

No policy better illustrates the gendered criminalization of poverty than the Personal Responsibility and Work Opportunity Reconciliation Act (PRWORA) of 1996, which replaced AFDC (Aid to Families with Dependent Children) with TANF (Temporary Assistance for Needy Families). PRWORA introduced lifetime welfare limits, work requirements without childcare support, drug-felony bans on food stamps and TANF, and mandatory paternity identification. It punished women for the conditions that often led to their incarceration and created new pathways into criminalization when sanctions spiraled into homelessness or child removal. Alleyne captures this reality with piercing clarity: "Locked up means locked out."

The Adoption and Safe Families Act (ASFA) of 1997, passed just one year later, dramatically expanded the state's power to permanently sever parental rights. It mandated termination proceedings when a child had been in foster care for fifteen of the previous twenty-two months—a timeline fundamentally incompatible with prison sentences. Most incarcerated mothers serve longer than fifteen months. As a result, thousands lost parental rights solely due to incarceration. Arditti emphasizes that ASFA transformed family separation from a temporary consequence into permanent erasure. Many mothers described this loss as a psychological death.

Faced with rising arrests and longer sentences, states built new women's prisons. This was not feminist progress, but the industrialization of punishment. Facilities lacked prenatal care, mental-health staff, or trauma-informed treatment. Strip searches, shackling during transport, and rigid disciplinary systems—designed for men—were imposed on women.

The 1990s also solidified the practice of shackling pregnant women during labor and childbirth. Abbott, Scott, and Thomas document how "heightened security culture" outweighed medical ethics. Mothers describe giving birth in restraints without family present, then surrendering newborns within twenty-four to forty-eight hours. One woman said, "I felt like my child was taken as punishment, not because I could not love her."

"There is growing evidence to show an increase in mental illness in all women separated from their babies. For imprisoned women, the risk of self-harm and suicide may be exacerbated." These separations produce profound psychological harm, uncertainty, and disenfranchised grief.

Missouri has since created a prison nursery program allowing some mothers to keep their infants for eighteen months. This is a positive development, though alternatives to incarceration remain urgently needed for women who have not committed serious offenses.

By 2000, the United States had the largest women's prison population in the world. The early 2000s entrenched this system even further. Despite rhetoric about rehabilitation, mandatory minimums remained, welfare restrictions persisted, ASFA continued to sever families, and prisons filled with women they were never designed to serve.

This era was defined by contradiction. Policymakers acknowledged women's distinct needs while simultaneously deepening their suffering. "Gender-responsive" corrections emerged, emphasizing trauma-informed care and reproductive health. On the surface, this appeared progressive. Yet, as Kilgore and feminist abolitionist scholars argue, these reforms often stabilized prisons rather than dismantling the punitive structures driving incarceration.

The 2000s also saw an unprecedented number of women entering prison with severe mental-health needs. Nearly 75 percent had histories of physical or sexual abuse, more than 60 percent had post-traumatic stress disorder, and substance-use disorders were widespread. Prisons—designed for male populations—were ill-equipped to respond. Trauma responses were punished as misconduct. Kilgore writes that prisons interpret trauma behaviors as rule violations, disciplining the very symptoms produced by the system.

Despite advocacy and litigation, shackling during pregnancy and childbirth remained widespread. Abbott, Scott, and Thomas classify these conditions as "institutionalized reproductive trauma," noting that the 2000s solidified—rather than reduced—these abuses. Automatic separation after childbirth remains nearly universal.

In the 2010s, reforms disproportionately benefited men. The opioid crisis ruralized women's incarceration, sweeping poor white women into jails unequipped to treat addiction. Prenatal criminalization surged. While public rhetoric softened, punishment remained. Heimer and colleagues describe this "divergent era" as one in which women's incarceration continued to reflect not crime trends, but poverty, addiction, and untreated trauma.

Women's incarceration represents a "carceral revolution" hidden in plain sight. It embeds punishment into women's bodies, relationships, and motherhood. It is not simply about crime, but about what a society chooses to fear and whom it chooses to punish. Taken together, these studies collectively demonstrate that the system is functioning as designed: criminalizing poverty, trauma, and survival while reinforcing racial, economic, and patriarchal hierarchies. It criminalizes the conditions it simultaneously produces—poverty, addiction, homelessness, untreated mental illness, and generational trauma—and then punishes the people most vulnerable to those harms.

For decades, public policy has asked prisons to do the impossible: treat addiction, cure mental illness, resolve domestic violence, stabilize families, and rehabilitate individuals—all while operating through fear, isolation, punishment, and deprivation. The results were predictable: suffering multiplied, families fractured, children traumatized, and cycles of poverty entrenched across generations.

Women know what needs to be done. Incarcerated mothers, formerly incarcerated women, survivors of violence, peer mentors, and community organizers have been building alternatives since long before policymakers took notice. The future of decarceration will not come from legislative chambers alone. It will come from the wisdom and lived expertise of those who survived the system. The fate of the children left behind depends on it.

Research Sources

*"vicious associates...good domestic...*Wikipedia contributors, "Chillicothe Industrial Home for Girls," 9 Jan. 2005.

*Indiana boasts the first prison...*James Kilgore, "Women's Prisons," *Understanding Mass Incarceration: A People's Guide to the Key Struggle of our Time* (The New Press, 2015).

According to the Prison Policy Initiative...prisonpolicy.org/reports/ pie2024women.html.

*The United States has 5% of the world's population...*James Kilgore, "A Snapshot of the System," *Understanding Mass Incarceration: A People's Guide to the Key Civil Rights Struggle of Our Time* (The New Press, 2015).

"In a 2005 study, more than half of the men's prison population... James Kilgore, "Women's Prisons," *Understanding Mass Incarceration: A People's Guide to the Key Struggle of our Time* (The New Press, 2015).

*Drug use among women...*Joyce Arditti, "Maternal Incarceration," *Parental Incarceration and the Family: Psychological and Social Effects of Imprisonment on Children, Parents, and Caregivers,* (NYU Press, 2014).

*"Today almost two-thirds of incarcerated women..." "Notably, 88% of fathers in state prisons...*Dona Playton, "The High Cost of Incarceration: A Call for Gender Responsive Criminal Justice Reforms for Women and Their Children," *Connecticut Public Interest Law Journal, Vol1.1, 2021.*

*As James Kilgore writes, the modern carceral system...*James Kilgore, "A Snapshot of the System," *Understanding Mass Incarceration: A People's Guide to the Key Civil Rights Struggle of Our Time* (New Press, 2015).

*"fractures the maternal identity at its core...*Joyce Arditti, "Maternal Incarceration," *Parental Incarceration and the Family: Psychological and Social Effects of Imprisonment on Children, Parents, and Caregivers,* (NYU Press, 2014).

*Abbott, Scott, and Thomas describe how carceral...*Laura Abbott, et al. "Compulsory Separation of Women Prisoners from their Babies following Childbirth: Uncertainty, Loss and Disenfranchised Grief," *Sociology of Health & Illness* 45.5. (2023).

*Erica Breuer's research shows...*Erica Breuer, et al. "The Needs and Experiences of Mothers in Prison and Post-Release; a Rapid and Thematic Synthesis," *Health and Justice* 9.1 (2021)

*"women become locked out...*Vanessa Alleyne, "Locked Up Means Locked Out: Women, Addiction, and the Criminal Justice System," *Women & Therapy*, Vol. 29.3–4, 2006.

*"a chronic form of anticipatory grief...*Joyce Arditti, "Maternal Incarceration," *Parental Incarceration and the Family: Psychological and Social Effects of Imprisonment on Children, Parents, and Caregivers,* (NYU Press, 2014).

*"the steepest period of growth for women's...*Karen Heimer, et al. "Trends in Women's Incarceration Rates in U.S. Prisons and Jails: A Tale of Inequalities." *Annual Review of Criminology*, Vol. 6.1, 2023.

*"Locked up means locked out...*Vanessa Alleyne, "Locked Up Means Locked Out: Women, Addiction, and the Criminal Justice System." *Women & Therapy*, Vol. 29.3–4, 2006.

*Arditti emphasizes that ASFA...*Joyce Arditti, "Maternal Incarceration," *Parental Incarceration and the Family: Psychological and Social Effects of Imprisonment on Children, Parents, and Caregivers,* (NYU Press, 2014).

*"the steepest period...*Karen Heimer, et al. "Trends in Women's Incarceration Rates in U.S. Prisons and Jails: A Tale of Inequalities." *Annual Review of Criminology*, Vol. 6.1, 2023.

*Facilities lacked prenatal care...*James Kilgore, "Women's Prisons," *Understanding Mass Incarceration: A People's Guide to the Key Struggle of our Time* (The New Press, 2015).

*"heightened security culture..."I felt like my child was taken as punishment..."There is growing evidence to show an increase in mental illness...*Laura Abbott, et al. "Compulsory Separation of Women Prisoners from their Babies following Childbirth: Uncertainty, Loss and Disenfranchised Grief." *Sociology of Health & Illness* 45.5. (2023).

*Missouri has since created...*Cora Palomar-Nelson, "The Pros and Cons of Expanding Prison Nurseries in the U.S." *ACE Research, Criminal Justice, Public Health, Department of Justice,* 28 July 2024.

*The 2000s also saw an...*Karen Heimer, et al. "Trends in Women's Incarceration Rates in U.S. Prisons and Jails: A Tale of Inequalities." *Annual Review of Criminology*, Vol. 6.1, 2023.

*Nearly 75% had histories of...*Erica Breuer, et al. "The Needs and Experiences of Mothers in Prison and Post-Release; a Rapid and Thematic Synthesis." *Health and Justice* 9.1 (2021).

*Kilgore writes that prisons...*James Kilgore, "Women's Prisons," *Understanding Mass Incarceration: A People's Guide to the Key Struggle of our Time* (The New Press, 2015).

*"Institutionalized reproductive trauma,"...*Laura Abbott, et al. "Compulsory Separation of Women Prisoners from their Babies following Childbirth: Uncertainty, Loss and Disenfranchised Grief." *Sociology of Health & Illness* 45.5. (2023).

*the 2000s solidified—rather than reduced...*Joyce Arditti, "Maternal Incarceration," *Parental Incarceration and the Family: Psychological and Social Effects of Imprisonment on Children, Parents, and Caregivers,* (NYU Press, 2014).

*"The opioid crisis ruralized...*Karen Heimer, et al. "Trends in Women's Incarceration Rates in U.S. Prisons and Jails: A Tale of Inequalities." *Annual Review of Criminology*, Vol. 6.1, 2023.

*"divergent era..."*carceral revolution...Karen Heimer, et al. "Trends in Women's Incarceration Rates in U.S. Prisons and Jails: A Tale of Inequalities." *Annual Review of Criminology*, Vol. 6.1, 2023.

*generational trauma...*Erica Breuer, et al. "The Needs and Experiences of Mothers in Prison and Post-Release; a Rapid and Thematic Synthesis." *Health and Justice* 9.1 (2021).

Daddy, Mom, Patty, Mary, and Frank, 1959

Jane, Patty, and Matthew, 1973

Patty, Carrie, Sarah, Jane, Bill, and Matthew, 1975

Carrie and Patty, 1976

Loran, Jace, Morgan, Carrie, Jane, Patty, and Zachary, 1993

Patty and Gary, 2004

Ann (Mom), Frank (Dad) and Patty, 2006

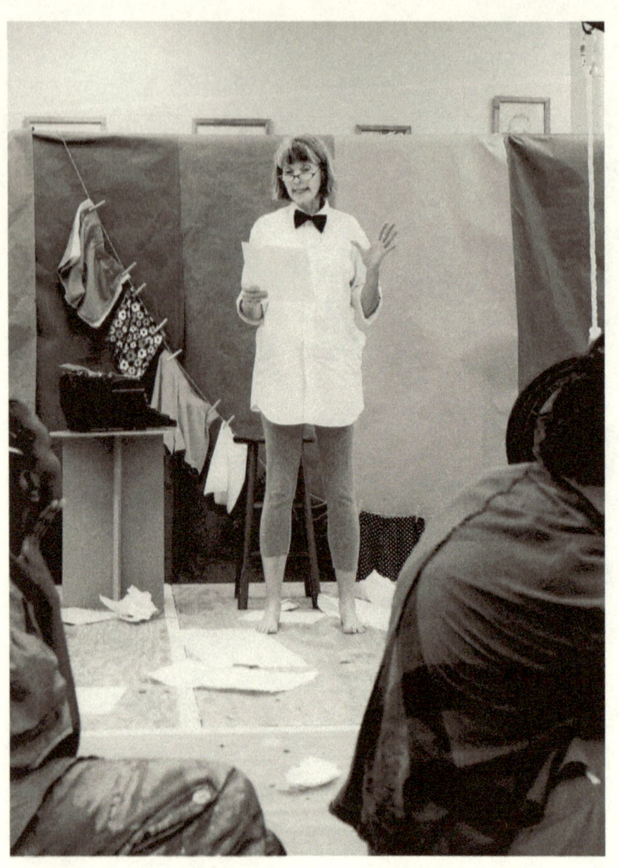

Patty in a Prison Performing Arts play, 2007

Patty, Jane, Abbey, Sarah, Callie, and Carrie, 2012

John, Jane, Patty, and Zachary, 2018

Tom, Patty, and Nancy, 2018

Patty at the Missouri Capitol Building thanking people who helped free her, 2025

Acknowledgments

Besides my former farm-girl sister-friends, Marsha Frantsen Kearns, Nancy Knudsen Besse, and Mary Stevens O'Roark Englert, I also wish to sincerely thank all the generous people who contributed to my survival—this includes, but is not limited to, the following, in no particular order:

Daddy and Momma, aka Wesley Frank and Edith Ann Slaughter, William Edward "Bill" Prewitt, Mary, Doug Longaker, Jesse, Justin, Frank Slaughter, Frankie, Betsy, Katie, Laura, Amanda, Sarah, Abbey, Megan, Will, Tom, Carrie, Callie, Drew, Jane, John, Zachary, Jace, Morgan, Allison, Patrick, Alyssa, Matthew, Gary Kirkland, Uncle Ivan, Aunt Marge, Stan, Linda, Yvonne, Josh, Granny and Grandpa Snow, Grandma and Grandpa Slaughter, Uncle Joe, Aunt Jean, Mother Squires, Carli, Heather, Tom, Aunt Pearl, Don, Mindy, Fred, Carolyn, Glen, Curt, Joyce, and crew, Uncle Russ, Aunt Laura Snow, Uncle Casey, Dot Prewitt, Jim Davis, Bob, Jan Eagleson, Will, Vi Knudsen, Tom, Linda Williams and clan, Kathleen Kennedy, Ira Griffin, Jim Brown, Linda McBride, Sue Pikey, Pamela Kline, Nan Rochberg, Alec Rosenblum, D.J. Allen, Stacie Lentz, Steve and Linda Hotmer, John Amman, Sage Corum, Matt Flener, Sam Jones, Janiece Moore, Miracle of Innocence, After Innocence, Missouri Professional Communicators, George Lombardi, Gloria, Paul Shy, Mickie Perry, Philip Cardarella, Bob Beaird, Deleta Williams, Dale, Marilou Whiteside, Helen Martin, Judy Henderson, Hugh Francis, Seamus Behan, Norma Streumph, Jimmy and Roselyn Carter, Sue Shear, Father Lou Dorn; Agnes, Bob Wilcox, Rachel Tibbetts, Courtney Bailey, Bryan Goeke, Daniel Kohl, J. Malcolm Garcia, Beth Charlebois, Barbara Baumgartner, Sean, Quinn O'Brien, Ruth Beamer, Cindy Ostmann, Mel, Jean Carnahan, Governor Parson, Professor Kevin Windhauser and all the Washington University professors involved in their Prison Education Project, Brian Banks, Lonnie Coombs, Dave

Parker, Jim Phillips, Sue Stewart, Jerri and Paul Austin, Jaye Wright, Jenee Lowe, Shamed Dogan, Donna Baringer, Jason Flom, Dr Phil McGraw, Dan Martin, Maggie Freleng, Stephanie Granader, Paige Bridgens, John Burnett, Lisa Boyd, Maureen Gorsuch, Hedy Harden, Jeff Humfeld, Laura Phillips, Siobhan Walsh, Jane Aiken, Brian Reichart, Greg Zlotnick, Tracy McCreery, Barbara Wall Fraser, Marcia McConville and family, Angie Ricono, Tony Messenger, Bill Deeken, April McLaughlin, Story Link, Bill Boucher, Nancy Bolin, Linda Walker, Theresa Harrigan, Patty, Sheena, Aisha Sultan, Elizabeth Townsend, Seth Gordon, Jamie Tomek, Jane Ponte, Lucy Freeman, Amy Sherrill, Tim Gustin, Juanita Stephens and children, Dr. Joe Kayser, Margie, Chels Fabian, June Pearse, Denis Shine, Paulette Bruch, Anna Shabsin, Kami Hancock, Jim and Sandy Lingua, Jake Louraine, and Susie DeVore Warren.

Some People Press would like to thank the following people:
Lakshmi and Hari Cianculli, Jay Platt, Marcy Freedman, Josh Donen, Miranda July, Beatrice Red Star Fletcher, Sarah Minnick, Kristi Garced, Gretchen Dykstra, J. Malcolm Garcia, Barbara Baumgartner, Elizabeth Charlebois, Brian Reichart, Hugh Carter, and especially Patty, Jane and the rest of the Prewitt family.

About the Author

Patty Prewitt was born and raised on a cattle ranch near Lone Jack, Missouri, and was first published in *Wee Wisdom Magazine* while in second grade. During her incarceration she won a PEN America writing contest and has had both prose and poetry published in *Wrath-Bearing Tree, The Massachusetts Review, The Tampa Review, Tacenda Literary Magazine, Cholla Needles,* and *Duende Literary Journal,* and has had two plays performed at the Kennedy Center. In December 2024, after over thirty-eight years of incarceration, Prewitt was released from prison. She now lives in Greenwood, Missouri, with family. Since her release, Prewitt has published her first book, gone skydiving, and earned her bachelor's degree from Washington University. *Trying to Catch Lightning in a Jar: Letters from Prison* and *A Little Person Like You Whose Mommy Goes to Prison* are available from Some People Press.

About Some People Press

Some People Press publishes autobiographies by formerly incarcerated writers, as well as books on art and other subjects. We challenge the idea that only certain people—with the right education, experiences, and connections—can be published authors. Instead, we encourage writers to use their existing skills and to write about what they know best, their own lives. All profits from sales of autobiographies are split evenly between the Press and the author. Some People Press is supported by book sales and contributions via Venmo @somepeoplepress.

Other books published by Some People Press

Hi Friend by Jess Hilliard

Smile Now, Cry Later by Terry James

Worth It! by Joey Lucero

How Long Is Five Minutes? by Arron Magar

The Blacksmith by Juliano Miller

Trying to Catch Lightning in a Jar: Letters from Prison by Patty Prewitt

A Little Person Like You Whose Mommy Goes to Prison by Patty Prewitt

untitled (Plaid Pantry) by David Rosenak

Enjoy the Ride! by William Shawn Tillman